IMAGES
of America

HUDSON

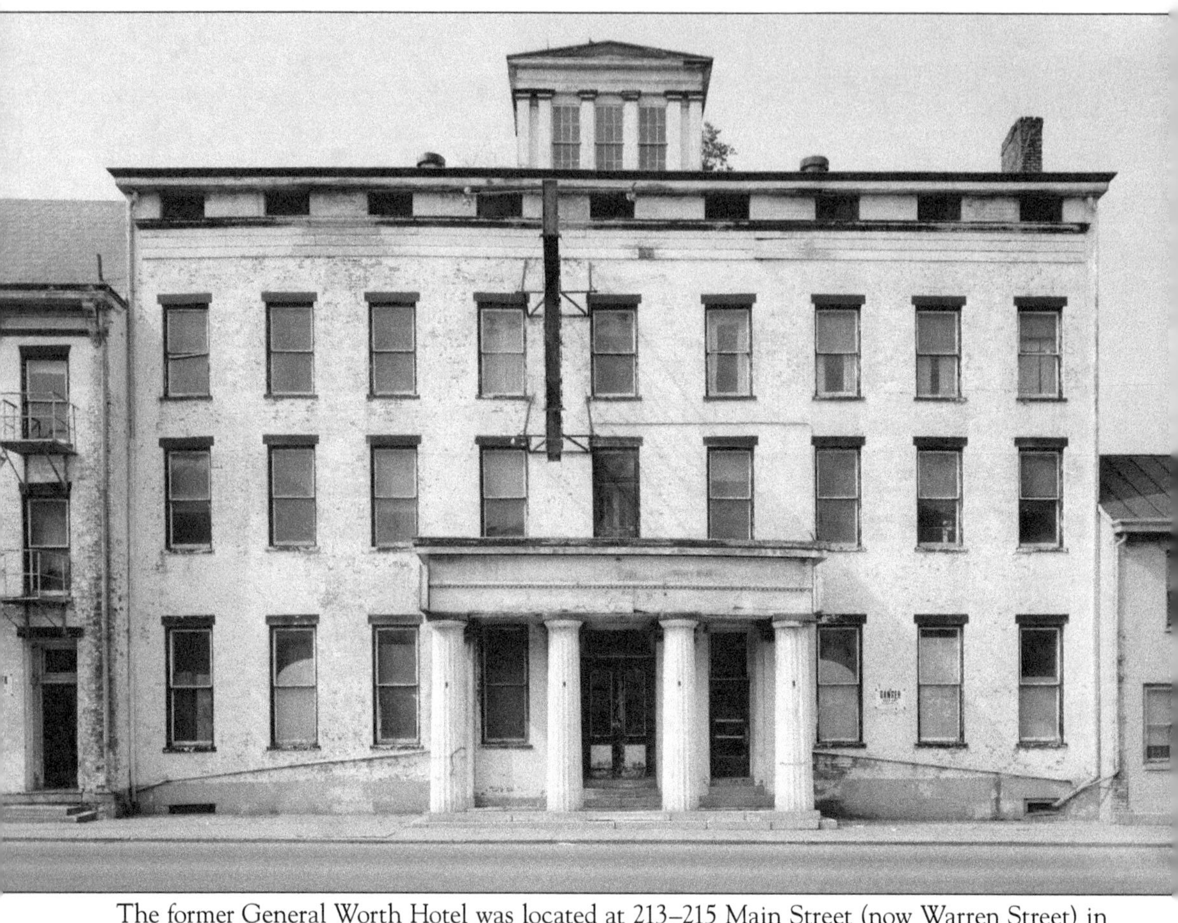

The former General Worth Hotel was located at 213–215 Main Street (now Warren Street) in Hudson. It was demolished in 1970. (Courtesy Library of Congress.)

On the Cover: The former Worth Hotel, on Warren Street in Hudson, is pictured here. (Courtesy Library of Congress.)

IMAGES
of America

HUDSON

Lisa LaMonica

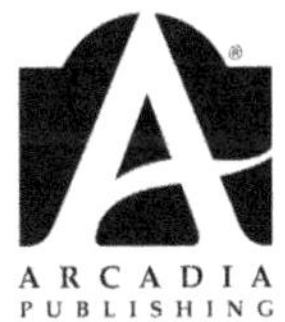

ISBN 978-1-5316-7390-1

Published by Arcadia Publishing
Charleston, South Carolina

Library of Congress Control Number: 2014939281

For all general information, please contact Arcadia Publishing:
Telephone 843-853-2070
Fax 843-853-0044
E-mail sales@arcadiapublishing.com
For customer service and orders:
Toll-Free 1-888-313-2665

Visit us on the Internet at www.arcadiapublishing.com

This book is dedicated to Hudson police officer William B. Wrigley III, who, at 35, lost his life on the bitter cold morning of January 24, 2014, in a car accident. He was a noble and protective person who will be so missed by many in Hudson.

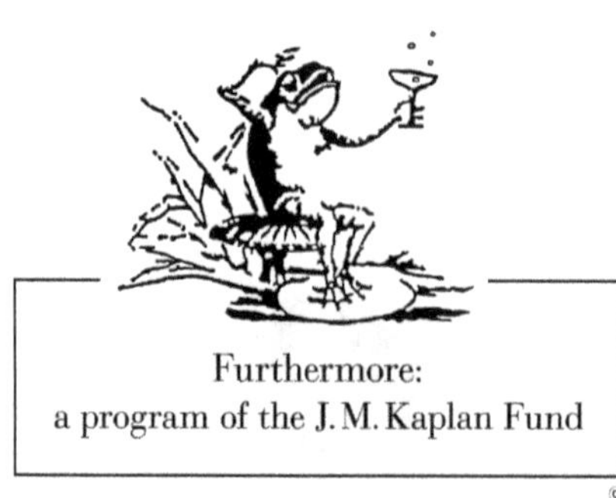

Furthermore:
a program of the J. M. Kaplan Fund

Contents

ACKNOWLEDGMENTS

Unless otherwise noted, all images appear courtesy of the Library of Congress.

Thanks to my son Patrick Robert Mason; Stephen Kent Comer, descendant of the original people of Columbia County, the Mohicans; Peter Stott; Rob Gelles; Tim O'Connor; Jon Meredith; the Hudson Fortnightly Club; and Historic Hudson.

Gratitude to the people who inspired me: John Craig, Emily Chameides, Vicki Kosovac, Tom D'Onfrio, and Joe D'Onfrio, for their enthusiasm and amazing contributions to the city of Hudson and the Hudson Area Library History Room.

INTRODUCTION

Hudson, with its scarlet past, is still intriguing today and in new ways. Discovered by tourists, celebrities, chefs, world-famous artists, motion pictures, and major magazines, Hudson is a go-to destination just two hours north of New York City. Hudson is a place of art, culture, and fine food. Visitors say that there is a palpable vibe, a vortex of creative energy. Hudson has the most self-employed people per capita in New York State. David Byrne of the band Talking Heads, in an October 2013 article for the *Guardian*, wrote, "If young, emerging talent of all types can't find a foothold in [New York City], then it will be a city closer to Hong Kong or Abu Dhabi than to the rich fertile place it has historically been. Those places might have museums, but they don't have culture. Ugh. If New York goes there—more than it already has—I'm leaving. But where will I go? Join the expat hipsters upstate in Hudson?"

Hudson historically became a haven for people leaving New York City for other reasons as well, including Frank Serpico. In 1971, Serpico, a Brooklyn policeman, was shot in the face during a drug bust. After a movie was made with Al Pacino cast as him, Serpico became one of the 100 most loved film heroes in history. The real Frank Serpico lives quietly here in the home he built on the Hudson River, frequenting area libraries and coffee shops to people-watch and visit with friends. He is working on a memoir.

This renewed interest in Hudson was not always the case. In the 1980s, for example, diners on Warren Street would go from the restaurant directly to the car and not linger anywhere. Hudson was seedy and dark. It was not considered very safe at all during those years. It was a time of decay and drugs. A Hudson drug addict knew it was time to quit when "the parking meters were singing and the street was waving."

William Kennedy's movie *Ironweed* was filmed here. Hudson locals had the thrill of being photographed with Jack Nicolson around vintage automobiles.

During the 1980s, the city slowly resurrected, starting with antique dealers on Warren Street and then "weekenders"—New York City visitors buying second homes in and around Hudson.

America's first art movement started in Hudson with the Hudson River School of painters, who captured the wilderness and fall colors before Hudson became known as a tourist destination. The painters themselves acquired wealth and fame during their lifetimes, leaving a legacy of romantic artwork.

The importance of Hudson's early history cannot be stressed enough, however. Much was learned from the Mohicans, and it is important to tell their stories as well. Around 1736, Mohicans left Claverack, Hudson, and the area that is now Columbia County, traveled east, and settled in what is now Stockbridge, Massachusetts. Despite the Massachusetts Court assuring Stockbridge Indians that their land would never be sold, the agreement was eventually taken away. Despite having the aid of Mohicans during the Revolutionary War, Massachusetts forced their relocation, first back to New York State, to Oneida, and then on to Wisconsin. It is important to know the prehistory of Mohicans inhabiting this vast region before they first began selling parcels of their land to early Europeans. They should be remembered and honored.

In September 1609, Henry Hudson arrived in the Catskills area at Stockport, riding in an Indian canoe to shore three days after his arrival, as he traveled up the river that was later named for him. The river was originally called the Mohicanituk, or "Grandmother," by the Mohicans.

The Hudson River was a constant resource for Mohican daily life. Yearly flooding of the Hudson created rich soil for Mohican agriculture. Mohicans feasted on bear, deer, moose, turkeys, pheasants, berries, cherries, nuts, and the ocean fish spawning in spring. Shellfish were plentiful. Mohicans tapped the trees and made maple syrup. Mohican ceremonies honored the seasons, like harvest time. Mohicans were powerful people.

Later, visitors purchased flats along Claverack Creek, in Greenport and Claverack. Abram Staats purchased a tract at the mouth of Stockport Creek (also known as Oosterhoeck, a Dutch description). The first actual settlement was around 1660, and there are records of a land purchase from the Mohicans by Jan Fransen van Hoesen at Claverack Landing (now Hudson). Later, in 1667, land patents were also granted to his widow.

It is important to think about the native Mohicans' friendly acceptance of these early visitors, showing them their way of life, their tools made of shells and stone, their food supplies and cooking methods, and their hunting techniques. Mohicans lived in one longhouse with round tops made of oak bark, containing large supplies of corn and beans from a previous year. When sharing a meal with the native Mohicans, Henry Hudson was given cooked corn and the meat of dogs and pigeons. In Hudson's journals, which are now lost, he wrote, "On our coming near the house, two mats were spread out to sit upon, and immediately some food was served in well made red wooden bowls; two men were also despatched at once with bows and arrows inquest of game, who soon after brought in a pair of pigeons, which they had shot. They likewise killed a fat dog, and skinned it in great haste, with shells which they got out of the water."

Author Shirley Dunn also wrote about a reassuring gesture by the Mohicans: "The natives broke their arrows and threw them into the fire so Hudson would not be afraid." Where would Hudson be without the Mohicans?

Journals kept at the time state that Henry Hudson also entertained some Mohicans aboard his ship *The Half Moon*. Fur trading with Mohicans would begin a year after Hudson left and returned to the Netherlands. The Dutch returned up the Hudson River every summer for furs. It was recorded that when Henry Hudson's ship departed the region for his homeland, an old chief was left "very sorrowful."

Mohicans were numerous and strong at the time of Henry Hudson's arrival on the Hudson River in 1609 and for about 20 or so years afterward. By 1664, the English had conquered the Dutch, and the Hudson Valley was mostly abandoned.

Mohican lands included what is now Vermont and south nearly to Manhattan Island, with land on both sides of the Mahicannituck (Hudson River), including Windham, and east into Massachusetts and Connecticut.

In 1984, historian Kenneth Mynter wrote in a Hillsdale newspaper, the *Independent*, "Indians were living here in this county before the building of the pyramids . . . at a time when our own ancestors were living in the New Stone Age in Europe."

Donald Shriver, president emeritus of the Union Theological Seminary of New York, and Stephen Kent Comer, the last lineal survivor of the Mohican Nation in the vicinity of Columbia County, added a historical marker alongside the long-standing "History of Columbia County" marker at the northernmost west-side overlook of the Taconic Parkway. The original marker tells of Henry Hudson's coming up the river in 1609 with no mention of Mohicans. After years of fundraising with a variety of state agencies, and with the help of St. Peter's Presbyterian Church in Spencertown, the men decided it was necessary to commemorate the Mohicans who had greeted Hudson and his crew. "Taconic" is a Mohican word, and thousands of the tribesmen lived in the valley at the time of the foreigner's first visit. Stephen Kent Comer said, "I can say that, when I came to this area 30 years ago, I was amazed to find virtually nothing about my people in their native land. It was as though we were a ghost people."

A ghost story known as "Spook Rock Road," having arisen from the Mohicans' involvement with Europeans, is retold here. Comer describes it as a "typical Indian" story that is actually a "White Victorian folktale interpreted as a colonialist explanation for the reason why the Original People seemed to 'melt away' at the encroachment of EuroAmerican society. In this case the young brave is symbolic of Native people presumably wanting to integrate into Colonial society but unable to do so because they cannot meet the requirements of White civilization. The Native peoples then destroy themselves because of their regrets and inabilities, rather than from any aggression on the part of the invaders."

Without Hudson's whaling history, Hudson might not have existed either. Seth and Thomas Jenkins, brothers from Nantucket, raised $100,000 and sailed up the Hudson River looking for property and means for their merchant business. They arrived at Hudson with an area deep enough for whaling ships.

Still known as Claverack Landing at the time of the American Revolution, Hudson got its name from the 30 proprietors of the town in 1784, most of which were part of a family that came soon after the Jenkins men. The Nantucket Navigators Company was formed, shipbuilders were found, and whaling began in Hudson.

Hudson became known as a great whaling port where sealing also occurred. The last ship left Hudson in 1844. Many a ship left Hudson heading out for whaling adventures in Europe and the Caribbean.

For 60 remarkable years, Hudson saw outstanding prosperity and entrepreneurial spirit. The Barnard Curtiss Company operated a whale-oil lamp lighting and candle factory near the present train station. Seal hides were important to Hudson because they prompted the creation of many tanneries, which turned the hides into shoe leather. Tanners Lane is still in use today, with many of its original buildings still standing. Whaling waned as whale blubber was gradually replaced by kerosene and other fuels.

In regards to smaller fish, the city of Hudson's riverfront used to supply hundreds of goldfish to the world's fair, including the Seattle World's Fair. Hundreds more went to Montreal, as well as the presidential palace in Mexico City. Hudson's locals remember a colorful character named Everett and his yearly order for 5,000 goldfish to be delivered to a New Jersey tropical fish dealer, who would then ship to customers around the world.

Hudson's history ranges from the last of the Mohicans, to whaling, to a red-light district that would receive notoriety as far away as Europe, to a multitude of factories in the Industrial Age, to modern times, with Hudson attracting celebrities and New York City chefs opening chic restaurants up and down Warren Street. There is little visible sign that Mohicans once trod here as the area's original people. Mohican history is mostly chronicled through English history now.

Hudson is a divided city, with very wealthy and very poor, as noted by Marina Abramovic, a superstar in the art world, on a recent visit to Hudson. She said, "I see very strong division between the poor and the rich neighborhoods. It's amazing; I don't even see the black people walking on Warren Street—it's like two parallel realities." This parallel reality is something Hudson is all too familiar with; in the past, respectable, accomplished citizens simply skirted around the many brothels and working girls circulating in town.

In October 2013, Stair Galleries, on Warren Street, set the world-record price for a Fabergé Hardstone Figure, which sold for an impressive $5.98 million at their auction. Found in a Rhinebeck, New York, attic, Nicholas II had commissioned Fabergé to produce this portrait figure of N.N. Pustynnikov, the personal Cossack bodyguard to the empress Alexandra. The figurine was then purchased at auction by Queen Elizabeth's jewelers, from London.

The architecture in Hudson still remains some of the most varied and interesting in the entire United States. Described as a "miracle city" and then a "finished city," Hudson, amazingly, has been able to reinvent itself a number of times, in part due to the entrepreneurial nature of its people.

One

HUDSON'S *TITANIC* SURVIVOR

Gretchen Fiske Longley was the daughter of a past Hudson mayor, Levi Longley. An orphan at age 12, Gretchen lived with her grandmother and maternal aunts at 751 Warren Street, in a house that no longer exists. She and her aunts Kornelia Theodosia Andrews and Mrs. John C. Hogeboom boarded the *Titanic* in Southhampton under ticket number 13502 and occupied cabin D-9. Gretchen opened a farewell letter from an admirer when she arrived in her cabin; it was a good wish for every day of the impending voyage, spelling out her name: "Good weather/ Refreshments/Every desire/Tommies to burn/Chocolate ice cream/Heavenly evenings/Entire meals/No regrets."

Upon the opening of the first *Titanic* movie, *A Night to Remember* (1958), Gretchen told a reporter that her aunts had taken her to Europe. After traveling in Italy and France, they booked a first-class return on the maiden voyage of the *Titanic*. At 11:45 p.m. on April 14, Gretchen was awakened by a loud crash. Outside her room, in the hallway, ice crystals had come in through a porthole, which a steward said were "no danger." The women went back to bed. After midnight, much commotion had broken out in the hallway. The women were told to put on life preservers as a precaution, which they promptly topped their nightdresses and fur coats with. The women rushed up to the deck, where crew members were filling lifeboats. The third boat had room for Gretchen, but she refused to go without her aunts. They left in the third, and last, lifeboat. As they were lowered 75 feet down into the icy waters below, the women noticed only one able-bodied seaman in their boat. So Gretchen pulled an oar until she was exhausted. At 2:00 a.m., they saw *Titanic*'s boilers explode. The ship's lights went out. The *Titanic* split in two and disappeared forever under the ocean. Gretchen said the shrieks were "blood curdling," as hundreds of people drowned. Eight days after the disaster, the women were back in New York. The *Newark Evening News* reported in their article "Three Still Suffer from Perils and Cold" that they were safely in the home of another aunt of Gretchen's. The women were not able to speak above a whisper.

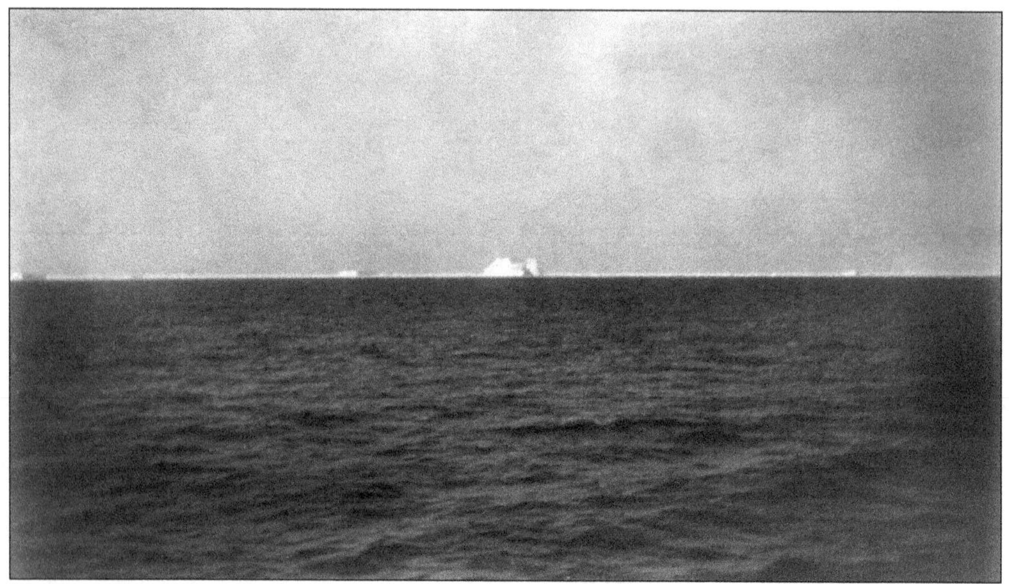

"Not even God himself would sink this ship," said an employee of the White Star Line at the *Titanic* launch in 1911. This is an eerie, ominous view from the SS *Carpathia*, a rescue ship for the *Titanic* survivors, of the fatal iceberg that sank the *Titanic*.

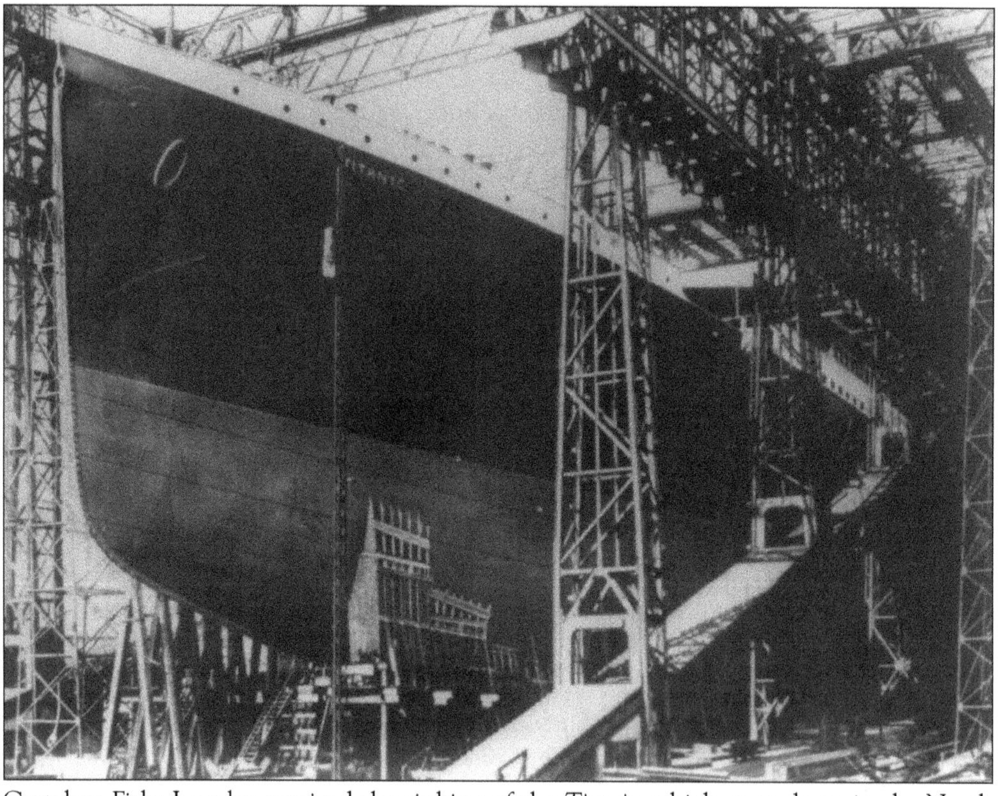

Gretchen Fiske Longley survived the sinking of the *Titanic*, which went down in the North Atlantic in April 1912 after hitting an iceberg. Her story is inspirational and seemingly without fear. Of the 1,500 passengers, only 713 would survive.

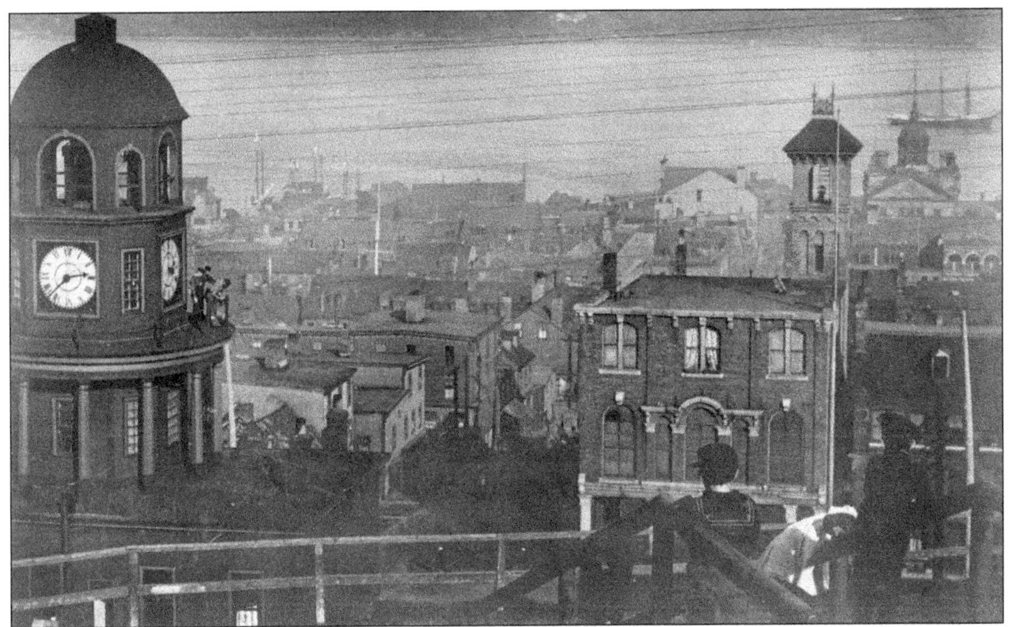

Halifax Harbor, seen here, is where *Titanic* survivors were taken. The women described their lifeboat pulling away as they saw "Major Butt and Colonel Aster" on the upper deck, with Colonel Aster waving a last farewell to his wife. Just 18 months after this unforgettable experience, Gretchen Fiske Longley married Dr. Raymond Leopold in Hudson. Almost three years later, Gretchen sailed to Bermuda, "just to see if I could do it."

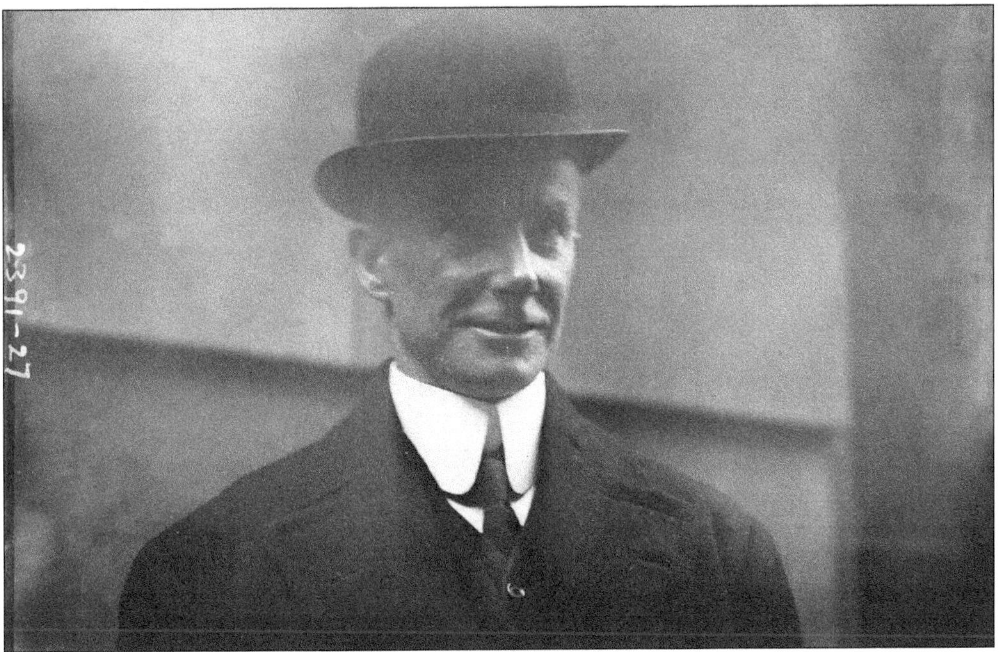

Capt. Arthur Henry Rostron of the *Carpathia*, who rescued survivors of the *Titanic*, is seen here. With mettle and moxie, Gretchen Fiske Longley sailed across the Atlantic 13 more times. She died peacefully in August 1965, in her stateroom on the SS *Constitution*, during a Mediterranean cruise. Her aunts are buried in Hudson's Cedar Park Cemetery.

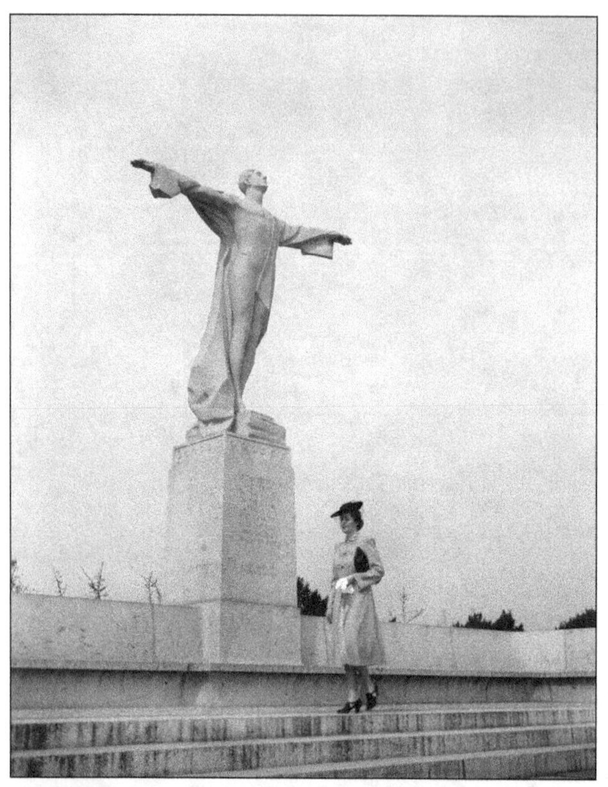

The Titanic Memorial in Washington is seen here in 1940 with Mrs. Lister Hill. The statue honors the men who gave their lives so women and children could be saved from the *Titanic* disaster. The 13-foot-tall figure is a partly clad male figure with arms outstretched. The statue was erected by the Women's Titanic Memorial Association.

Capt. Arthur Henry Rostron of the *Carpathia* receives a trophy from Molly Brown for service rescuing *Titanic* victims. At dawn, *Carpathia* appeared on the horizon. After seven hours in the water, Gretchen Longley's boat reached the rescue ship. Survivors were hauled aboard like livestock, with ropes around their waists, their fingers and toes frozen, and their throats hoarse with cold. The Hudson women refused a stateroom, seeing survivors in worse condition.

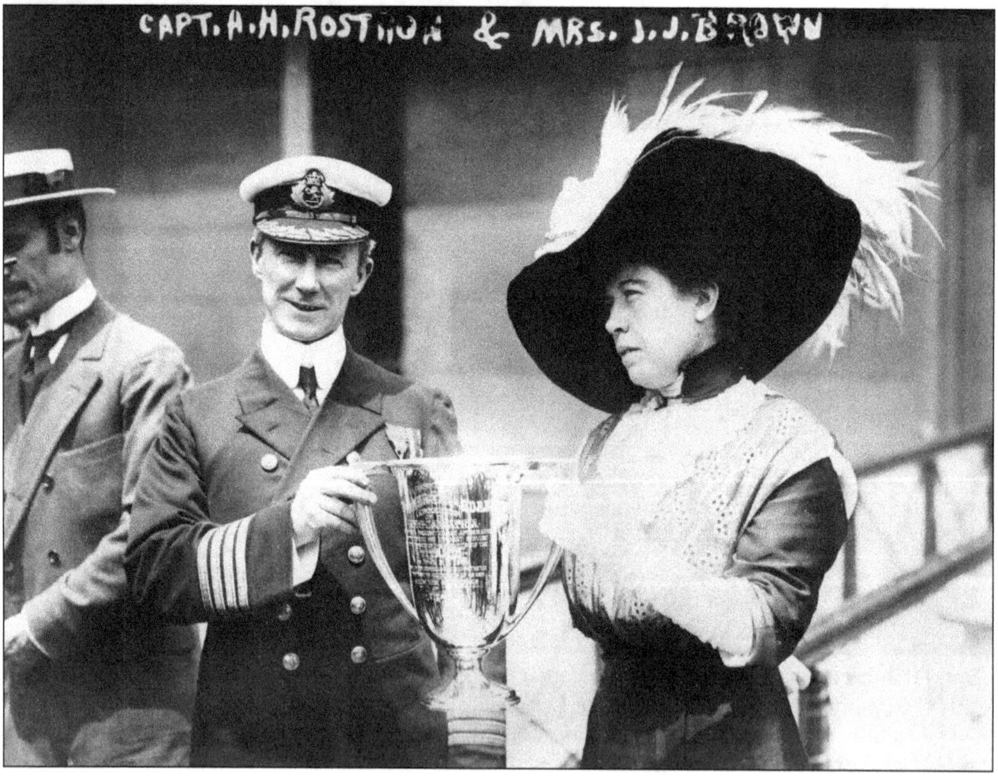

Two

Stockport

"History is my whole life, because it's about people," said Viola Williams, Stockport historian.

Until the 1830s, Stockport was part of Hudson. James Wild's five-story cotton mill was there. Wild, born in Stockport, England, imported raw cotton from slave states, which was then turned into textiles. Ruins of the mill can still be seen from the Route 9 bridge and the Columbiaville gorge. Stockport was an area diverse in mills, with shipping, cloth, paper, and other goods being produced there. Peter Stott's extensively researched book *Looking For Work* is a valuable resource and a necessary addition to a collection of Columbia County history. Stockport contains an octagon house that is reputedly haunted by a member of the once prosperous Smith family.

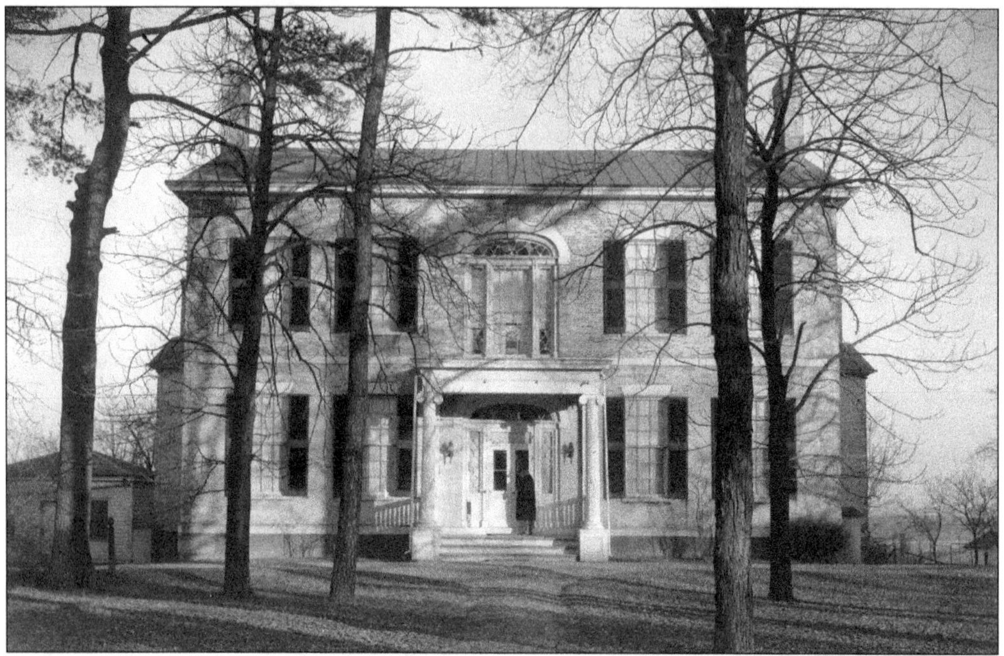

The Lathrop House in Stockport, photographed here in 1936, features 19th-century French scenic wallpaper depicting a very Western version of a Chinese landscape. It is now in the Cooper-Hewitt paper collection. The house was built in 1815 by Nantucket descendant and sea captain Seth G. Macy.

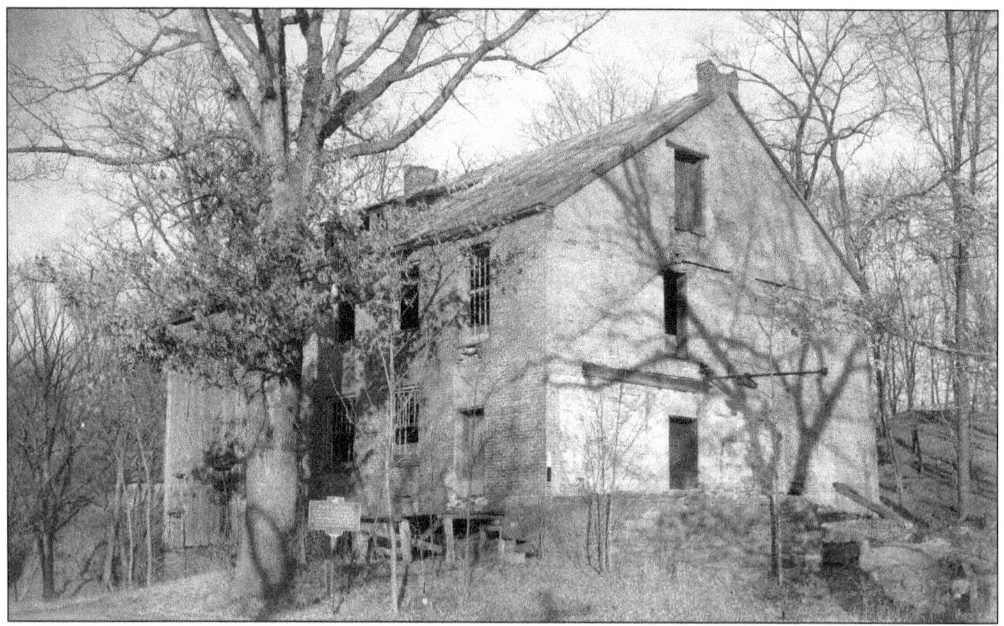

This is a southwest view of Print Works. According to Capt. Franklin Ellis in 1878, "In the year 1852, Mr. Rensselaer Reynolds co-partnered with Mr. Benjamin, and purchased the 'Marshall Print-Works,' in Stockport, then occupied by Roome's tobacco-factory. The firm engaged in manufacture of a new loom just invented by Mr. Reynolds, now and for many years past known as the Empire loom, proceeded prosperously till Dec. 10, 1858."

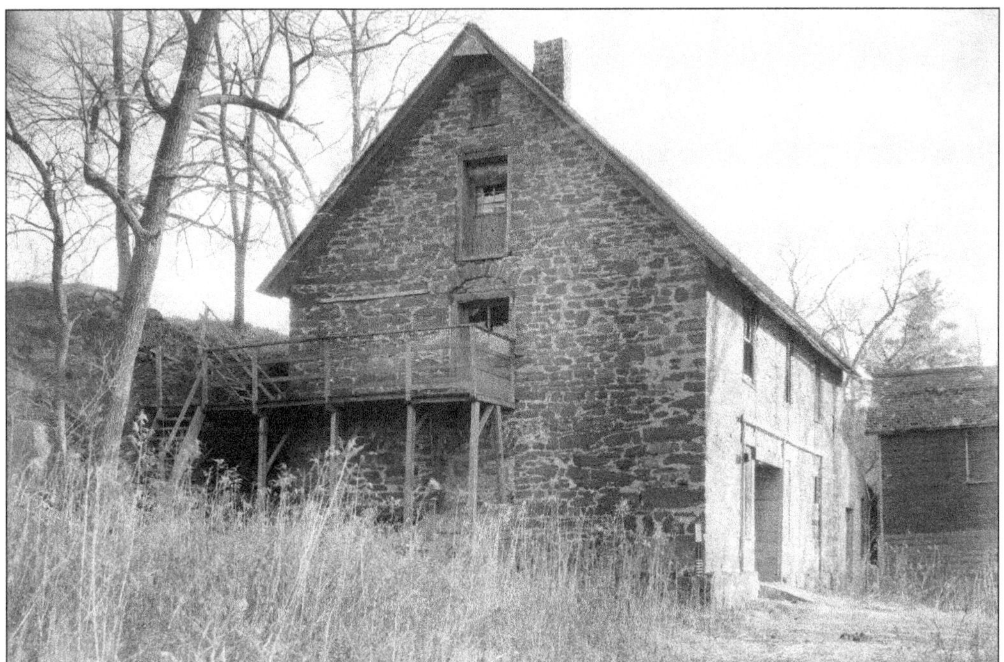

This north view of Stone Mill in Stockport was taken in 1936 looking upstream. Until 1833, Stockport was part of Hudson. It was noted for its early manufacturers and its waterpower. Stockport was originally a Mohican village, and it is believed to be a spot where Henry Hudson may have landed.

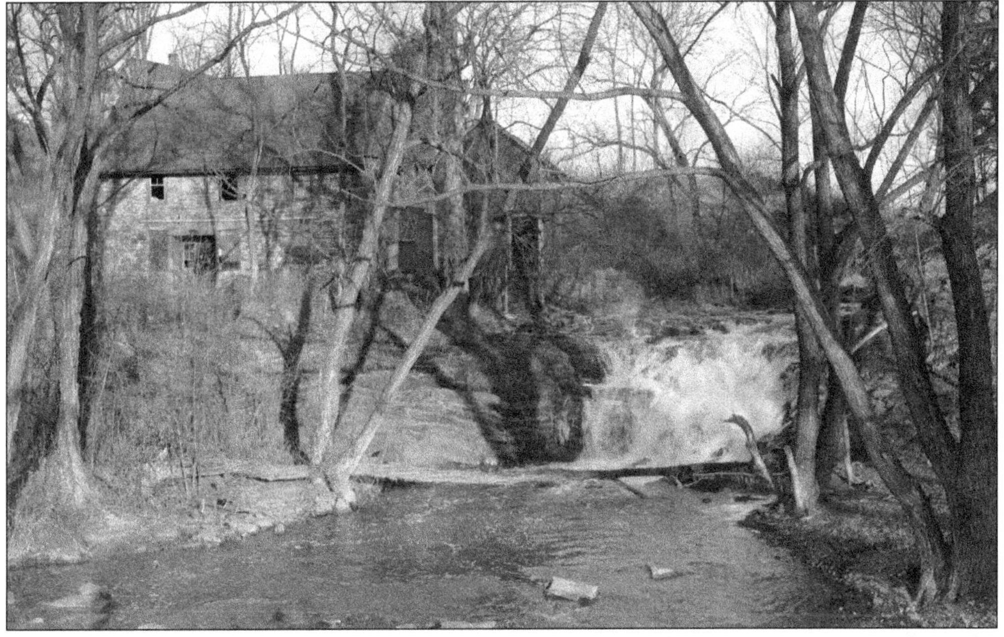

Shortly after Henry Hudson's departure and subsequent death by mutinous crew members, the Dutch established farms, mills, and trading posts in Stockport. Ethnological objects from an archeology dig there exist at the New York State Museum in Albany. Stockport Creek empties into the Hudson River. Fossils of trilobites from the Cambrian period have also been found there.

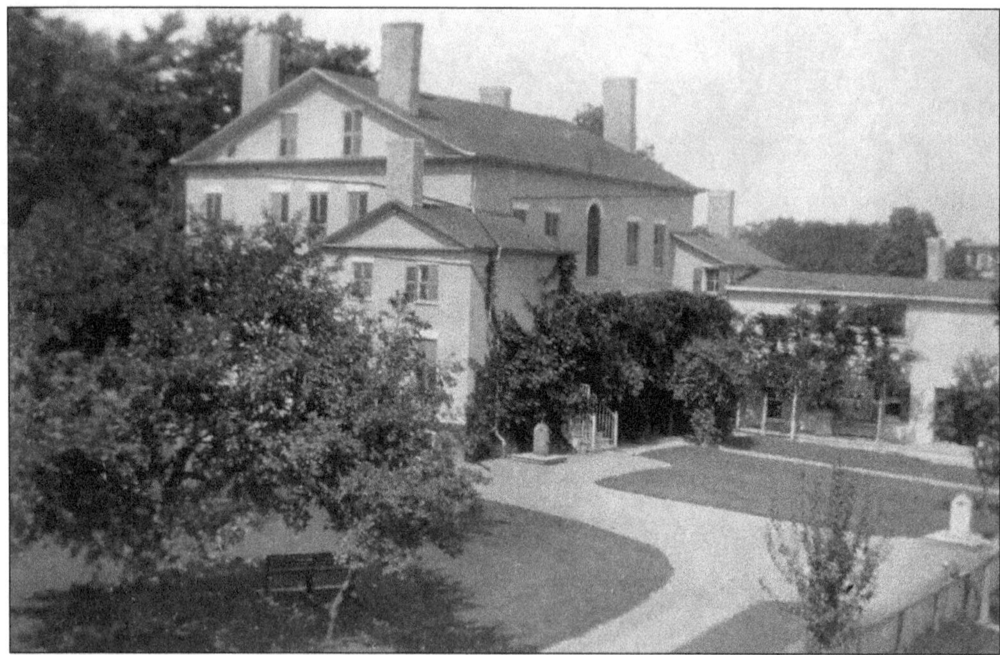

This postcard is titled "South End" and is one of seven matching views of the Lathrop House. The caption on the reverse of the postcard reads, "Front of Lathrop House. The house was built by retired sea-captain Seth G. Macy, 1815. Captain Seth seems to have used up all his fortune in building his house, forced to sell within a few years."

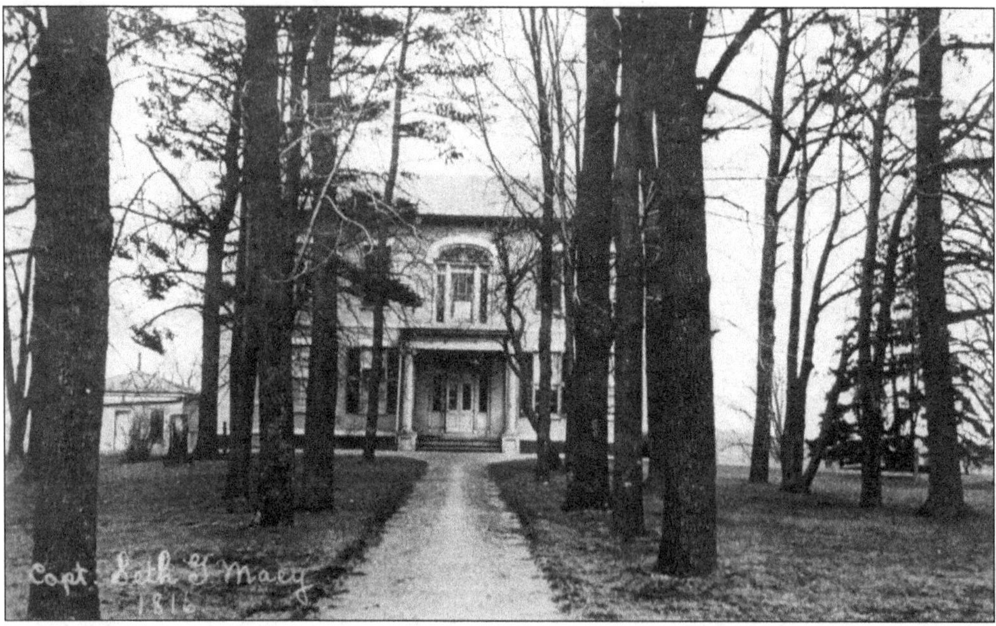

In 1905's *Old Time Wallpapers*, Kate Sanborn wrote, "The name 'Seth's Folly' still clings to the place. In 1853 Janet's father bought the house. By singular coincidence, Janet noticed the wallpaper the same as in the house in Albany where she was born. In the 1870s Janet visited a hunting lodge belonging to the King of Saxony, and found in the Chinese Room the exact same wallpaper." (Courtesy Peter Stott.)

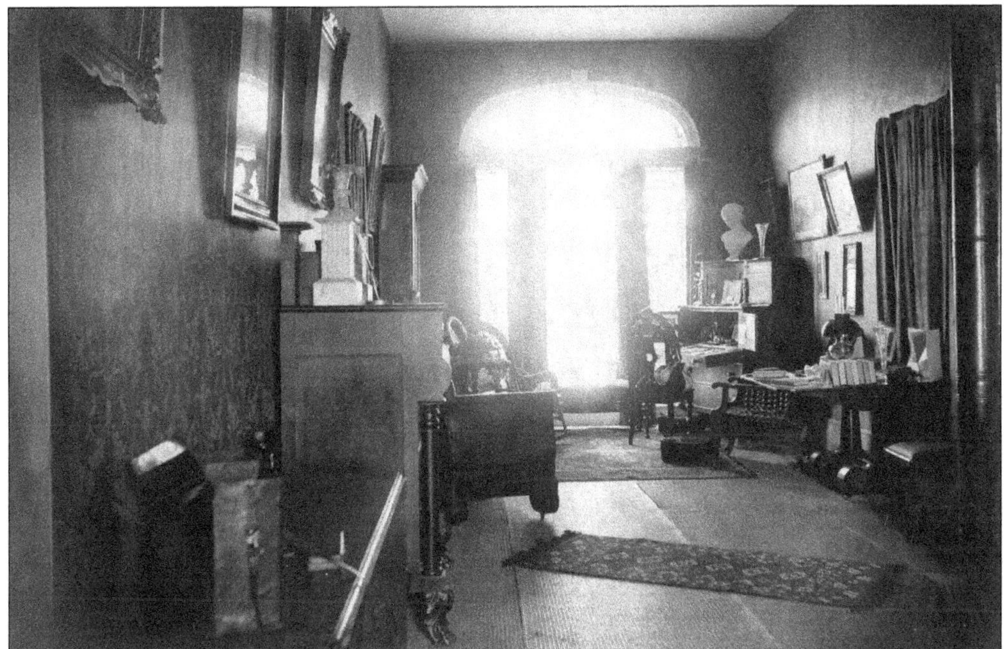

The upper hall at Lathrop House is seen here in 1895. In *Old Time Wallpapers*, Kate Sanborn wrote, "The Wallpapers described would seem to be the finest examples of continuous scenic papers still extant." On one of Capt. Seth Macy's trips on a merchant ship, he brought back the supplies for this foreign wallpaper.

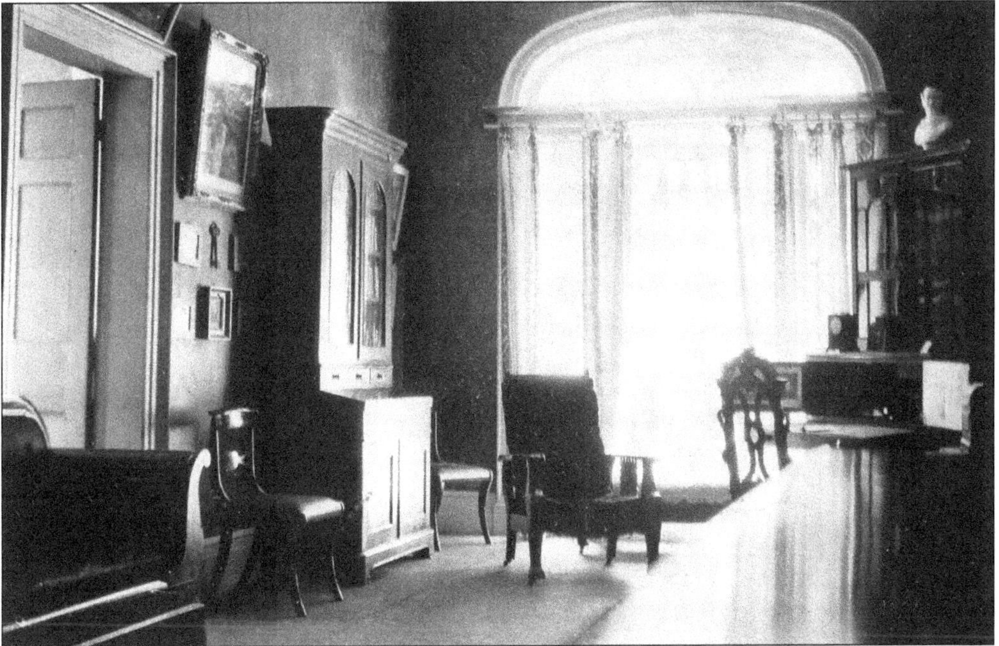

According to Nancy McClelland in 1924's *Historic Wallpapers*, "The paper is sepia printed from hand blocks 18 inches square. Scenes represented are Chinese, but faces and figures evidently not drawn by a Chinese artist. It is probable that the paper was done either in Holland, England, or France." (Courtesy Peter Stott.)

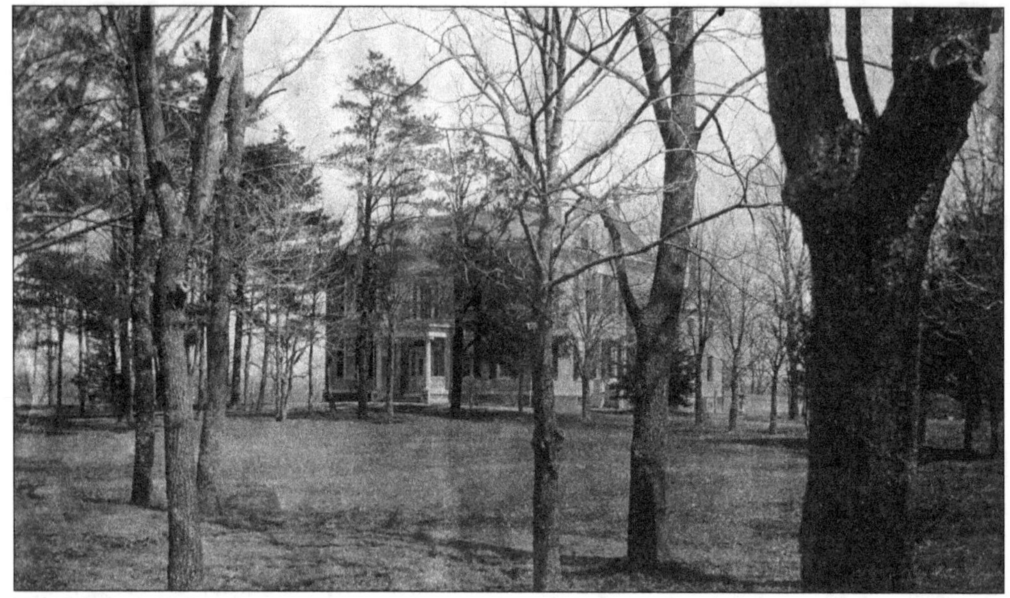

The Lathrop House is seen here in an original cyanotype image, possibly of Marian Hooker's, in 1895. An 1846 James E. Johnson painting shows Lathrop children Robert "Roby," age 6, and Janet on the stair. The records of the Church of St. John the Evangelist (Stockport) and St. Barnabas (Stottville) burials reads, "Lt. Robert Dunlop Lathrop, of 159th Regiment, New York State Volunteers, killed in battle at Irish Bend, St. Mary's Parish, Louisiana. April 14, 1863. Son of Capt. Gideon Lathrop."

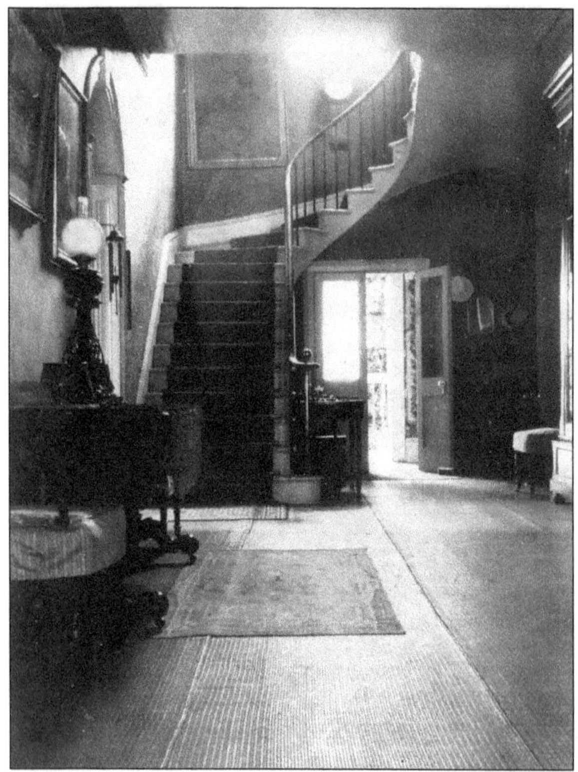

The lower hall at Lathrop House is seen here. Robert "Roby" was initially buried near the site of the battle he died in, in Franklin, Louisiana. Capt. Gideon Lathrop traveled to Louisiana after his death, and Roby's body was brought home and buried in "Grandfather Dunlop's lot" at Albany Rural Cemetery. Gideon Lathrop's diaries, which recount the loss to the family, are at the Columbia County Historical Society in Kinderhook. (Courtesy Peter Stott.)

Along with the diaries of Capt. Gideon Lathrop (1805–1877, seen at right), the Columbia County Historical Society has the James E. Johnson portrait of the captain's son Roby (age 6) and his sister Janet Andrews Lathrop. It depicts Roby pointing in the distance to his father's steamboat, possibly the *North America*. The "Grandma Lathrop" reference is to Gordon Stott's great-grandmother, Gideon's widow, Elizabeth Dunlop Lathrop (1815–1895, seen below). Note the Chinese wallpaper. (Courtesy Peter Stott.)

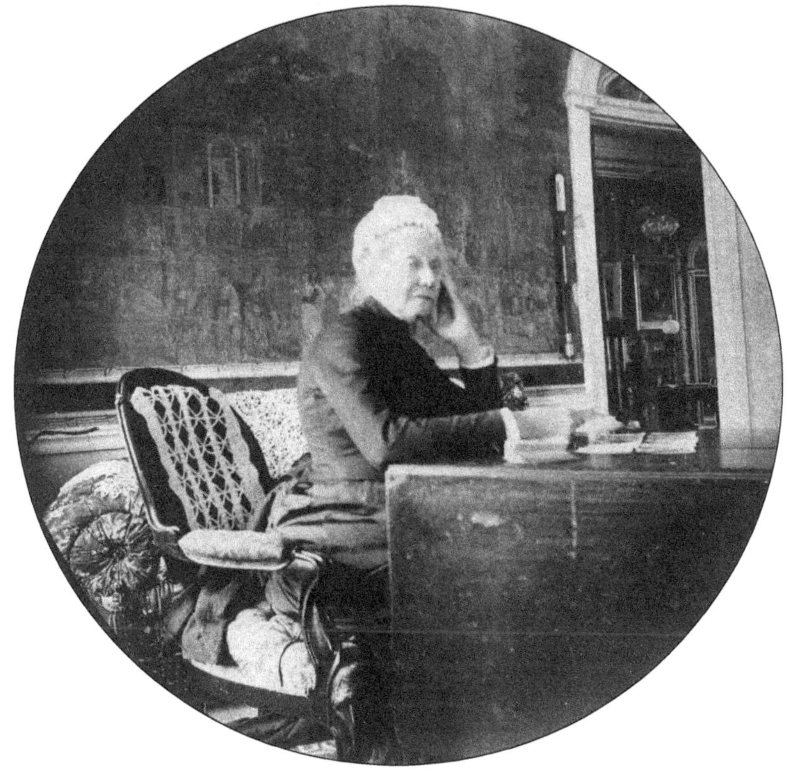

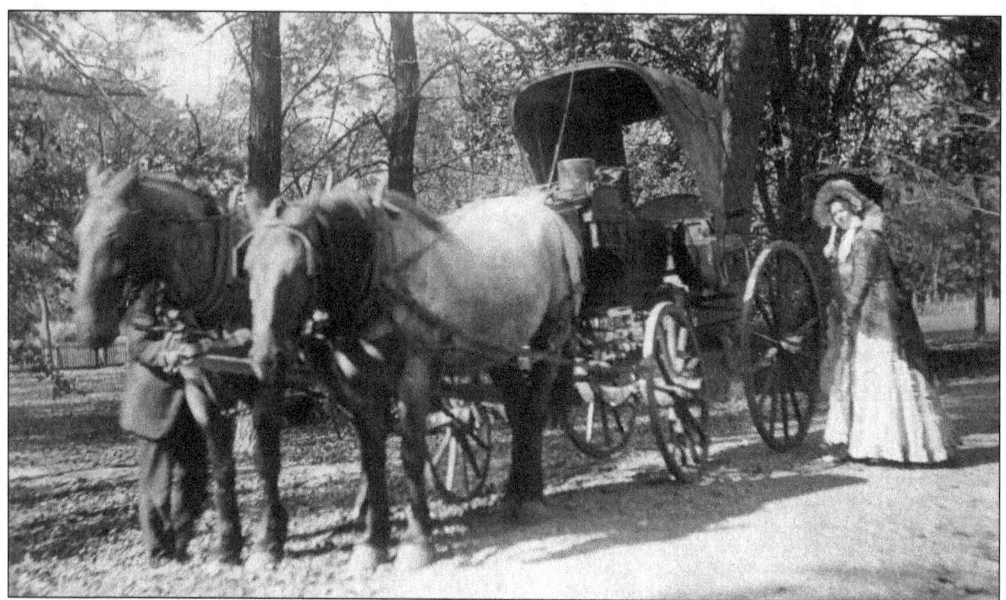

The caption for this photograph reads, "Old coach Stockport house, Aunt Florence Lathrop in it." This is a reference to Florence Campbell Trenholm Lathrop (1868–1957), the wife of "Uncle Alex," the youngest of the five children of Gideon Lathrop. Also written on the reverse is, "Elizabeth Dunlop Lathrop on porch at Stockport with Uncle Alex's dog 'Grouse.' "

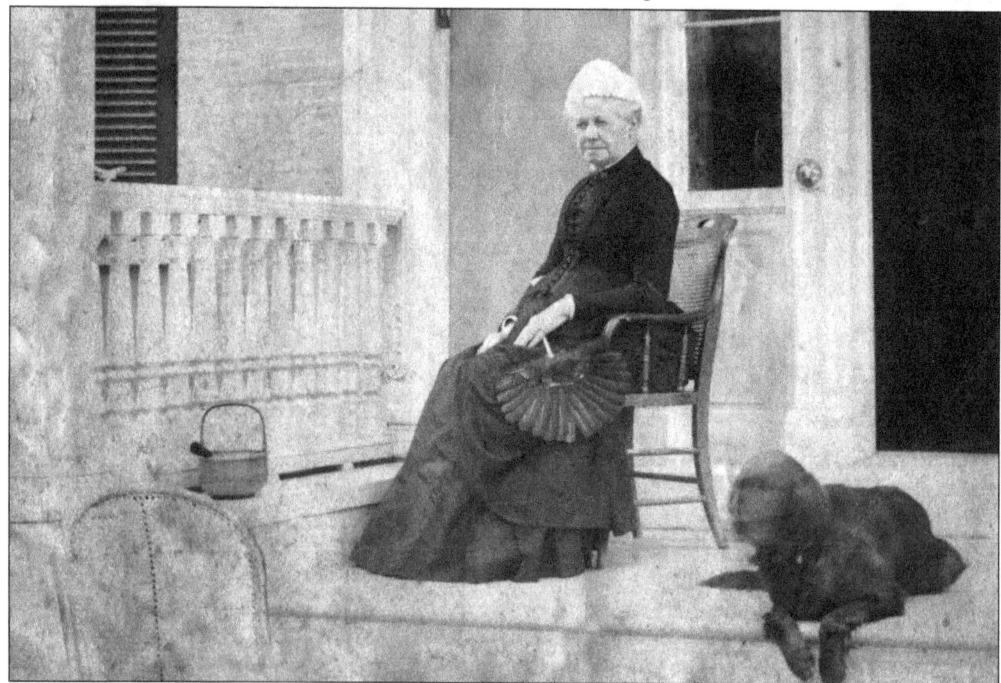

An 1884 Lathrop family diary includes the following: "Elizabeth was daughter of Robert Dunlop, who came from Scotland and settled in Albany. After marriage to Gideon Lathrop 1837, they lived a few years in Vermont, where Helen Elizabeth and Robert Dunlop were born. By 1843 they had removed to Albany where Janet Andrews and Archibald Dunlop were born. They settled in Stockport." (Courtesy Peter Stott.)

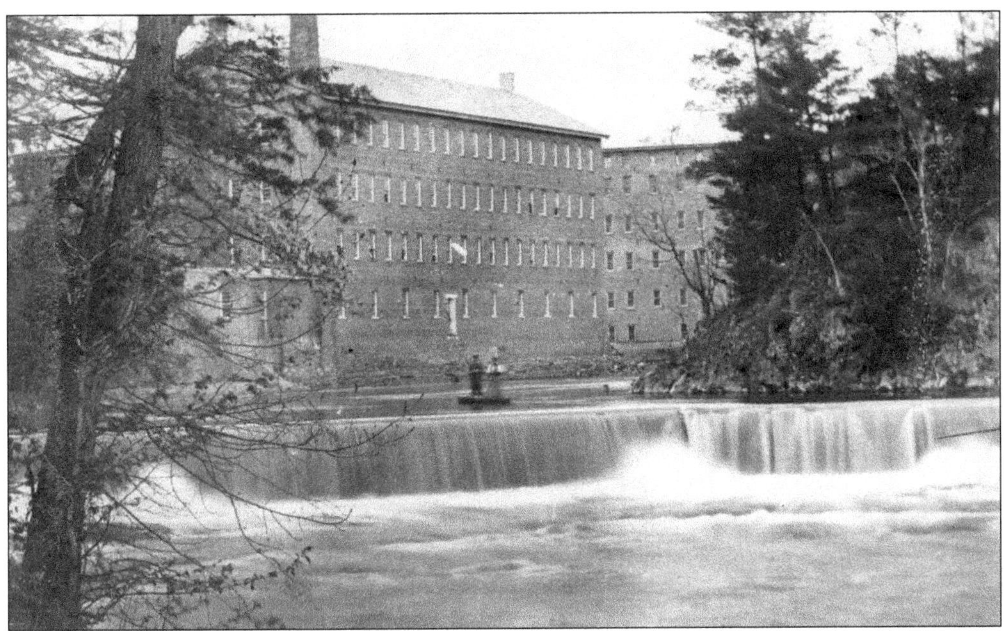

The former Stottville Mills are seen here, with two figures standing near the falls. Stottville enjoyed prosperity from 120 years of textile manufacturing powered by water from the creek. Jonathan Stott's mills produced felt from wool, supplying Union army uniforms during the Civil War. Augustus Juilliard, who later endowed the Juilliard School of Music in New York, bought the mills, and his firm successfully ran them through World War I. (Courtesy Jon Meredith.)

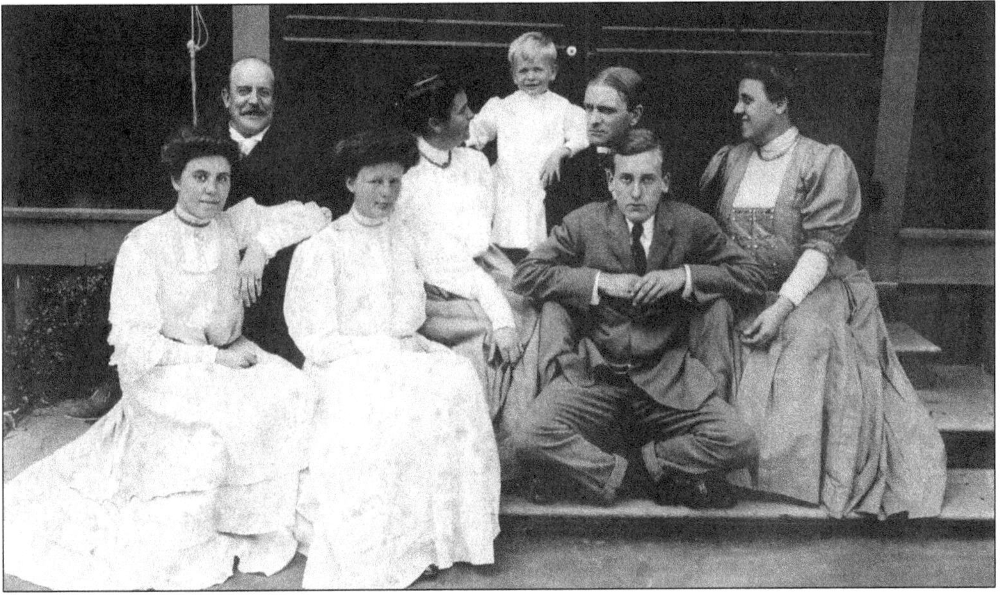

Helen Elizabeth "Lizzie" Lathrop Stott (1837–1907) was the daughter of Capt. Gideon Lathrop. In 1856 in Stockport, she married Francis Horatio Stott, son of woolen mill owner Jonathan Stott, who operated mills in Stottville. The family's strong Stockport connections brought strong links between St. Barnabas in Stottville and the Church of St. John the Evangelist in Stockport, where Francis Stott was a vestryman. Helen is buried in the cemetery of St. John the Evangelist. (Courtesy Peter Stott.)

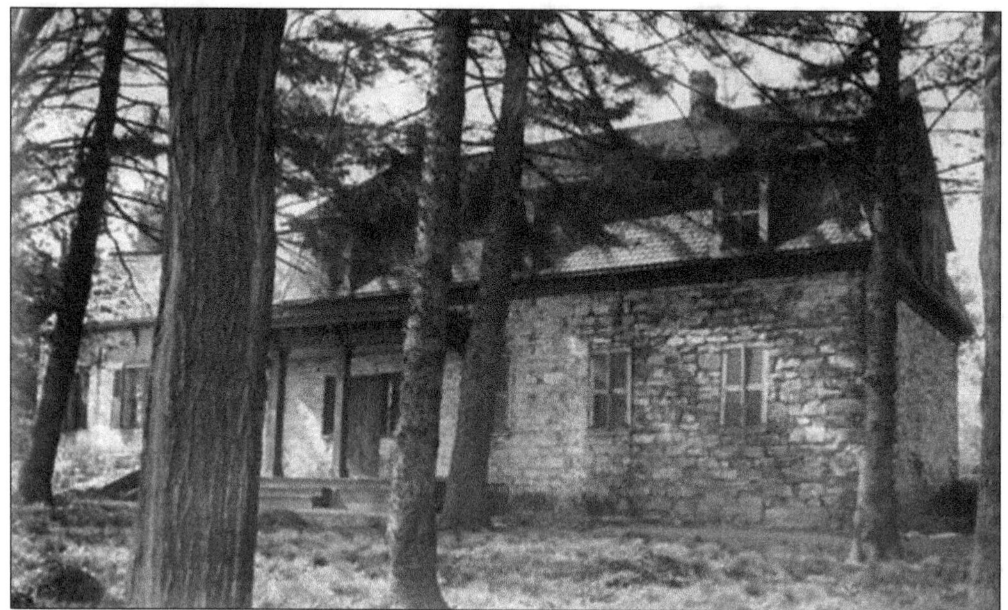

The Abraham Staats House, constructed in 1665 with three-foot-thick stone walls, was burned by Indians but quickly rebuilt. It still stands today on Station Road. Staats's original tenant was killed and his wife was carried off by Indians. The Staats House is located near the Columbiaville bridge and the nearby railroad tracks. Stockport was originally included in the Powell and Kinderhook grants made to Maj. Abraham Staats in 1667.

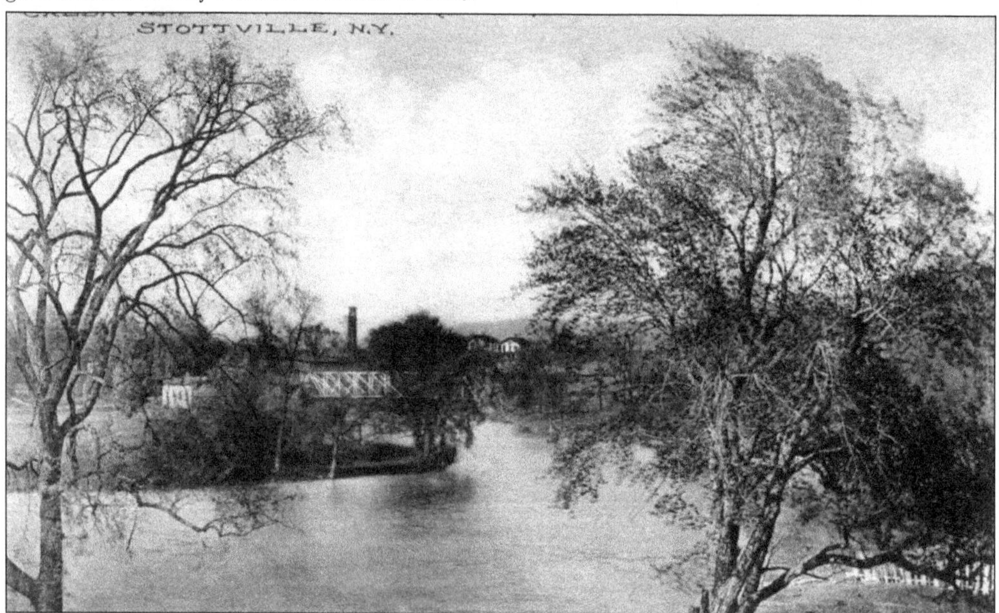

This 1914 hand-colored postcard shows a creek view from the old stone quarry in Stottville. Major Staats was the surgeon to the West India Company and the garrison in Albany in 1643. He was among the earliest immigrants from Holland to America and had a fur-trading business. The Abraham Staats House is the oldest home in the county. Capt. Franklin Ellis reported in 1878 that 25 bushels of Indian artifacts had been found near the house, including axes, arrowheads, and other items. (Courtesy Historic Hudson and the author.)

Three

OLANA

An artist's home is his sanctuary. Olana was Frederic Church's sanctuary, cocoon, and retreat from the world after the heart-wrenching loss he faced as a parent losing a child. He and his wife grieved the loss of their two children to diphtheria in 1865.

Church achieved fame throughout America for his art, living a very well-traveled, wealthy existence. A student of Thomas Cole, he made his professional debut as an artist at New York's National Academy of Design at age 19, and he was fully accepted as a member by 23. He was, and still is, the youngest painter ever to do so. Thousands of people lined the block paying to see his work when it was exhibited.

America's first art movement started here, in Hudson and the Catskills. The Hudson River School was not a guild or college, but rather a group of kindred souls who painted in a similar style. Thomas Cole is known to be its founder. Cole and Church were friends who sometimes traveled together, and Church was the only Hudson River School painter to study with Cole. Their subjects were mostly surrounding landscapes. Cole, an English-born artist, was used to autumn colors being much drabber than in the Catskills during fall. When Queen Victoria viewed Jasper Cropsey's *Autumn–On the Hudson River* in London, she could "not believe her eyes." Being told by the queen that he must be exaggerating, Cropsey had fall leaves shipped to England to convince her that these colors did exist in the Hudson Valley in fall. Words used to describe the composition of some Hudson River School paintings have included wild, dark, eerie, hallucinogenic, foreboding, exaggerated color, tranquil, calm, and with a sense of hope. This art movement dominated American art for most of 50 years. By the 1870s, though, Hudson River School painters drew criticism for being too "literal and grandiose" in depicting American landscapes.

Curators of art have called Olana "the single most important artistic residence in America and one of the most significant in the world." Olana should be seen and felt in person to appreciate the creative genius that went into designing its opulence: intricate details, collections, and views. When he could no longer paint as he neared the end of his life, Church worked on his masterpiece: Olana.

Leaving a lasting artistic legacy, Frederic Church and fellow Hudson River School painter Sanford Robinson Gifford were among the original founders of the Metropolitan Museum of Art in New York City.

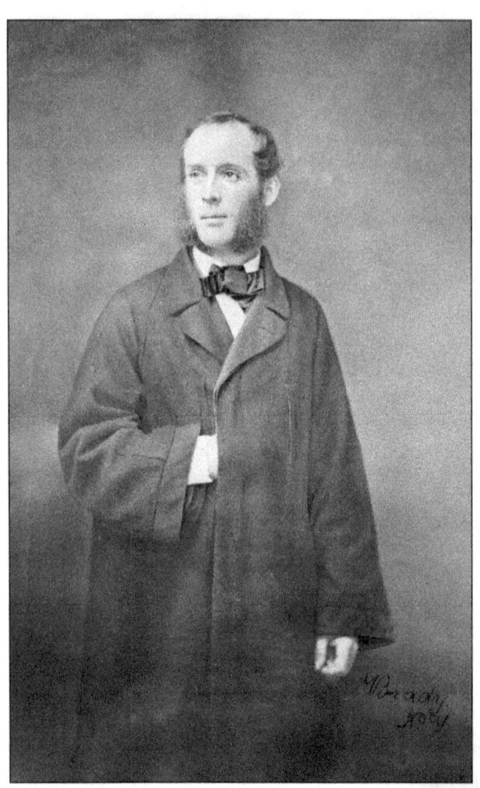

Frederic Edwin Church moved to Hudson in 1860 and then built his home, Olana, his version of a Persian villa, after many trips to the Far East. Church made many paintings from his exceptional hilltop views of the Hudson Valley, in all seasons. With an inspirational view to this day, Olana still attracts many painters and photographers capturing their own perspectives.

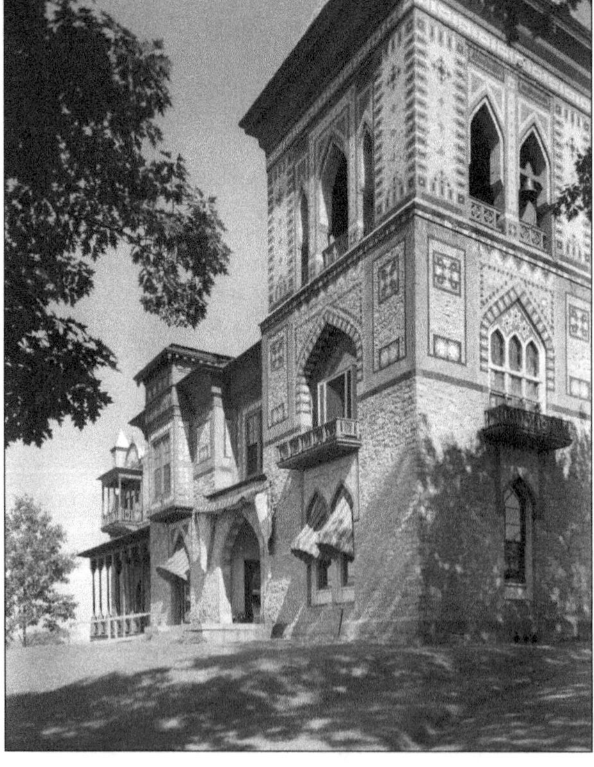

At Olana, on Mount Merino, the first and only pothole of its kind known in America was found, similar to what have been found in the Swiss Alps. This hole was eight feet in diameter and over 25 feet deep, with a hard slate bottom and sides as smooth as if they had been artificially polished.

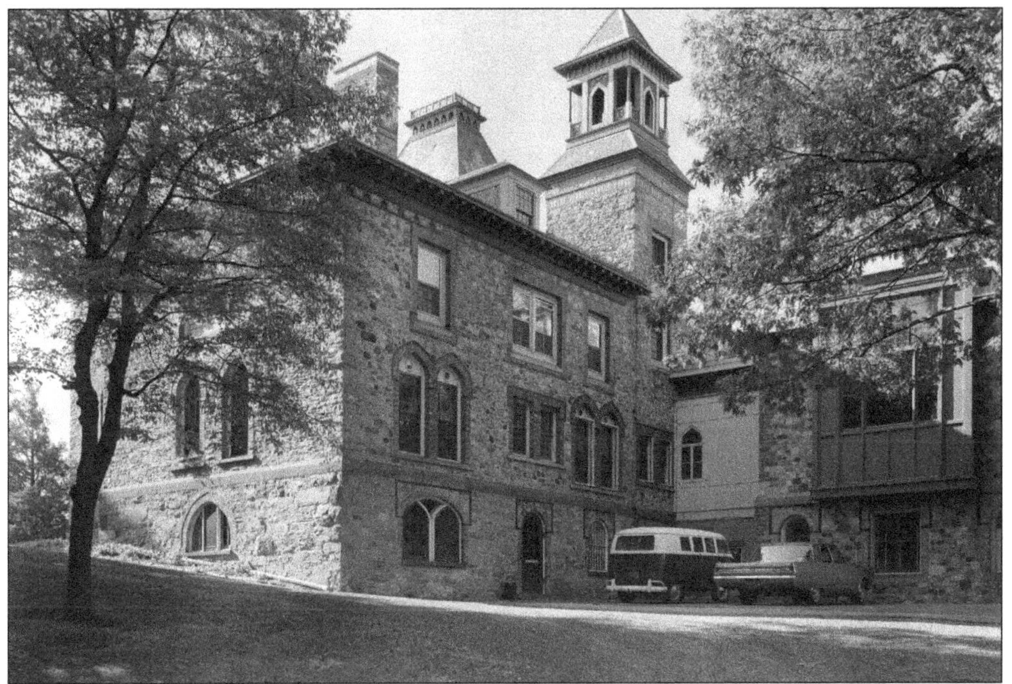

This is a rear view of Olana, the home and estate of Frederic Church. It is now a New York State Historical Site and National Landmark. Church's paintings characterized "a calmness and sense of hope," according to the Olana website.

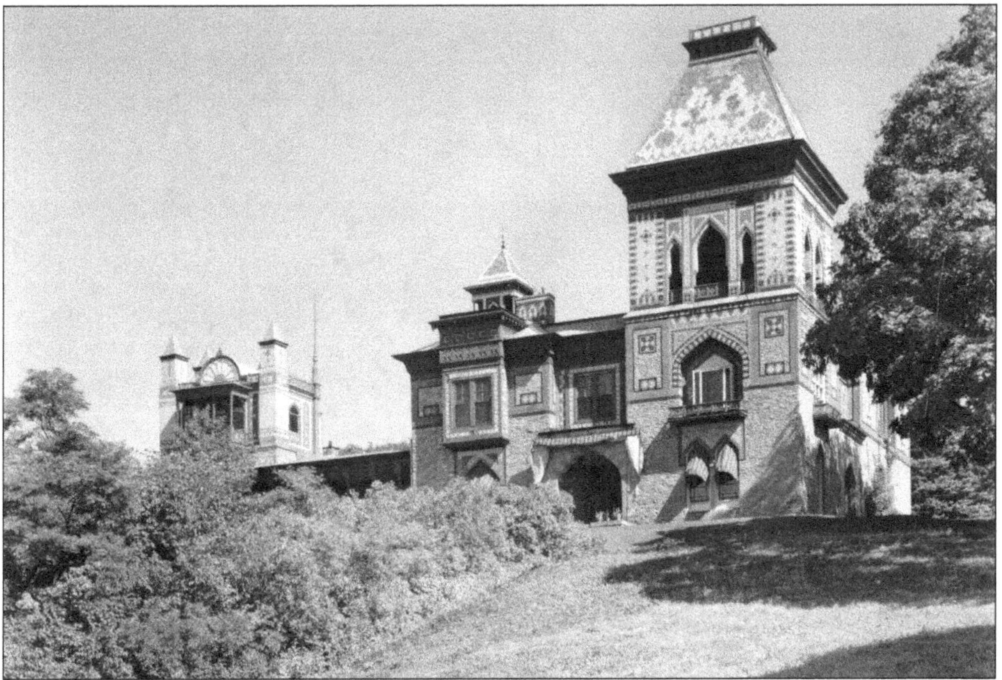

This is a general southwest view of Olana facing Route 9G. Church's wife, Isabel, named the estate Olana. It is an old Latin name for a place in Persia. Built up high on a hill near Hudson from 1870 to 1891, Olana appears as a fortress.

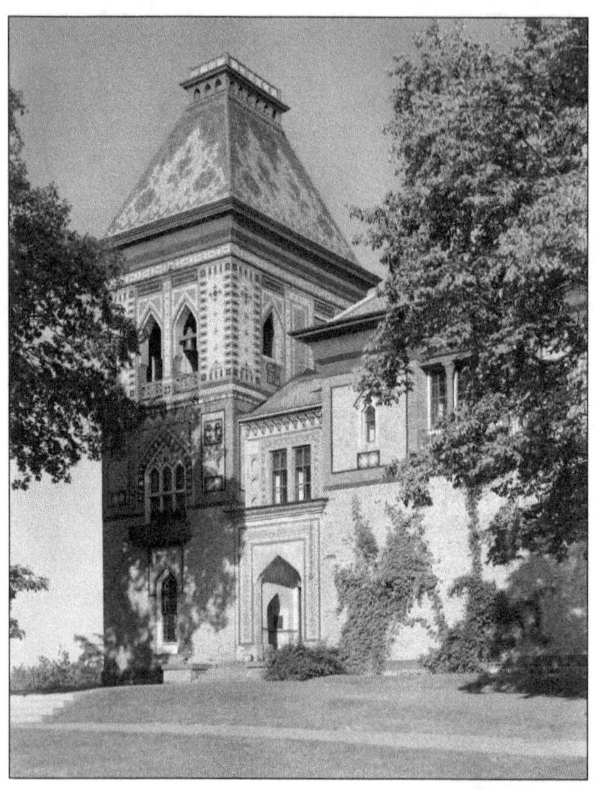

This southeast view shows the front elevation of Olana. Church called his home and creation "the Center of the World." With stunning views of the Catskill Mountains, the Taconic Hills, and the Hudson River, the 250-acre estate and house are Church's masterpieces.

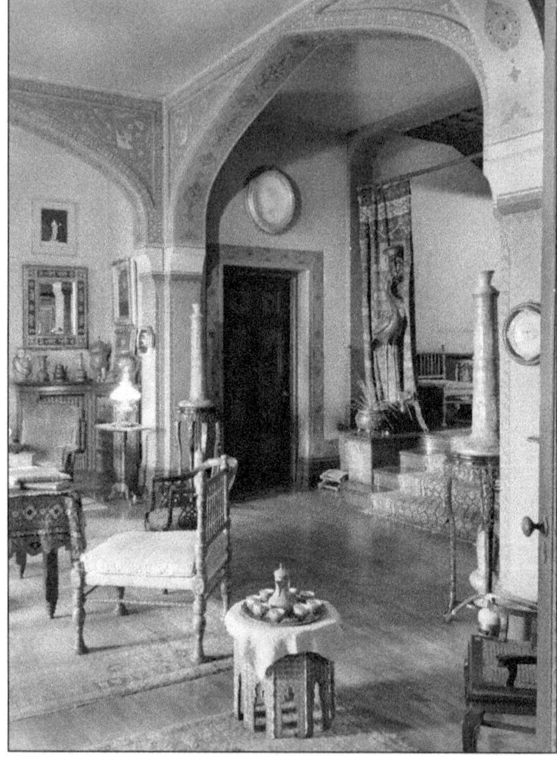

The court hall at Olana is on the first floor. In the fall of 1872, Church and his wife and children moved into the second story of the house while work and decoration was done to the main floor. The Churches collected thousands of objects from their travels to furnish Olana. Colors in the court hall's walls and stencils are yellow, purple, red, coral, salmon, gold-brown, and green.

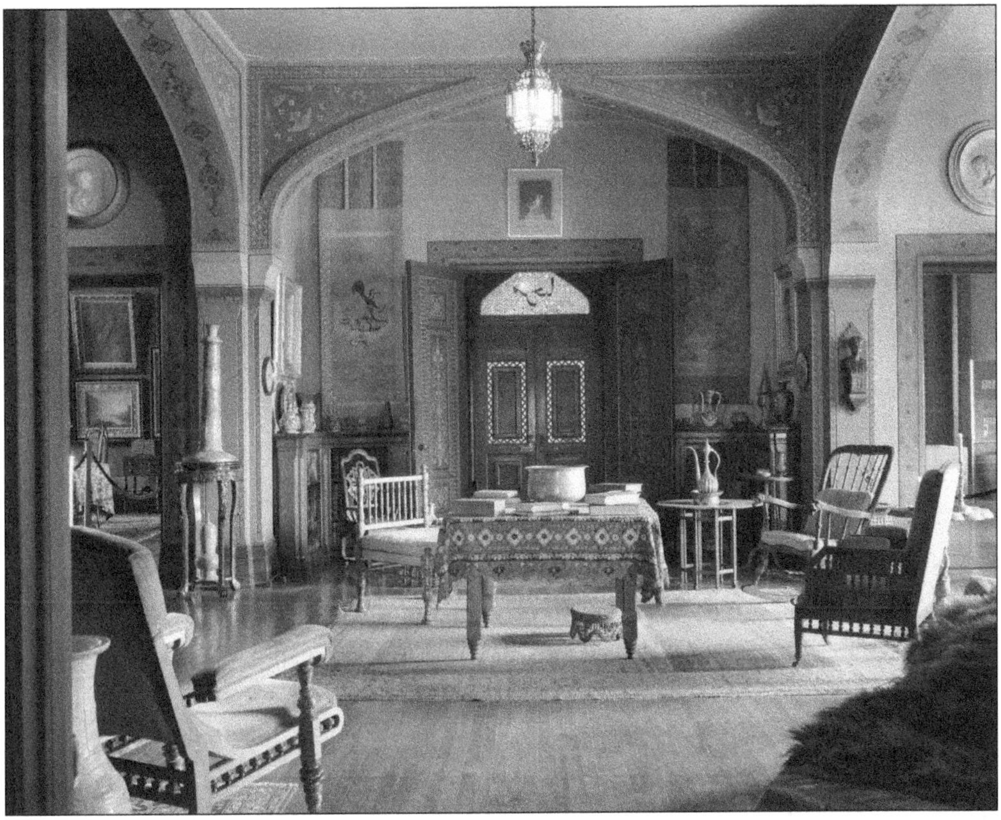

The court hall at Olana is seen in this photograph looking toward the main entrance. It includes a detail of the mantel at Olana. The contents of the house, acquired by Church over a 30-year period, include furniture, tapestries, bronzes, rugs, paintings, sculptures, and a host of other objects from past civilizations and religions.

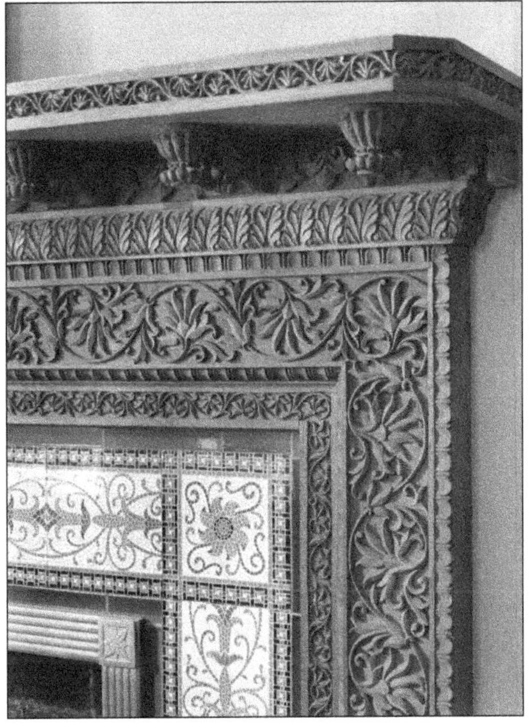

The color scheme and stenciling designed by Church in 1870 remain today. In 1889, Church closed his New York City studio of 30 years and shipped the contents to Olana. This included a gilded Buddha, a polychromed Madonna, ancient armor, fragments of the Parthenon, and stones from Petra. At first glance, the interior resembles the chamber of King Tutankhamun. There is some speculation that Church may have unintentionally created a tomb-like fortress after the loss of his children, akin to a gathering of possessions for the afterlife.

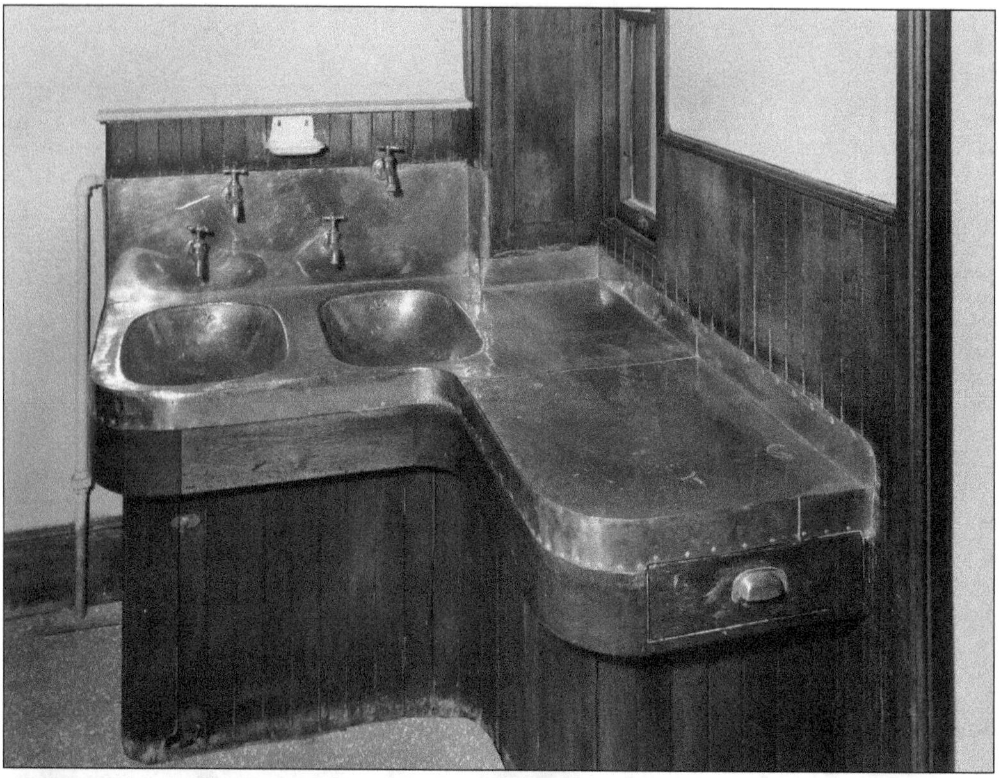

This east-facing photograph shows the sink in the butler's pantry. Tours at Olana include the servants' quarters, which are unrestored and include interpretive panels and the history of the four or five servants who worked there. Also described is how the household was run and managed to allow the Churches and their guests the comfort and lifestyle they were accustomed to.

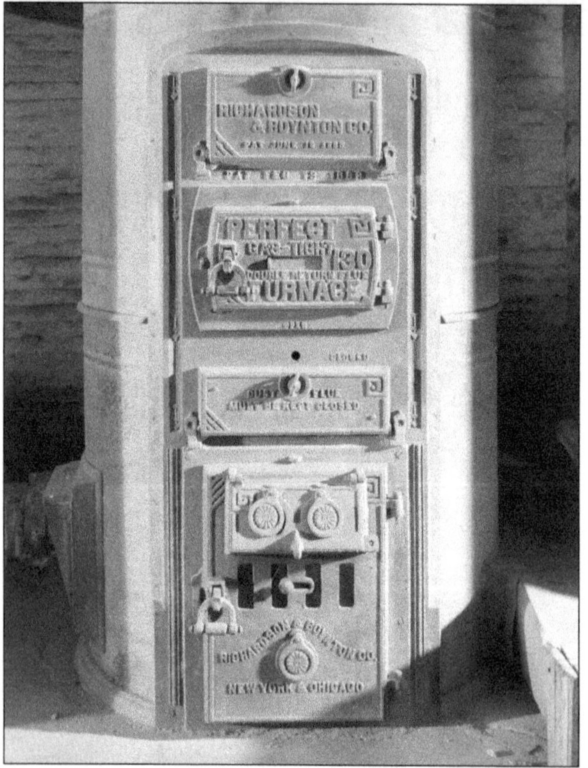

This is the wood-burning hot-air furnace in the basement at Olana. When Church died in 1900, the house was left to his son, whose wife ordered the servants to dust all the belongings but not move any of them. The Olana Partnership previously maintained cramped offices on the second floor and held meetings in the servants' dining room before the Cosy Cottage on the estate was restored to house the partnership.

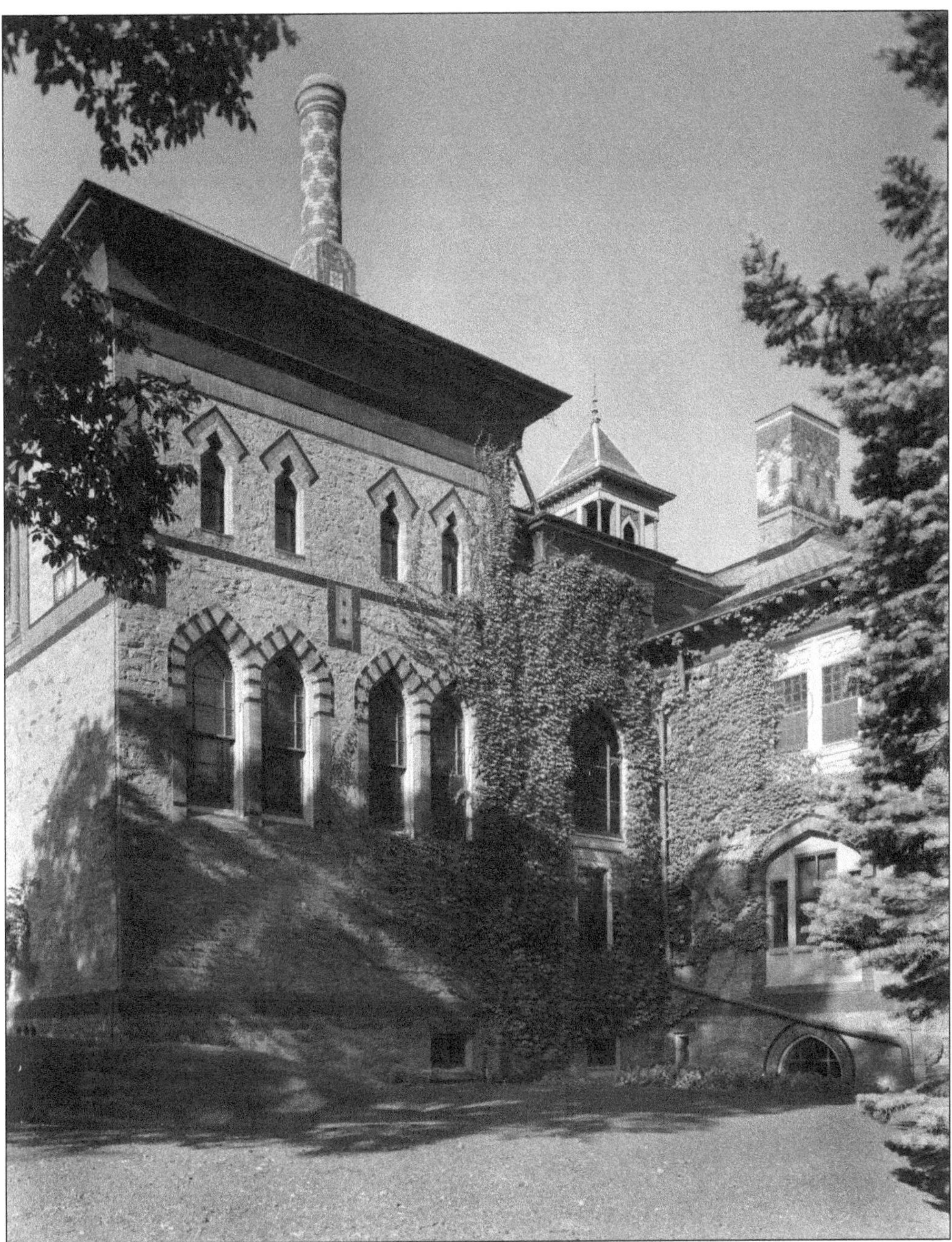

This photograph shows the rear side elevation at Olana. Church said, "I designed the house myself. It is Persian in style, a Feudal Castle adapted to the climate and the requirements of modern life. The interior decorations and fittings are all in harmony with the external architecture. It stands at an elevation of six hundred feet above the Hudson River and commands beautiful views. The noble River expands to a width of over two miles forming a lakelike sheet of water which is always dotted with steamers and other craft. Almost an hour this side of Albany is the Center of the World—I own it—I am all alone . . . enjoying a nice wood fire and thinking how thankful I ought to be to have travelled and returned with my family all well."

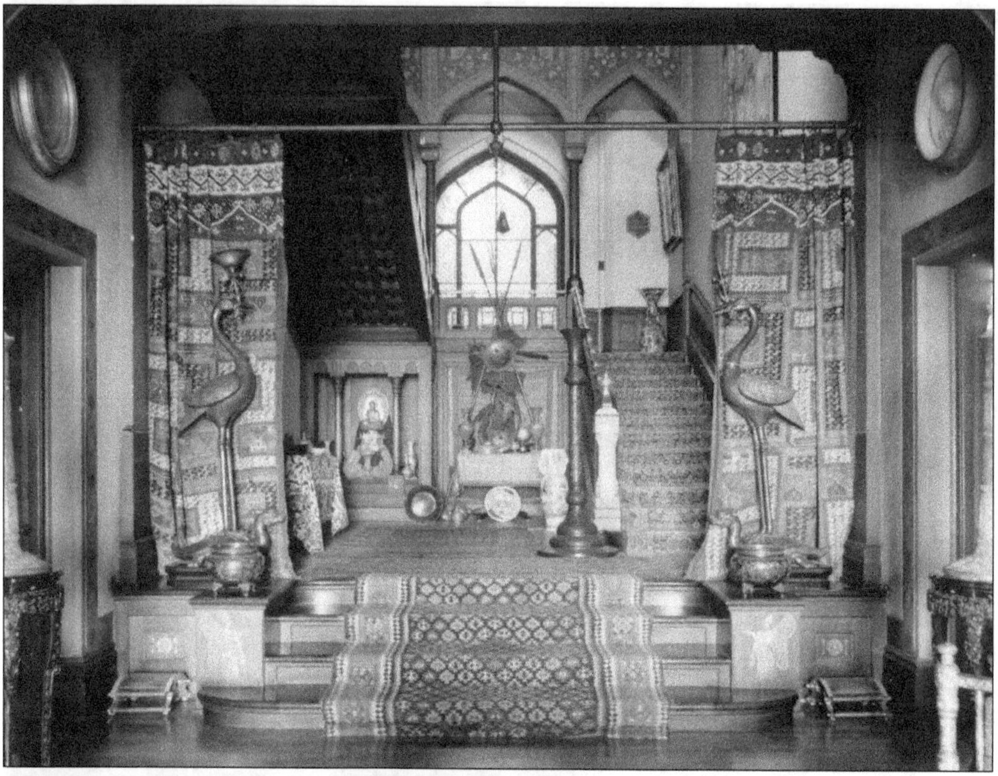

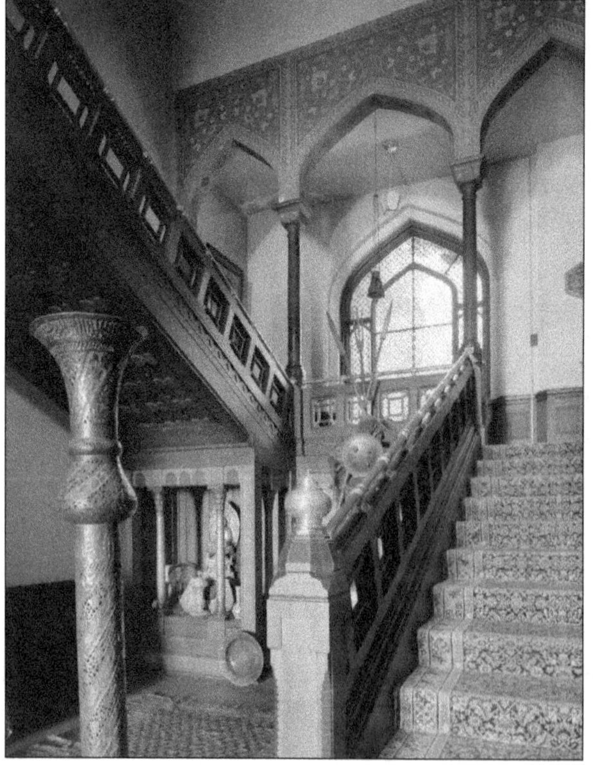

The main staircase and detail from it, from the court hall to the second floor, are seen in this northeast view at Olana. The court hall and its landing were sometimes used by the Church family and guests as a theatrical performance space and stage, with the children acting out skits. The colors on the vast Islamic arches are repeated throughout the house. The completion of woodwork and painted decoration on the first floor required at least four years.

Colors were derived from Church's own palette. They were unusual and difficult to produce, but they had to be meticulously used by contractors in stenciled patterns for doors and moldings. A vast collection of sketches for both stencils and color swatches remains, possibly inspired by a house seen in Damascus. The court hall organizes the house both spatially and visually, and it is the artistic center as well.

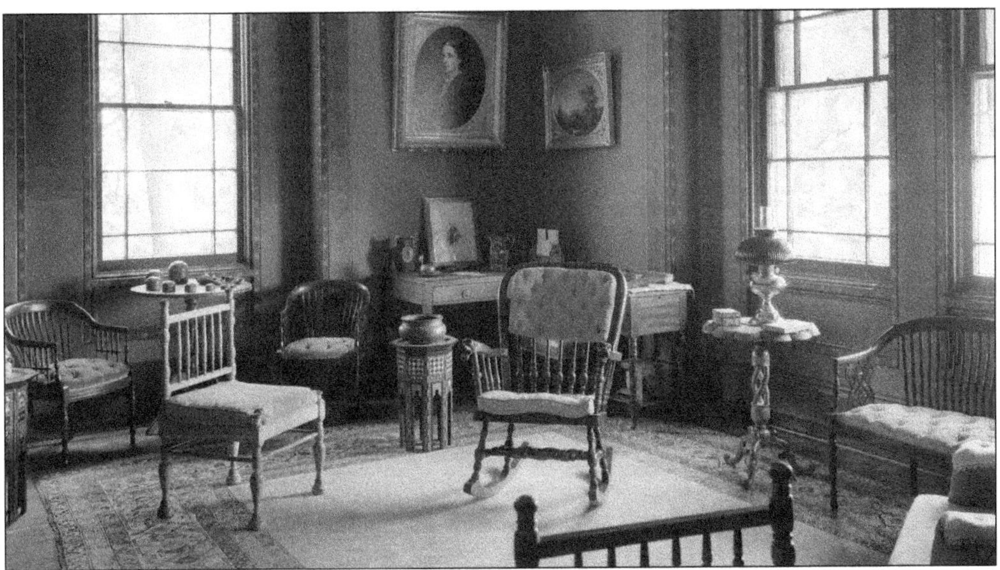

The parlor at the south corner of Olana on the first floor is seen here. Church prepared hundreds of architectural sketches. Many contain drawings of elements such as moldings, finials, staircases, brick and tile patterns, and geometric or leaf and floral designs for the stencils to cover interior walls and exterior cornices. The walls were canvases, and each window in the house was a frame to encapsulate a landscape painting.

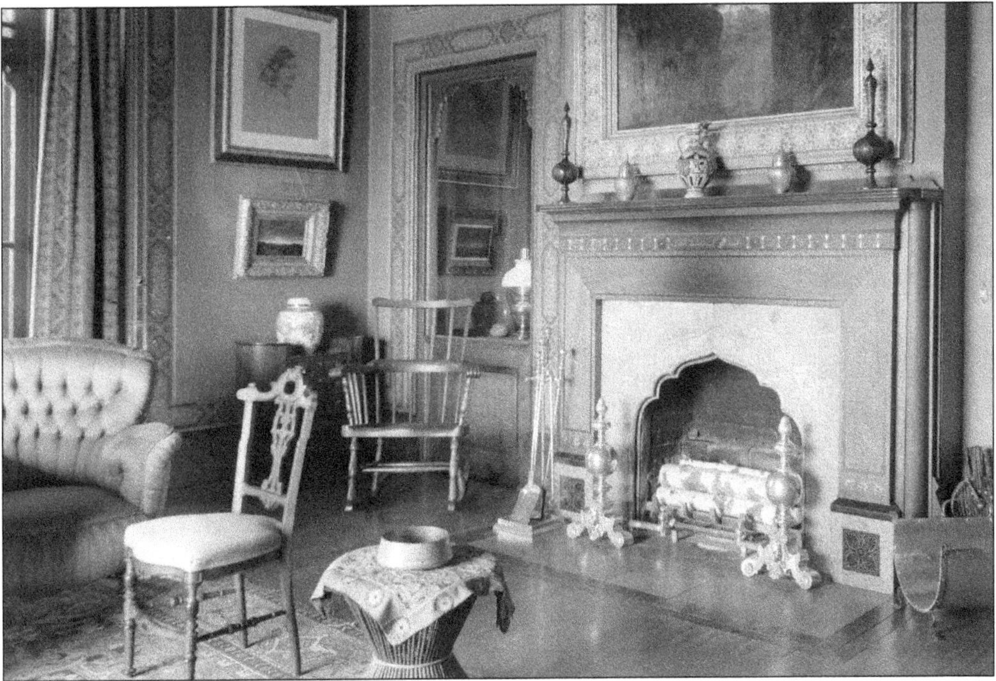

The first-floor sitting room in the west corner of Olana is seen here. This image from the early 1900s shows a differently furnished room than is seen in other, later publications. The mantel clock and the drapes here are missing in later photographs. Those photographs also show George Baker's 1860 painting of Church's future wife, Isabel, in this room, although it must have been elsewhere in the house at one time.

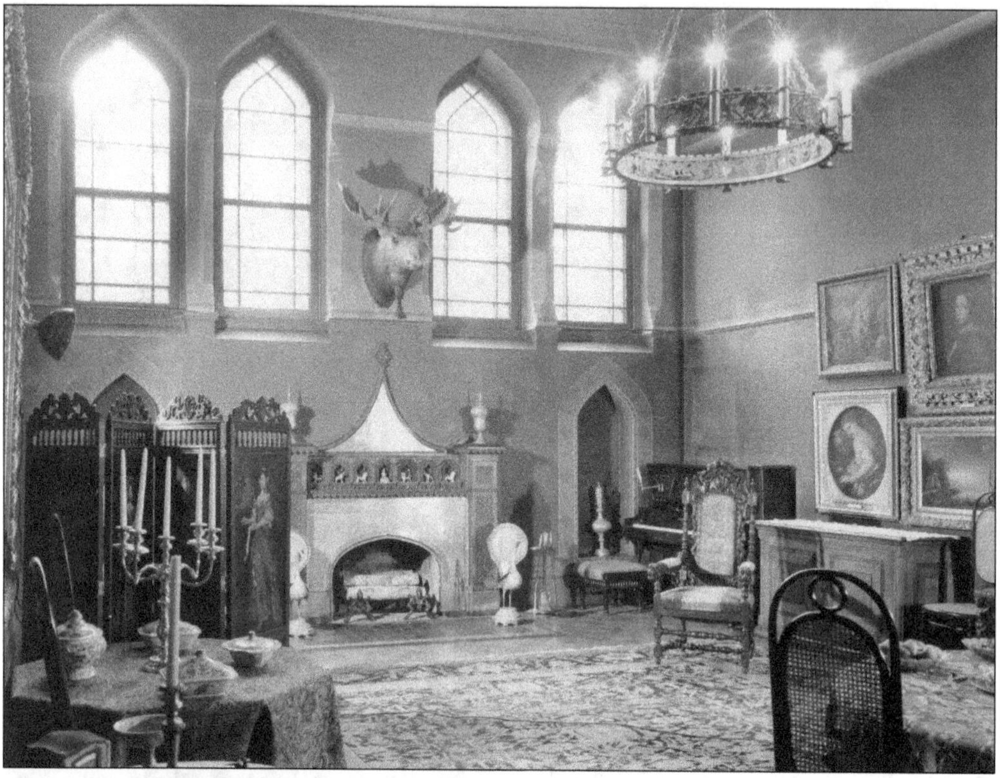

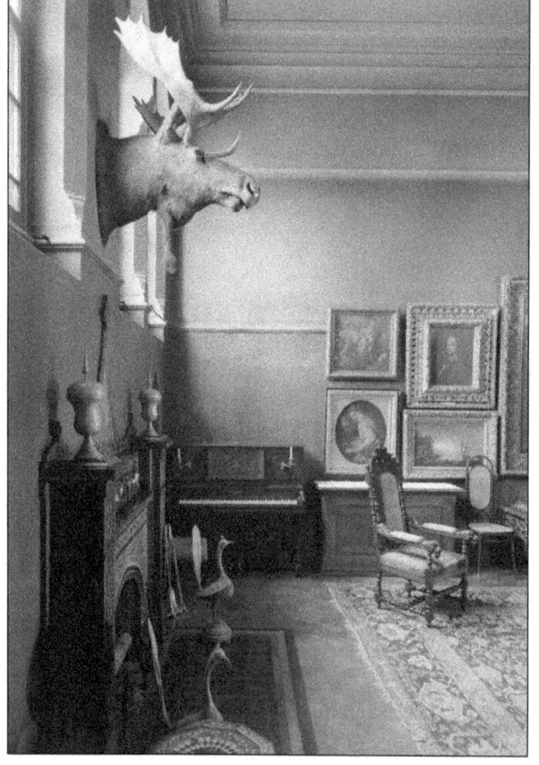

The dining room at Olana is seen here in a southeast view. This image from the early 1900s shows a mounted trophy animal and a chandelier, which are not shown in later photographs of this room in other publications. Robert and Emily de Forest's 1884 image *Dining Room Picture Gallery, Olana, October 11* also does not show the chandelier. Most images do show the small, beautifully ornate, wood-inlay table.

Rooms were furnished with esoteric items such as painted Kashmiri tables and chairs, Shaker rockers, rococo revival furniture inherited from Church's father, Persian and Syrian metal ware, South American birds, butterflies, Turkish rigs, and furniture made from Church's designs. Objects within the house are not considered valuable but rather visually appealing. In Damascus, the Churches had visited the home of an English aristocrat whose parlor may have served as the inspiration for theirs.

At right is the library looking towards the dining room, and below is the dining room mantel and alcove. In a letter to artist John Ferguson Weir, Church wrote, "I hope to be in New York in a week or so—but a Feudal Castle which I am building—under the modest name of a dwelling house—absorbs all my time and attention. I am obliged to watch it so closely—for having undertaken to get my architecture from Persia where I have never been—I am obliged to imagine Persian architecture—then embody it on paper and explain it to a lot of mechanics whose ideal of architecture is wrapped up in felicitous recollections of a successful brick school house or meeting house or jail." The Oriental motifs were extracted from books on Persian architecture that Church bought for his library.

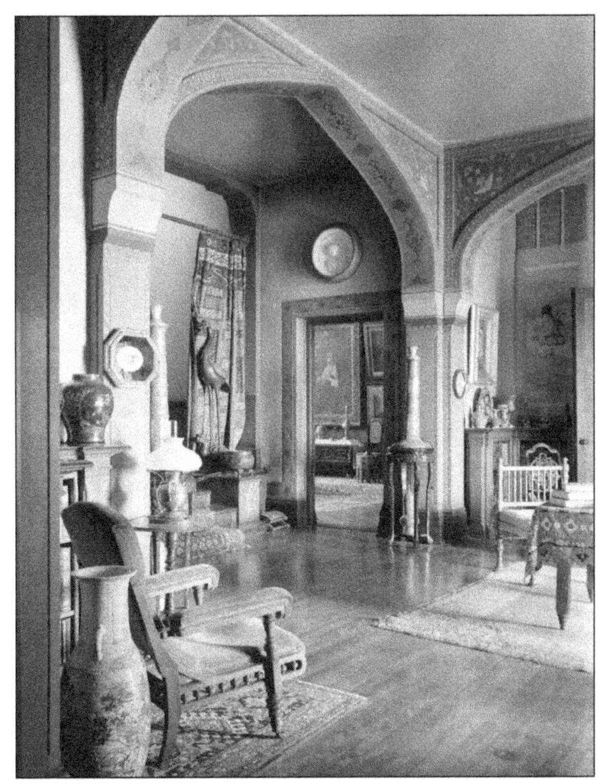

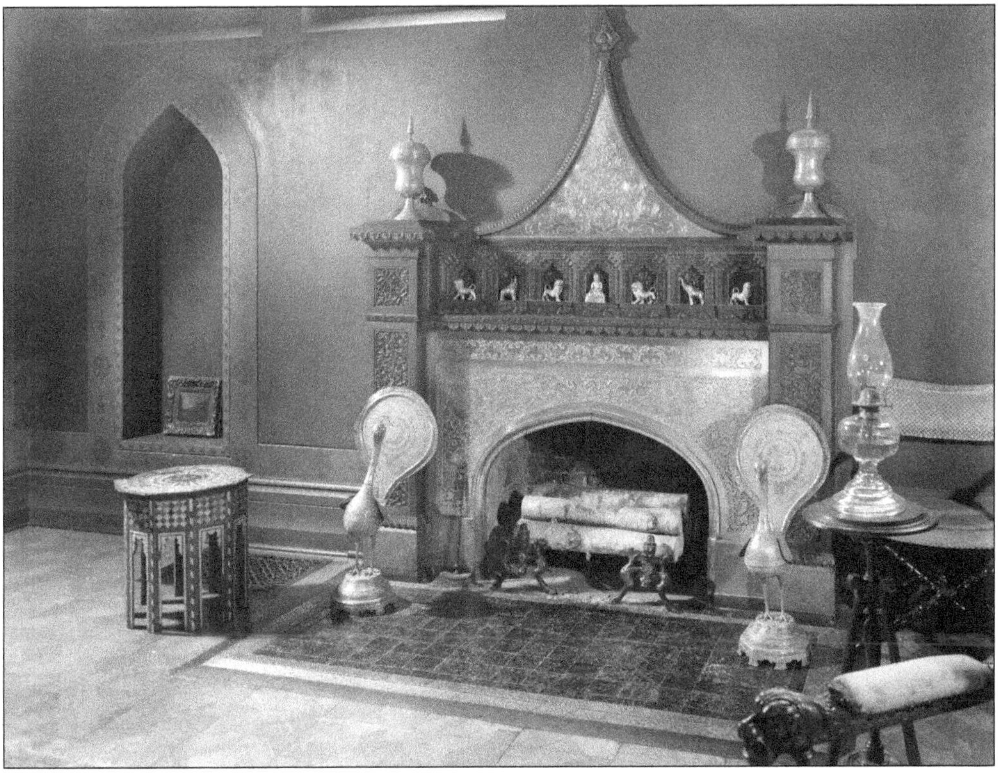

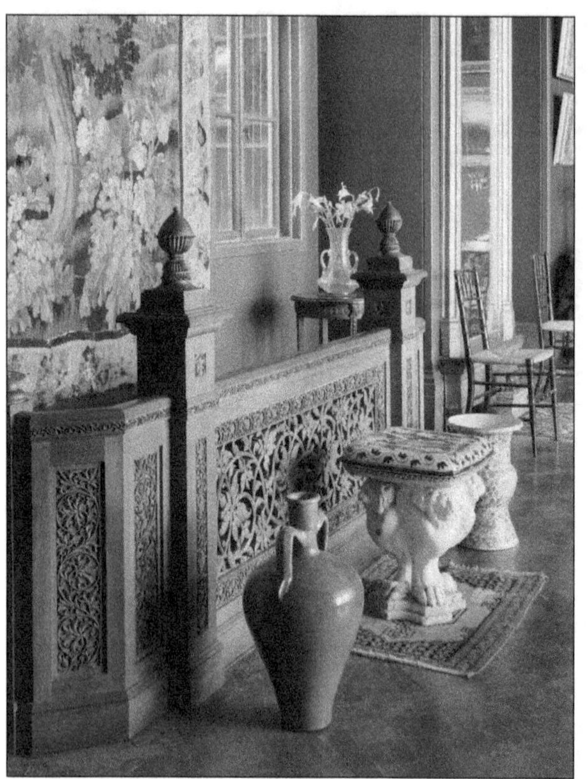

Seen here are the stair railing in the gallery, looking east, and the interior of the studio from the south, on the first floor at Olana. In 1888, Church became unhappy with his rheumatism and because of the waning interest in the Hudson River School painters, as the popularity of the Barbizon painters increased, he turned his creative energies to the construction of a studio wing at Olana.

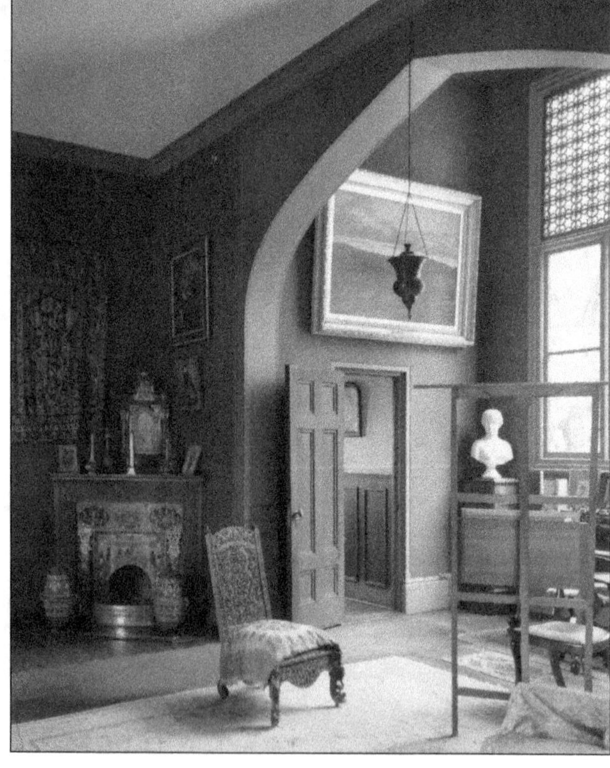

After closing his New York City studio, the new studio wing at Olana took three years to complete. The cost ran to $30,000. Since Church now did less drawing, he had to explain more to his contractors about what he wished his studio to encompass. This new project would give him a renewed interest and energy to paint. The new studio wing gave Church back his bliss.

The studio fireplace in the north corner of the first floor is seen at right, and the bathroom located at the northwest corner of the studio, looking south, is seen below. In a letter to a friend, Church wrote, "I inaugurated the New Studio—it is perfect. Filled with enthusiasm I attacked my first canvas and an iceberg scene is the result, the best I think I ever painted and the truest." The studio incorporates a view of the Catskills framed by a gilded Moorish window. According to a friend of Church's at the time, the studio "reflects Church's creative brilliance, his artistic achievements, his knowledge and appreciation of the world around him, and his devotion to his chosen career."

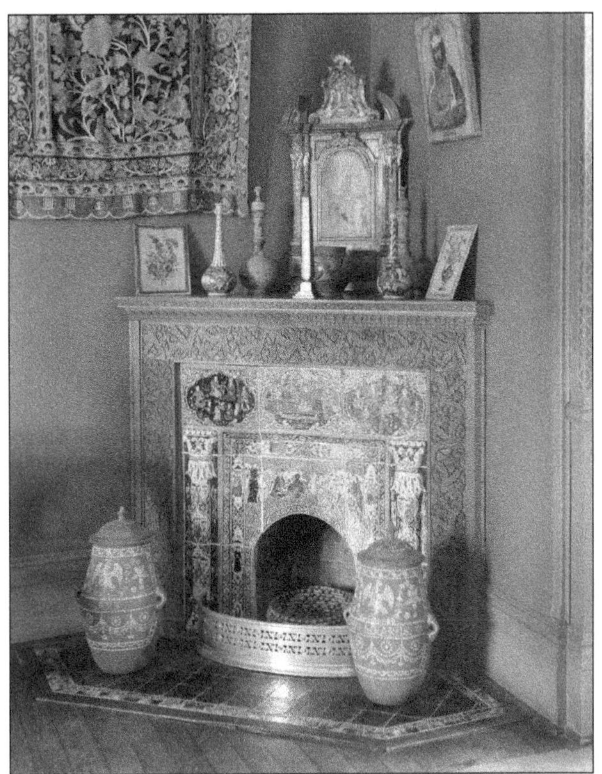

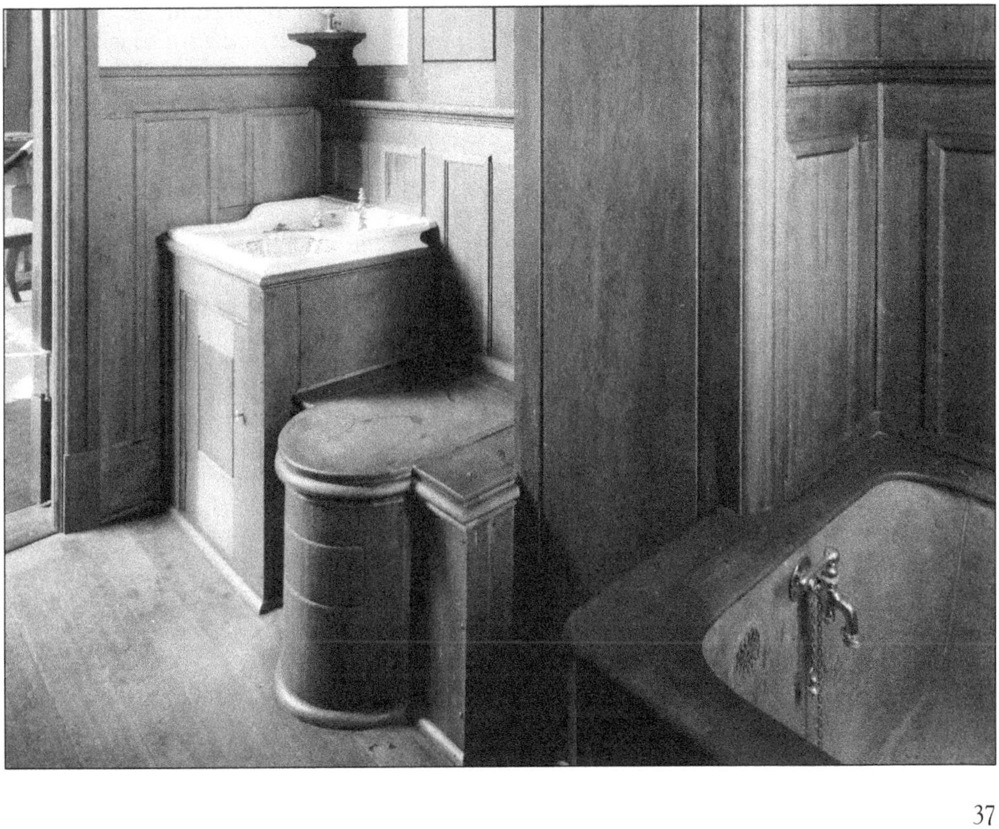

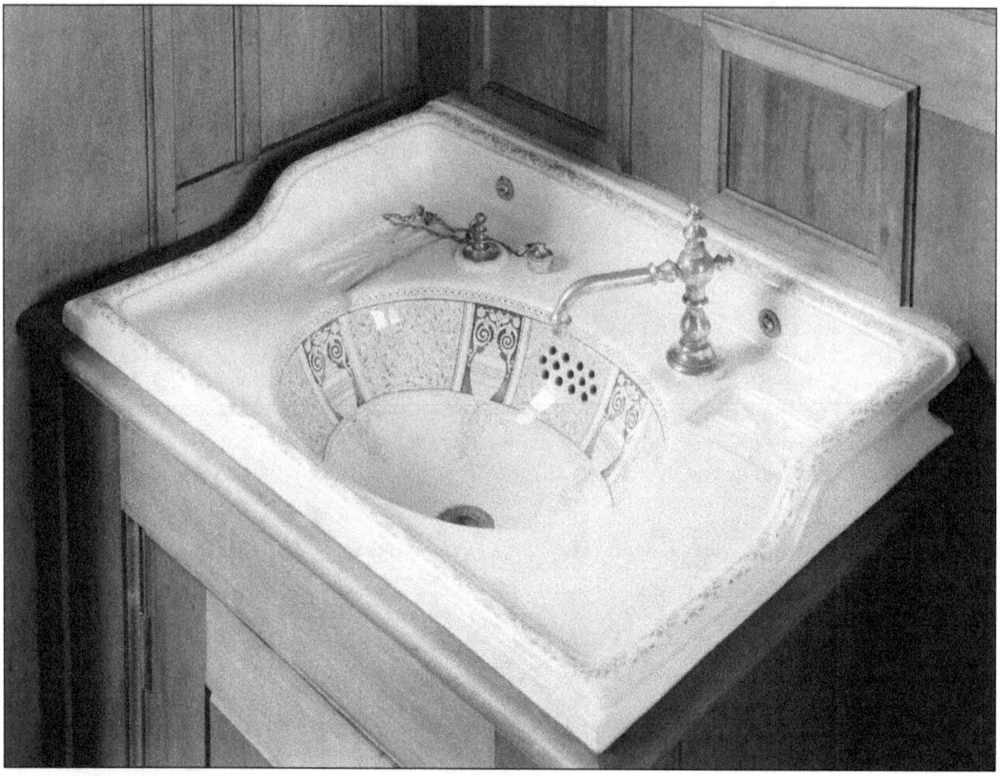

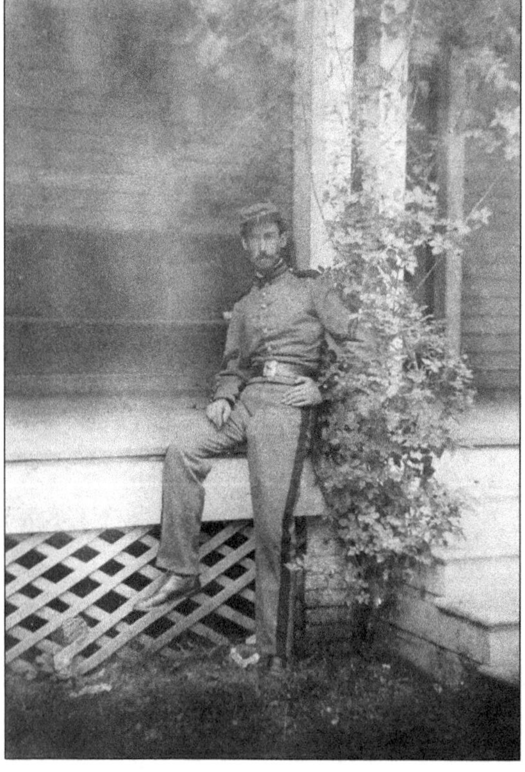

The washbowl in the bathroom in the northwest corner of the studio is seen above. Note the faucet, which turned on and off by swinging the spout left and right. Pictured at left, Sanford Robinson Gifford was born on July 10, 1823, in Greenfield, New York, but spent his childhood in Hudson. He was the only Hudson River School painter to grow up in Hudson. He and Church were among the founders of the Metropolitan Museum of Art in New York City. The image shows Gifford in 1861 as a soldier in the Union army. A prolific artist, Gifford created 700 paintings during his career, and he is regarded as a painter of Luminism, an offshoot of the Hudson River School characterized by an aerial view of its subjects with an emphasis on light and the hiding of brushstrokes, unlike, for example, Impressionism.

Four

EARLY ORIGINS OF THE POLICE AND FIRE DEPARTMENTS

According to Edward Moore of the Hudson City Police Department, "The Hudson City Police Department traces its beginnings to the cold winter's evening of January 5, 1788 when the City Council approved the formation of a 'Night Watch' to preserve order in the city. Since then the Department has evolved into a modern and effective police force. We are proud and confident of our abilities to maintain an orderly environment where citizens may live safely in peace and be secure in their possessions. Our police are mindful that we must serve our citizens in a professional manner, and it is to these people that we are ultimately responsible."

Often during the dark winter season, locals find themselves indoors and taking for granted the enjoyment, warmth, and safety of their homes. During the 1780s, nighttime in winter was often a time of impending doom for citizens of Hudson, where safety was lacking. In those days, streetlamps were only lit on nights with no moon and only lit until midnight, giving criminals free reign. As Hudson grew as a seaport with its whaling ships traveling the world, crime and its consequences grew with it. With so many people coming in and out of Hudson daily, robberies and rowdy drinking were a big problem, creating fear. At that time, the city was not fortified with locks, safes, or window latches, which are taken for granted today. On January 5, 1788, a group of Hudsonians volunteered to form a "Nightwatch" to "protect against thieves and fires, and to preserve and protect order in the city during the night." Originally, the Nightwatch was four citizens for each night, beginning at 9:00 p.m. and continuing until daybreak. Each nightwatchman was provided a large oak club that he would bang against the walkways or horse hitching posts, calling out the hour and an "all's well." In those days, a nightwatchman was empowered to question anyone out at "unreasonable hours" and to confine a suspect in the watch house until daybreak.

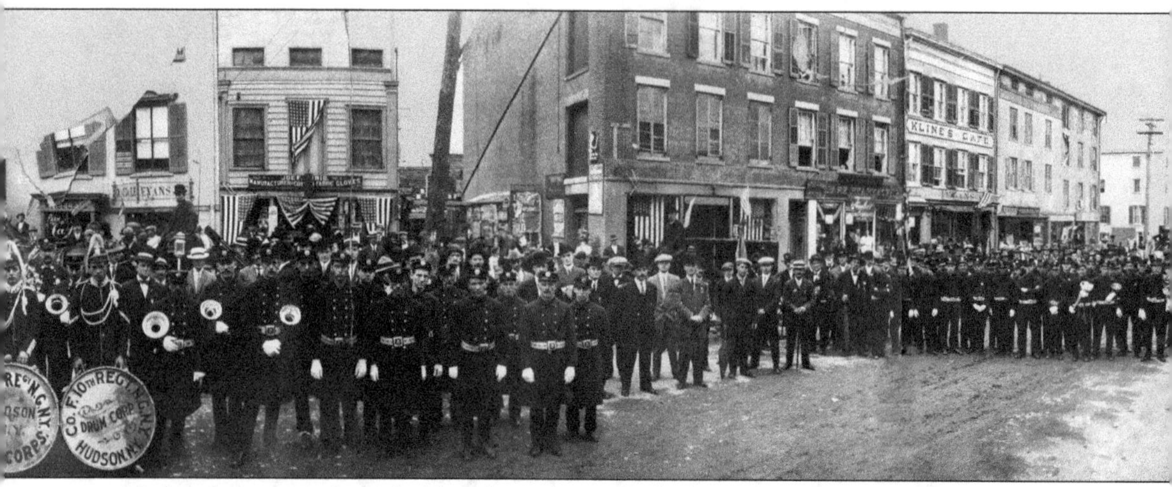

Hudson loves a parade, and its love for such goes back a long time. Since 2010, many more annual parades have come to the city of Hudson. Seen here is the New York National Guard Drum Corps sometime between 1868 and 1880. The photograph was taken on the corner of Warren and Seventh Streets and shows Company F, 10th Regiment, New York National Guard (center), the Hudson Band (far left), and the police and firemen (far right). (Courtesy Historic Hudson.)

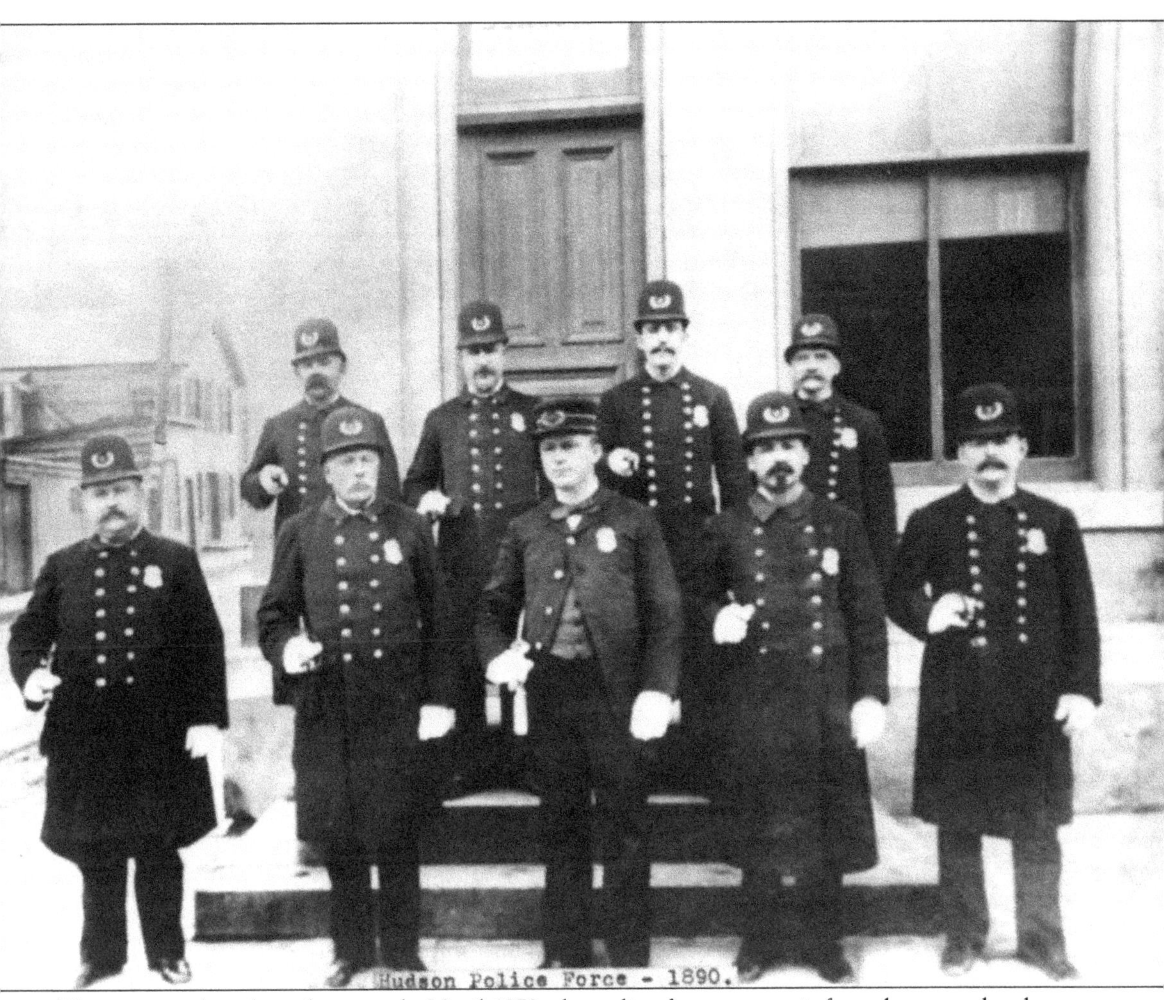

This is an early police photograph. Until 1872, the police force was an informal one, under the jurisdiction of the common council, a force which consisted of four constables elected annually, one from each ward. As the constable was not empowered to arrest without warrant, and patrol was not a function required of him to perform, he was not usually at hand when trouble occurred. On the off chance that he was on hand, he had to stop to obtain a warrant from the justice before making an arrest. These delays impaired the effectiveness of immediate detection and apprehension of criminals and, according to Mary Wend in 1960, "made him entirely dependent upon public cooperation—something Hudson has never been notable for." (Courtesy Hudson Area Library.)

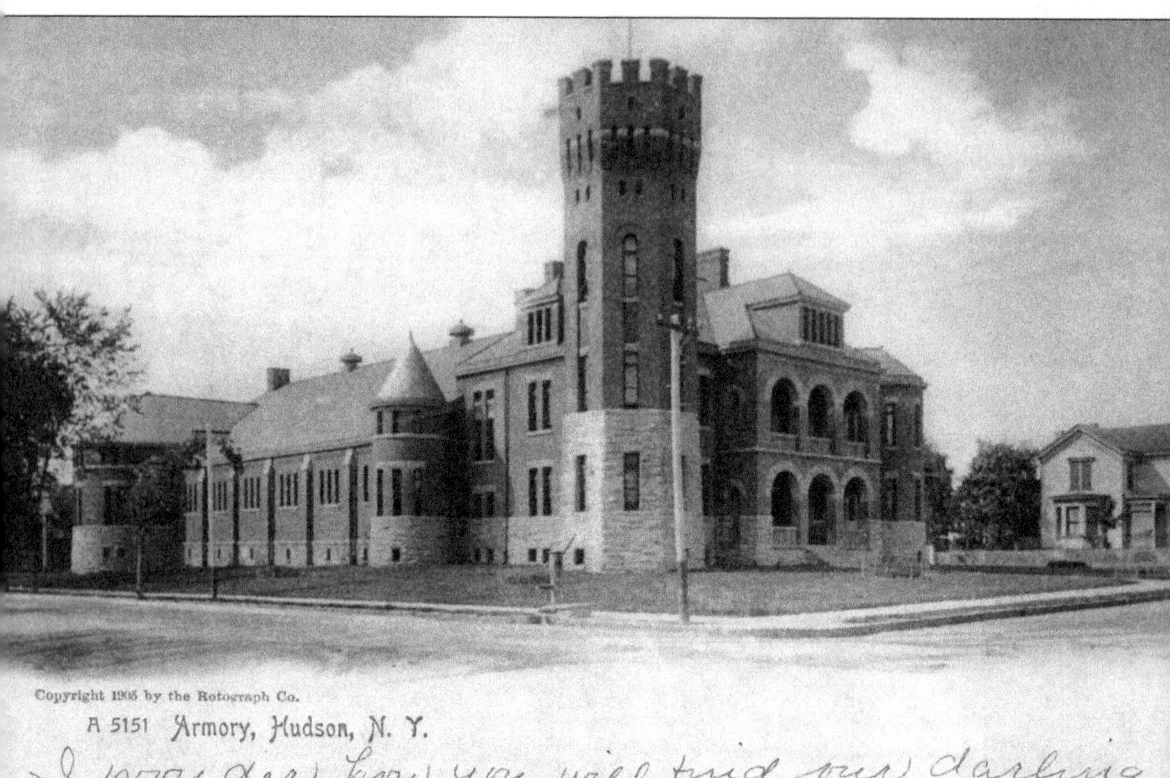

The Hudson Armory is seen here in 1906. It was at the corner of Fifth and State Streets and was built in 1898. Archival video footage of the December 31, 1928, Hudson Armory fire shows a vintage fire pumper and efforts to save the building. Most of the drill shed was destroyed by fire in 1921. Closed in the 1970s and owned privately, it was the future site of the Hudson Area Library. It functioned as an armory for New York State National Guard units, and community events such as proms, auto shows, and Harlem Globetrotters basketball games were also held there. Units at the armory engaged in conflicts during the Spanish-American War, the Civil War, World War I, and World War II. Units received much local appreciation for assistance in 1900 while enforcing a quarantine order during a smallpox outbreak in Stockport. In 1917, a unit was dispatched to the Catskills to protect the reservoirs that supplied New York City's drinking water after a German plot was uncovered to poison it. (Author's collection.)

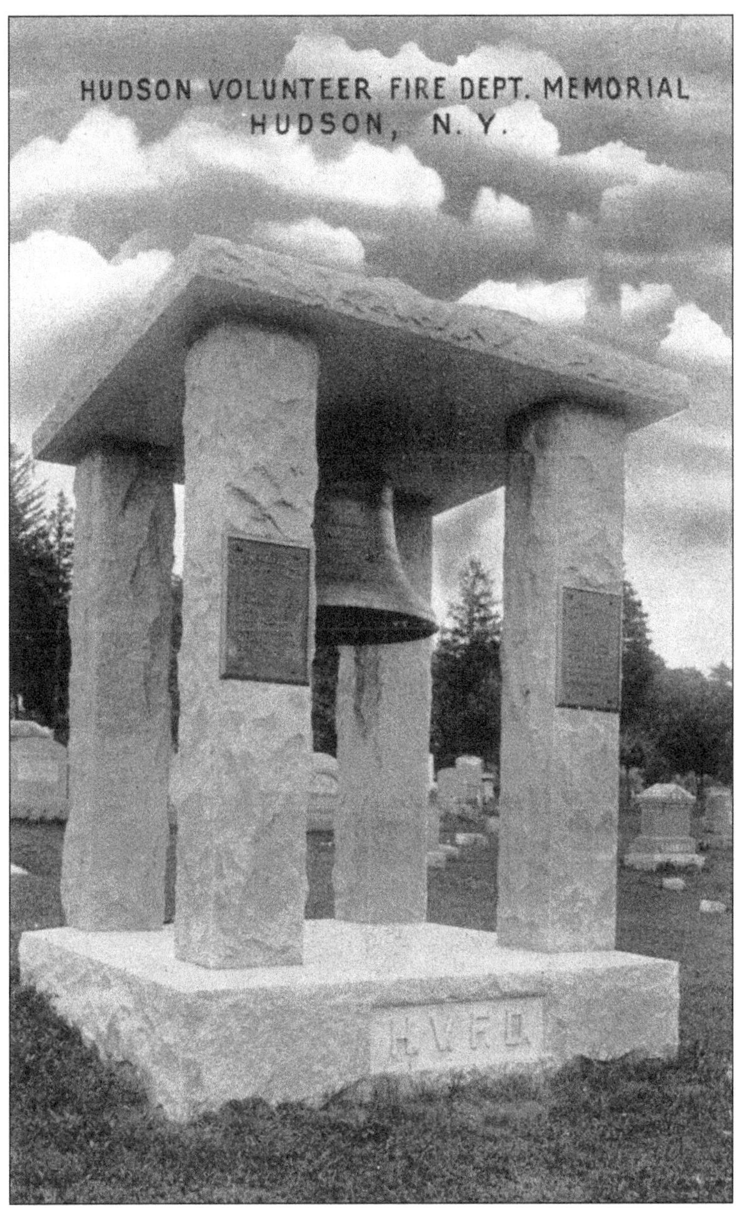

This is a 1935 postcard of the volunteer fire department memorial in Hudson. H.W. Rogers Hose Company, the second-oldest volunteer fire company in New York State, was originally chartered in 1794. The oldest volunteer fire company in New York State is also a Hudson unit: the J.E. Edmonds Hose Company No. 1. In a speech in January 1914, county clerk Milton Van Hoesen said, "Hudson had its first fire in 1793, when the office of the *Hudson Gazette* and the bookstore of Asafoel Stoddard were burned. There was no fire extinguishing apparatus, no firemen's organization, and no adequate water supply. This fire proved a warning and at the next session of the Legislature a petition was presented asking for authority to organize fire companies. The desired act was passed March 19, 1794 ordaining that the Common Council appoint Fire Wardens in this city, whose duty it was immediately upon cry of fire, to repair the place. Then it was further directed that in case of fire the inhabitants of the city should place lighted candles in the windows of their homes so that inhabitants could pass through the streets in greater safety."

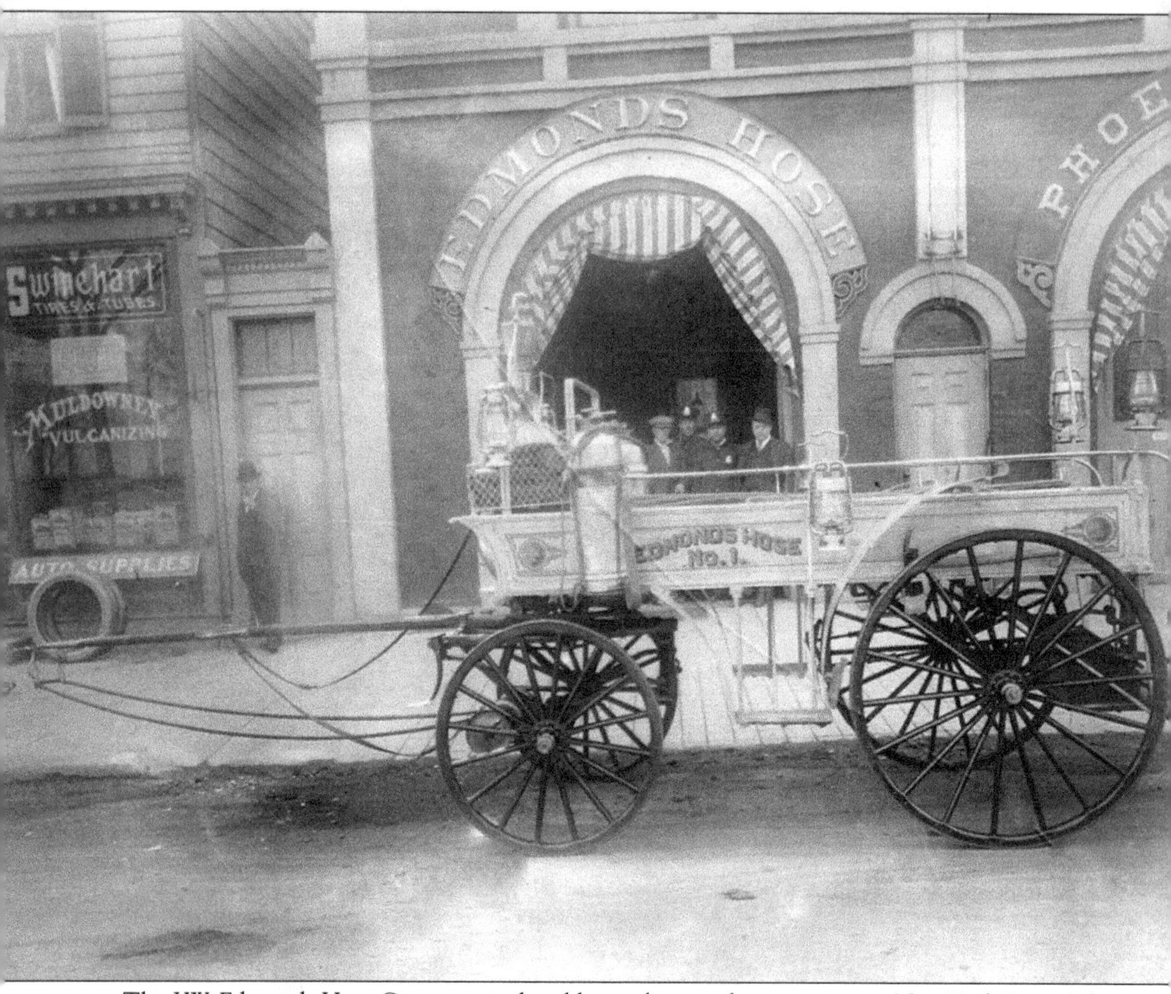

The J.W. Edmonds Hose Company is the oldest volunteer fire company in New York State. The fire company once had an apparatus with the likeness of J.W. Edmonds painted on its exterior. The fire pumper was made by A and Jones on South Front Street in Hudson. A fireman from the second-oldest fire company, the H.W. Rogers Hose Company, once had a dog that followed him to fires and even climbed a ladder to the top of a burning building to join his master. (Courtesy Historic Hudson and Hudson Area Library.)

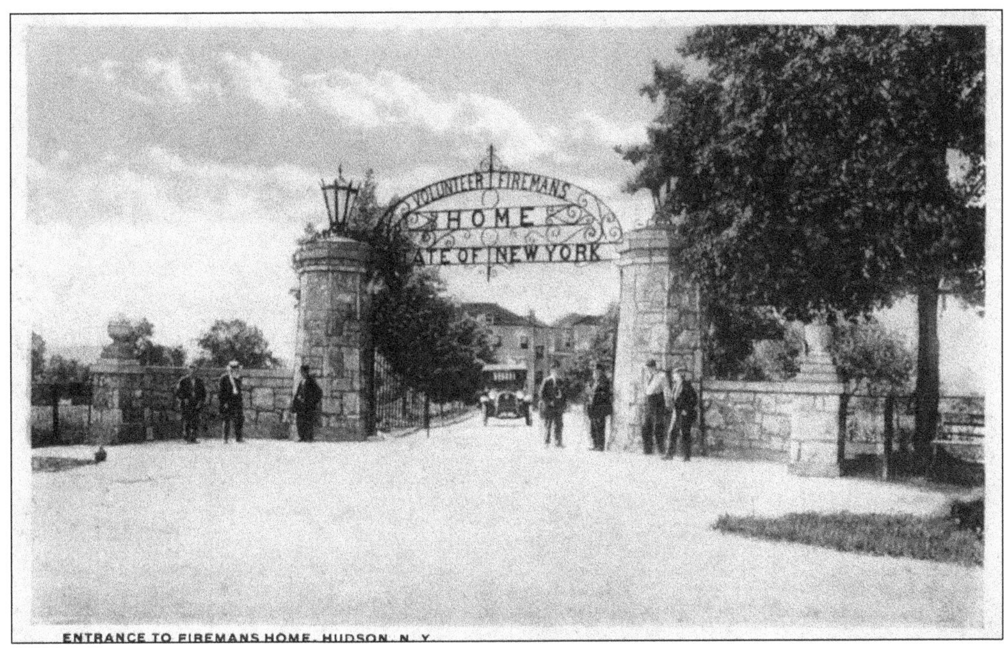

The Fireman's Home for the State of New York, seen here, also houses the American Museum of Firefighting. It is run by the Fireman's Association of the State of New York (FASNY). The Fireman's Home is the first old-age nursing home for firemen in the country. According to the FASNY website, "In 1941 FASNY purchased an adjacent one hundred twenty acre farm. The Firemen's Home now had over three hundred acres under cultivation with Home members doing much of the agricultural labor." (Both, author's collection.)

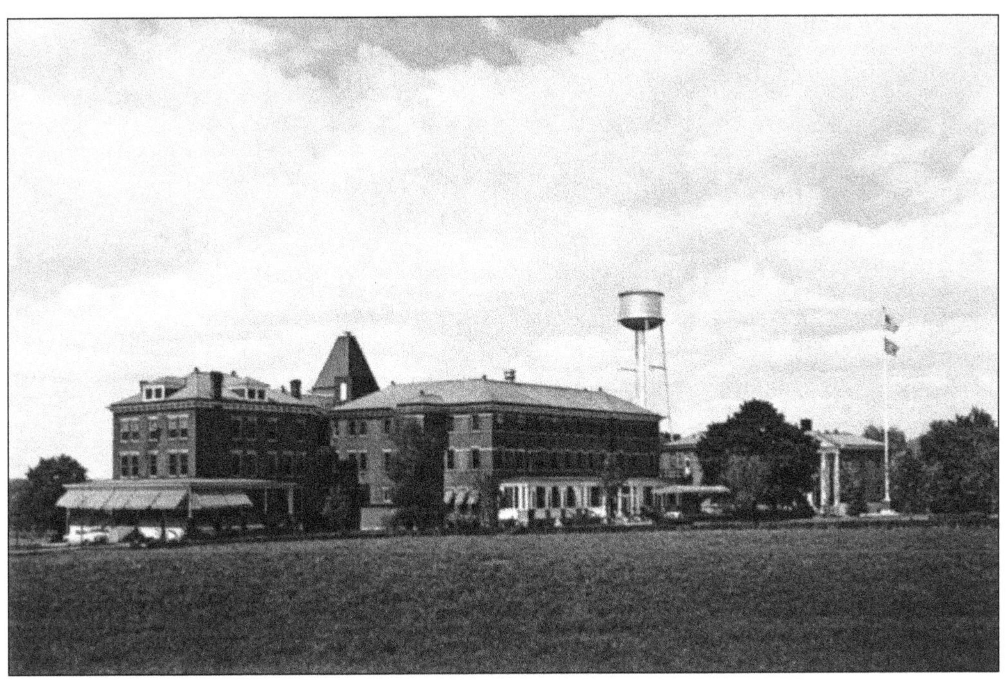

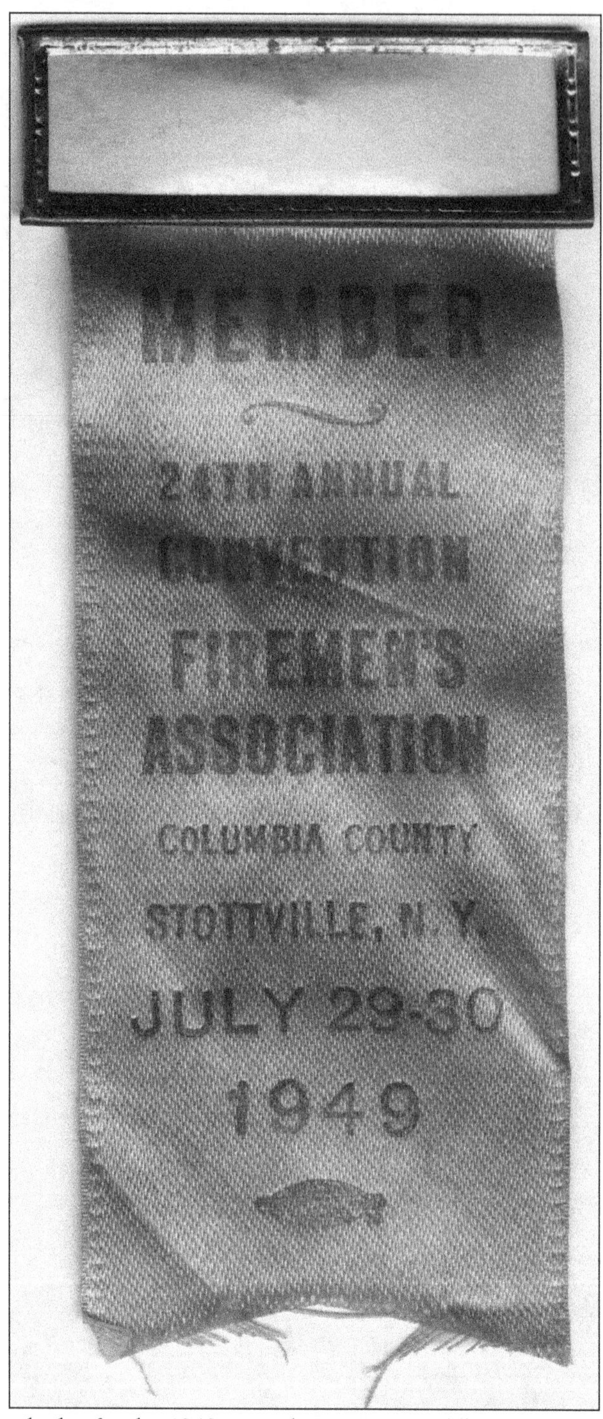

A Stottville member badge for the 1949 annual convention of the Fireman's Association is seen here. According to the FASNY website, "Farming operations ended in 1967 with sale of all equipment and livestock." In the 1800s, firehouses were social meeting places for the community. Today, FASNY's Museum of Firefighting houses the best collections of firefighting relics in the world. (Author's collection.)

Five

THE MASONS

The Masonic Club of Hudson was originally organized on January 14, 1899, with its purpose chiefly being for social reasons. The first meeting was held at the John McKinstry house on December 18, 1786. McKinstry was captured and taken prisoner at the Battle of Cedars in 1776. He went on to open the city's first tavern, on Warren Street. Saved by Captain Brant, a Mohawk chief, McKinstry was spared from being burned at the stake. A painting of Captain Brant stills hangs in the Robert Jenkins House at 113 Warren Street. Captain Brant's last visit to John McKinstry and the Hudson Lodge in 1805 attracted much attention.

The oldest public institution in the city of Hudson is the Order of Free Masons, organized only three years after the proprietors' arrival, many of whom had been Freemasons in Massachusetts and Rhode Island. The club quarters included a reading room, among other amenities, for members seeking a fraternal social structure. In 1795, the proprietors gave the Masons the land at the corner of Third and Union Streets on which to build their temple, under the condition that it could never be used as a tavern. The lodge was built within one year.

In 1826, the disappearance of one its members and the ensuing backlash nearly destroyed the Masonic organization throughout New York State. William Morgan had planned to write an expose of the Masons and give their secrets away. Morgan then disappeared, and people were led to believe, truthfully or not, that he was kidnapped, taken to Canada, and killed.

In 2007, the Hudson lodge merged with Widow's Son Lodge No. 135 in Livingston. The Hudson lodge had been sold in the 1990s. The lodge was named for the chief architect of King Soloman's Temple, Hiram Abiff, who was called the widow's son.

The lodge is now more active in the community, sponsoring programs at the Chatham Fair and providing two annual nursing scholarships to students at Columbia Greene Community College.

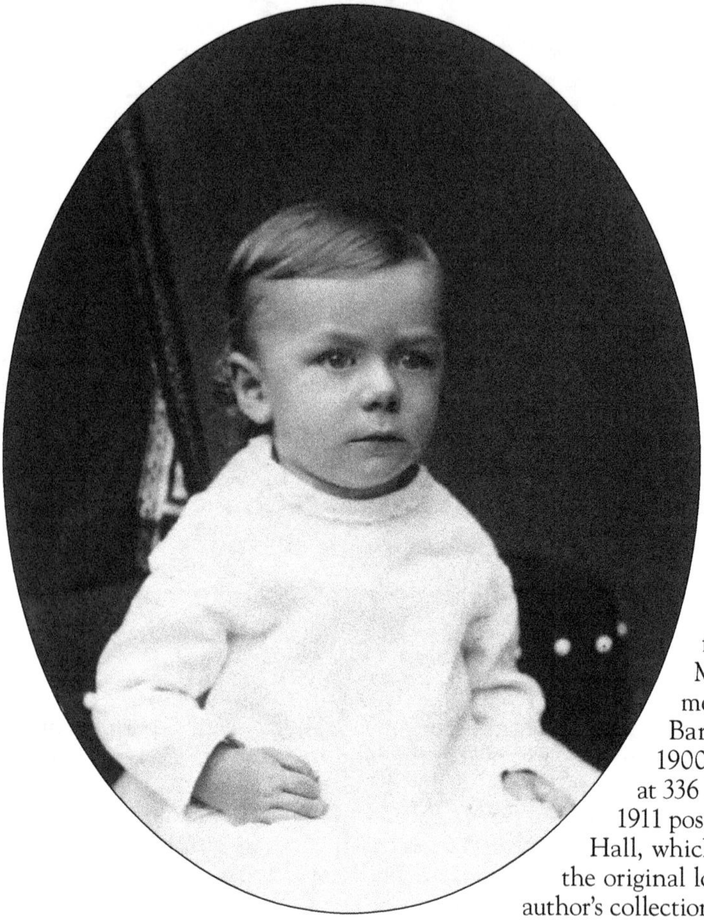

The Forshew Studio image at left is of Robert G. Patrie, former master of the Hudson Masonic Lodge. Patrie was a member of the New York State Bar Association in the early 1900s. He also had a residence at 336 Fulton Street, Jamaica. The 1911 postcard below shows St. John's Hall, which was built on the ruins of the original lodge after it burned. (Both, author's collection.)

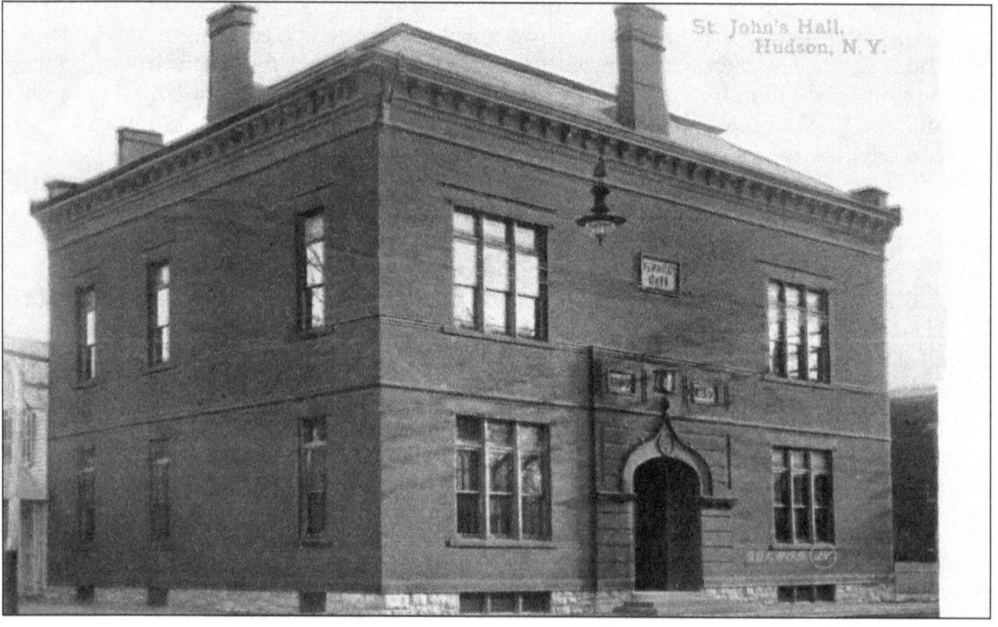

Six

The Hudson Fortnightly Club

The Hudson Social Reading Club was organized on January 22, 1879, with 50 members. It was created for social purposes at the height of the 19th-century social club era. The club reconvened the following autumn, on the evening of November 10, 1879. In her 1909 book *History of the City of Hudson*, Anna R. Bradbury wrote, "The literary menu was prepared by a committee who announced the fortnightly feast of reason and flow of soul." Bradbury stated that the club's formation was at the mention of "Miss Mary Gifford."

On November 5, 1888, the club was reorganized and renamed the Hudson Fortnightly Club. There were a few changes, most notably the omission of gentlemen, as well as the decision to hold meetings in the afternoon versus in the evening. A membership in these clubs was considered at the time to be a necessary and proper part of a well-rounded middle- and upper-class lifestyle. Original meetings were held in the homes of its members, in the parlors of prominent families' mansions in the neighborhoods of Allen Street and Willard Place. A high tea followed the business meeting, with all the required silver service, bone china, linens, floral decorations, and fine cuisine and a dress code that included hats and gloves. Today, the meetings are given to a more casual attire and meeting place, in the central location of a church hall. Some traditions of the club are still retained today, however, with a formal business meeting followed by a receiving line, where the hostess and the committee greet members and the day's guest speaker. A tea still follows, poured in the formal style, while sandwiches and sweets are passed by the hostess and the committee.

This club is one of a small group of social clubs having made the transition from the 19th century into the 20th and 21st. The club's ability to transcend three centuries is due to growth and change with the times and the needs of its members, as it continually seeks new sources of education and enrichment.

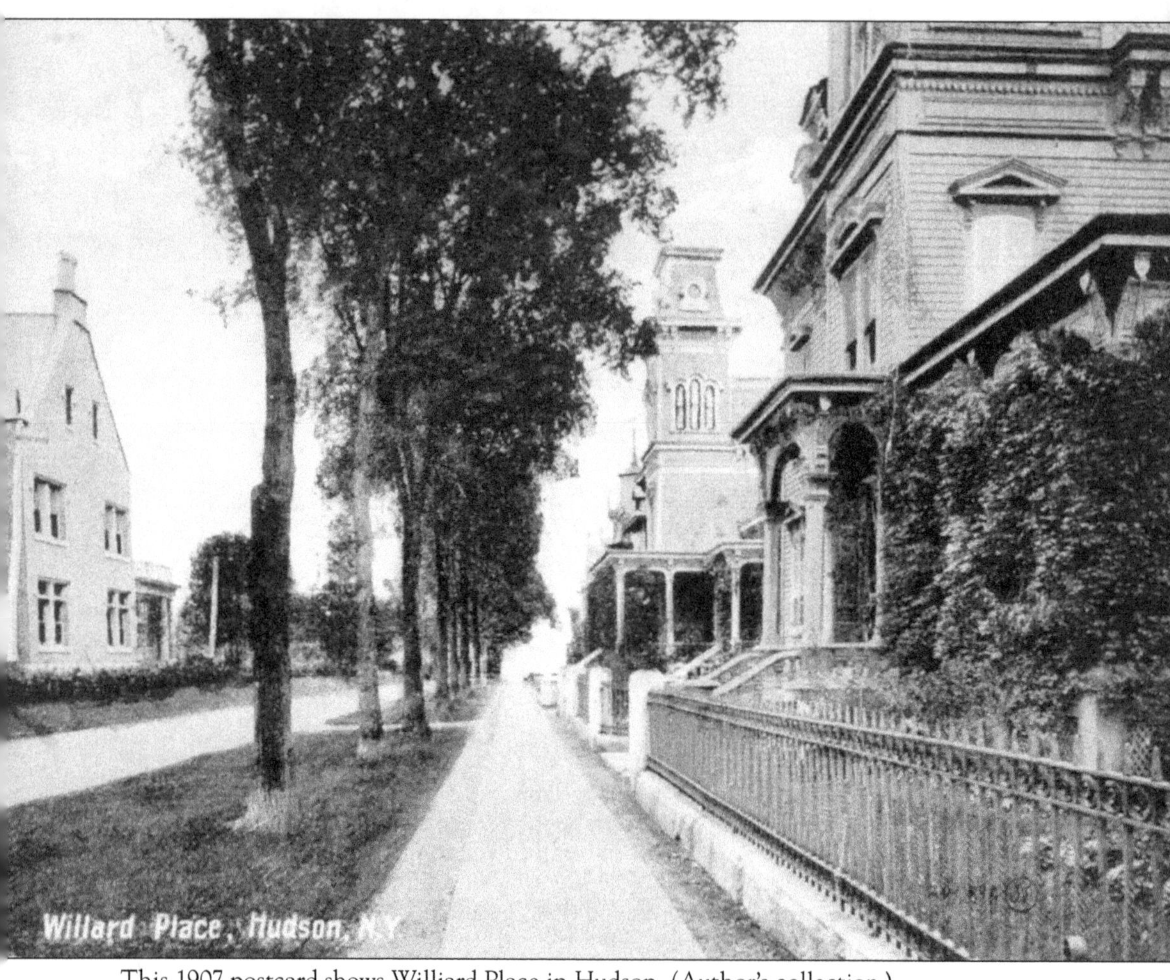

This 1907 postcard shows Williard Place in Hudson. (Author's collection.)

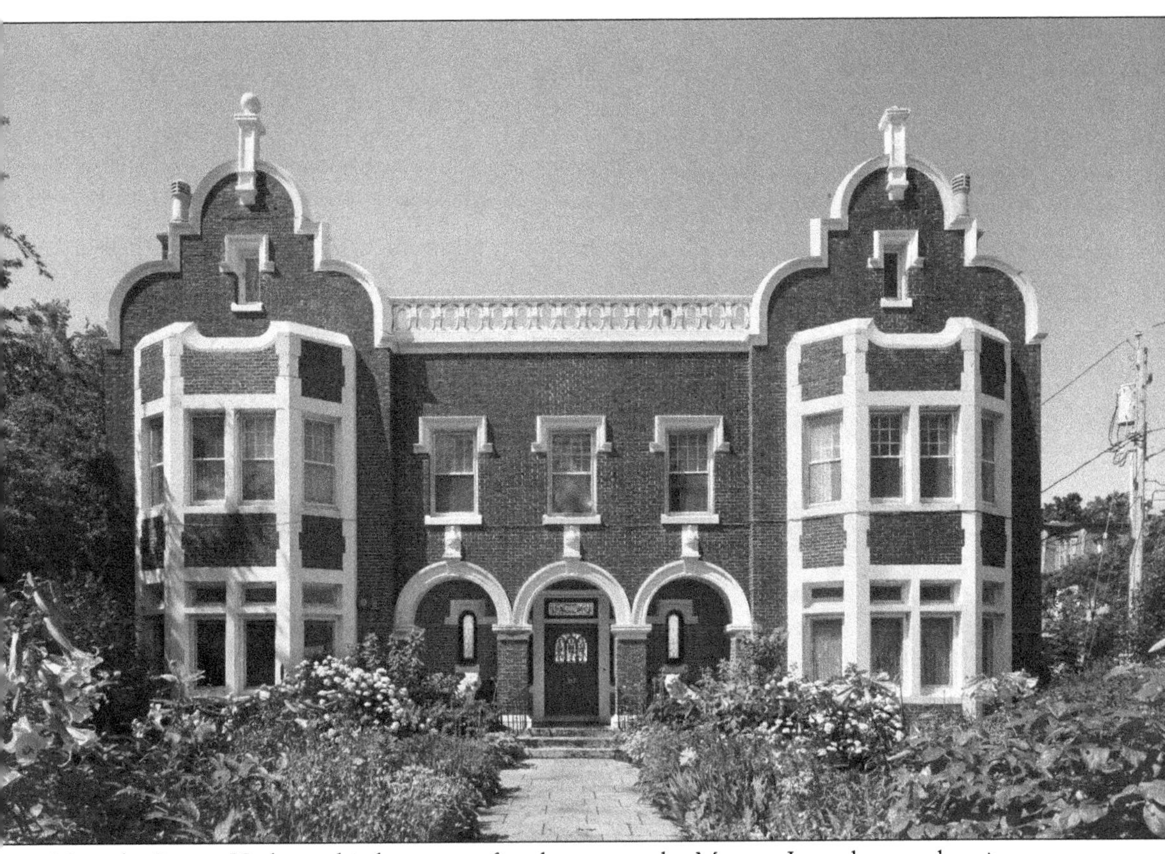

Now the Inn at Hudson, this home was first known as the Morgan Jones house when it was completed in 1906. It was designed by architect Marcus Reynolds and is considered his finest and richest house. It was later known as the Scovill Mansion when the Scovill family moved there around 1918. Morgan Jones's mother, Mary E. Morgan Jones, and his sister Mary E. II were Hudson Fortnightly Club members from 1914 to 1916 and undoubtedly entertained fellow club members here. Morgan Jones's profile is listed in *New York State Men: Biographic Studies and Character Portraits*. His family had two servants, Anna M. Krick and Mary A. Connors. The house is considered by many to be the most beautiful in Hudson, and it was very modern for its time, with electricity, gas lighting fixtures, and an efficient heating system. (Courtesy Windle Davis.)

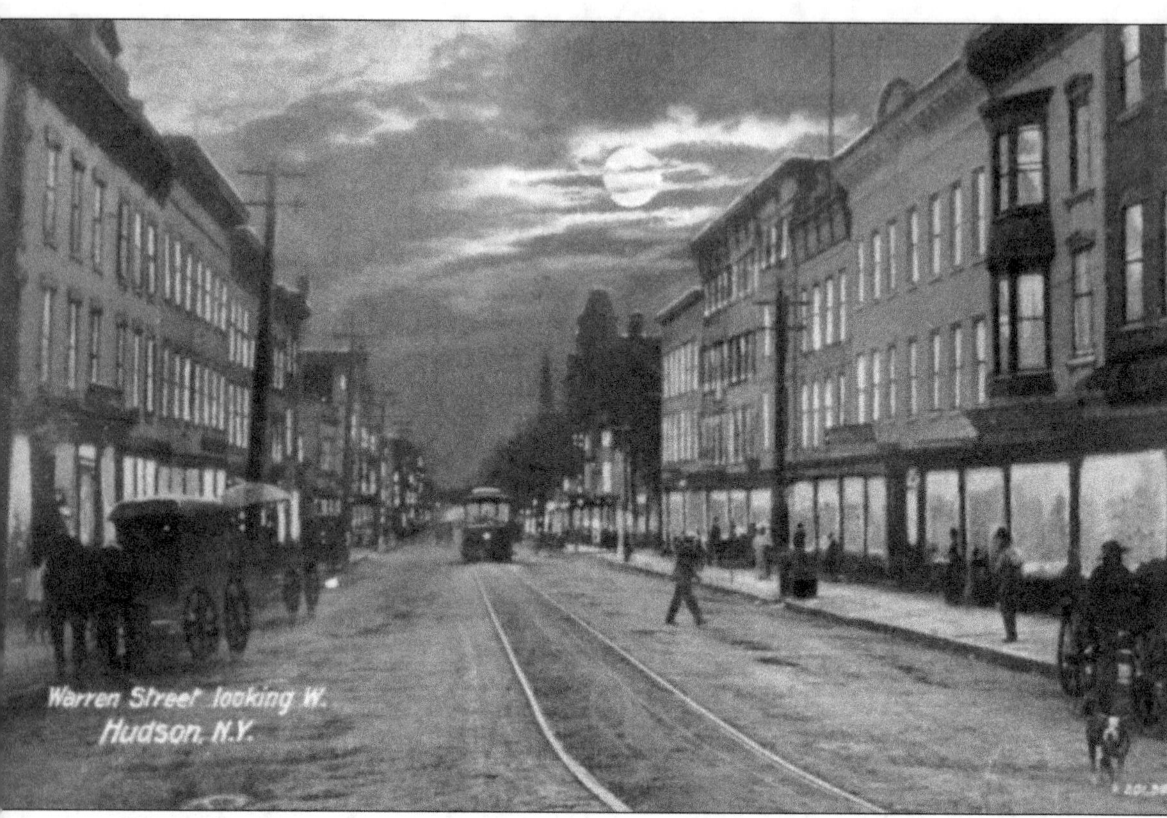

Warren Street is seen here at night. Robert Alfred Scovill became a resident of Hudson early in life, worked as a clerk either at the Bank of Hudson or the Columbia County Bank, and married Elizabeth Dakin of Hudson, "a lady of surpassing beauty, which she maintained until quite advanced in years," according to the *New York State Men: Biographic Studies and Character Portraits*. She was a Hudson Fortnightly Club member from 1926 to 1964. Inside the front entryway today hangs the 1935 painting *Diamond Street*, by artist Betty Wose. The interior of the house is richly adorned with chestnut, a wood used for staircases, woodwork, and moldings. (Courtesy Jon Meredith.)

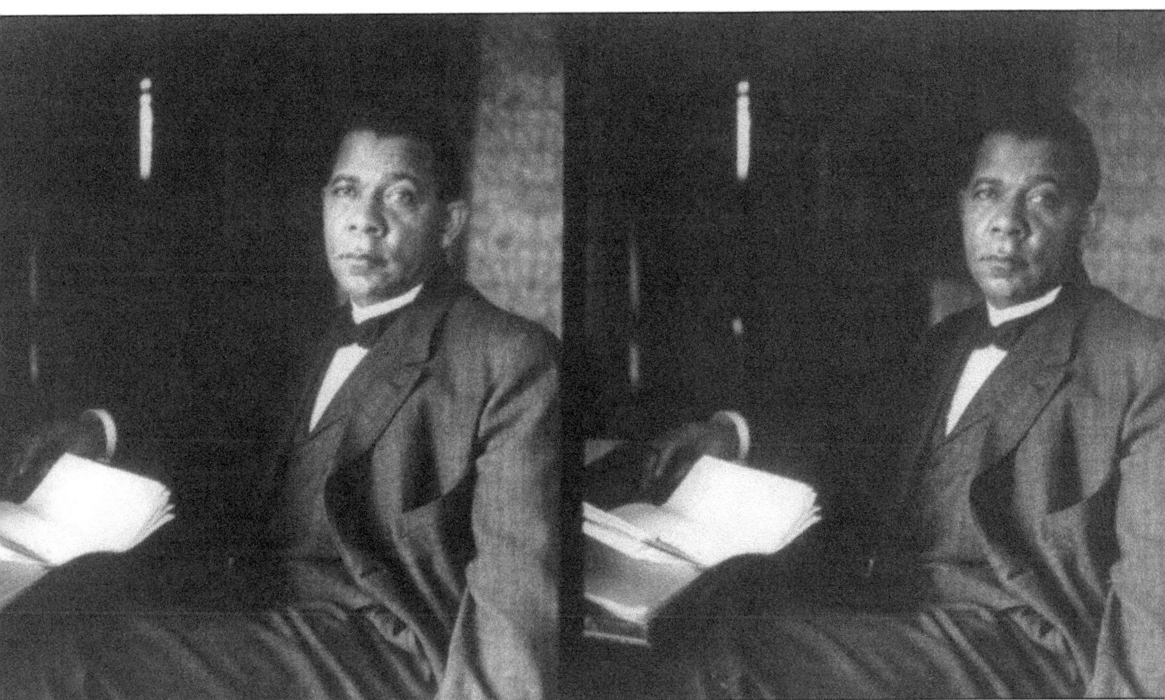

Mrs. Scovill's room was what is now known as the Pink Room, overlooking the front of the house and giving her a good view of arriving guests. According to *The Hudson Fortnightly Club: A Garland of Memories, 1888–1988*, the Hudson Fortnightly Club, "taking note of the plight of the black race, [made] a concrete gesture by sending money to Booker T. Washington" (seen above) and the famous Tuskegee Institute.

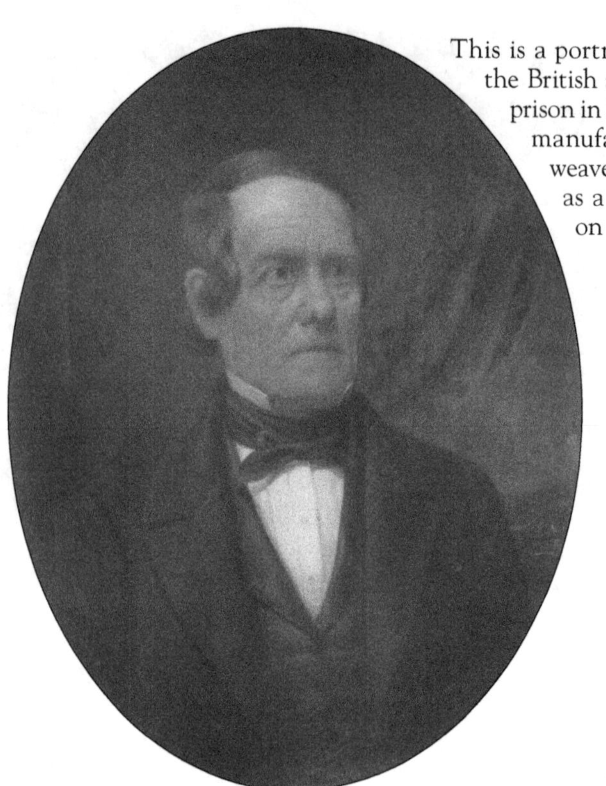

This is a portrait of Jonathan Stott. A member of the British army, in 1814, he was sent to military prison in Pittsfield, Massachusetts, where a loom manufacturer visited in search of English weavers. Jonathan, having learned the trade as a child, volunteered and was released on parole.

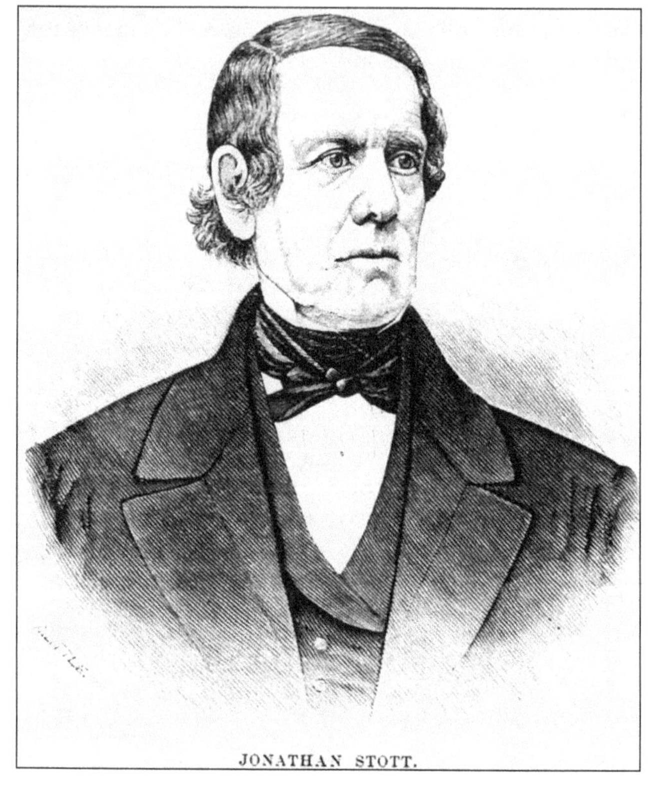

JONATHAN STOTT.

Jonathan Stott went into business with his own looms in Hudson. Securing necessary waterpower, he purchased mill privilege in Springville (now Stottville) in 1828. His financial backer was politician Elisha Williams (1773–1833). By the time of his death in 1863, the Stott woolen mills were famous for fine-quality flannels. Large contracts for military uniforms for the Union army brought real prosperity to Stottville. Jonathan Stott is buried in Hudson City Cemetery, Section 2B. Julia Stott, the wife of Jonathan's grandson, was a member of the Hudson Fortnightly Club from 1893 to 1922. (Courtesy Peter Stott.)

Seven

Sea Captains and Whaling

Hudson's many sea captains have romantic and harrowing tales to tell. Capt. Judah Paddock was shipwrecked and taken prisoner by Arabs. There is an account of the ordeal in *A Narrative of the Shipwreck of the Ship Oswego: On The Coast of South Barberry*. Henry Hudson, later killed by a mutinous crew, never again saw the river that was eventually named for him. Capt. Alexander Coffin, in 1744, returned consignees, people who had engaged in the Boston Tea Party, back to London. The Alexander Jenkins House on Joslen Boulevard in Greenport is reputed to have been a station on the Underground Railroad for slaves escaping from the South, with a tunnel leading to the Hudson River from there. Jenkins and Seth G. Macy were agents in the Hudson Whaling Company. Seth Jenkins corresponded with Thomas Jefferson on wine production and the whaling industry after Jefferson visited Hudson. The well-known phrase "there she blows" came from the lookout person on a ship, who would cry out from the crow's nest "there she blows" when spotting a whale's spout and the spray of moist warm air released from the whale's blowhole when it surfaced to breathe. A lesser-known whaling phrase was "chimney's afire," referring to a heavily bleeding whale exhaling a fountain of blood and water.

Newspaper articles at the time illustrate the prosperity of whaling. On May 3, 1837, the *Poughkeepsie Telegraph* reported, "Hudson, N.Y., April 25th, 1837—The whale ship *Martha*, Capt. Riddle, came up to this city on last Thursday having on board 1400 barrels of sperm oil worth 40,000." Tragedy was also reported on. On January 31, 1838, the *Poughkeepsie Telegraph* headline "A Hudson Whale Ship Ashore, Disaster" included the following story: "The whale ship *George Clinton*, of Hudson, Capt. Barret, Master, from the Pacific Ocean, with a full cargo of sperm oil bound to this port went ashore on the night of Thursday last, in a thick fog, at Little Egg Harbor. When boarded, no person was found on board, the captain and crew having previously left her. We cannot obtain further particulars." A total of 1,450 barrels of sperm oil were saved. The Barnard Curtiss Oil Company, processing whale oil, seal skins, and candles, stood near what is now the Amtrak train station.

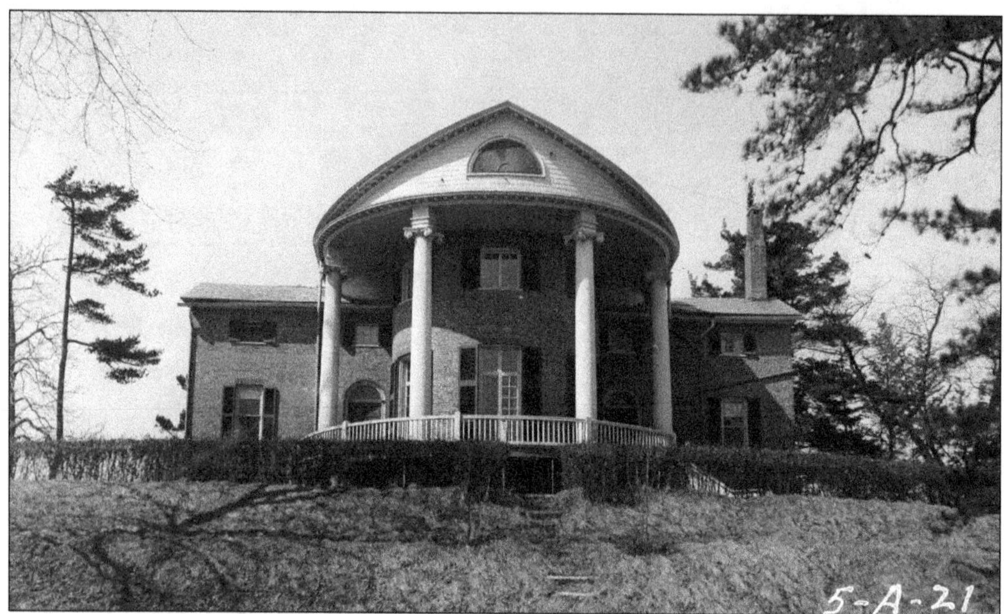

Seen above is the Turtle House in Greenport. The house was formerly part of Penton Hook Farm and was built by Capt. Job, or Joab, Center, with columns that were masts of a ship. Folk mythology at the time said that the "devil cannot corner the people who live in the house," due to its being round in part or in whole. Seen below is a captain's walk at the Historical Society of Nantucket, Massachusetts. Widow's walks, also called captain's walks, which are railed rooftop platforms, are found atop many fine Hudson homes. They were common on 19th-century North American coastal houses. A romantic explanation suggests that the platform was used to observe incoming ships on the Hudson River for returning lovers and husbands from sea voyages.

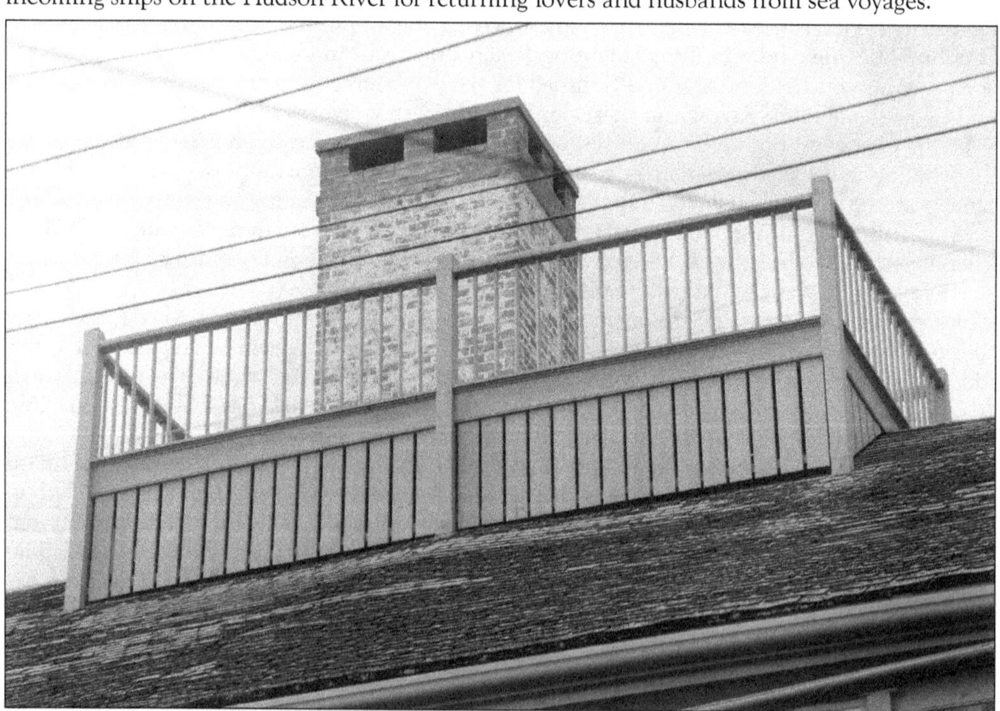

The lower jawbone of a whale is shown here on Warren Street in the 19th century. Children were known to hide in it when avoiding their parents. Local bakers would make ship biscuits known as "hard tack," which were kept for long voyages at sea. (Courtesy Hudson Area Library; gift of Carmen Ciancetta.)

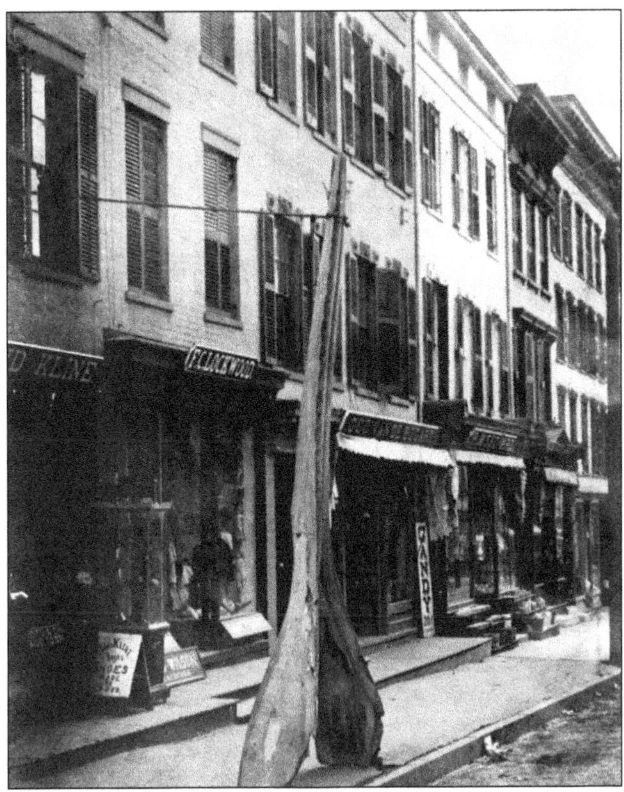

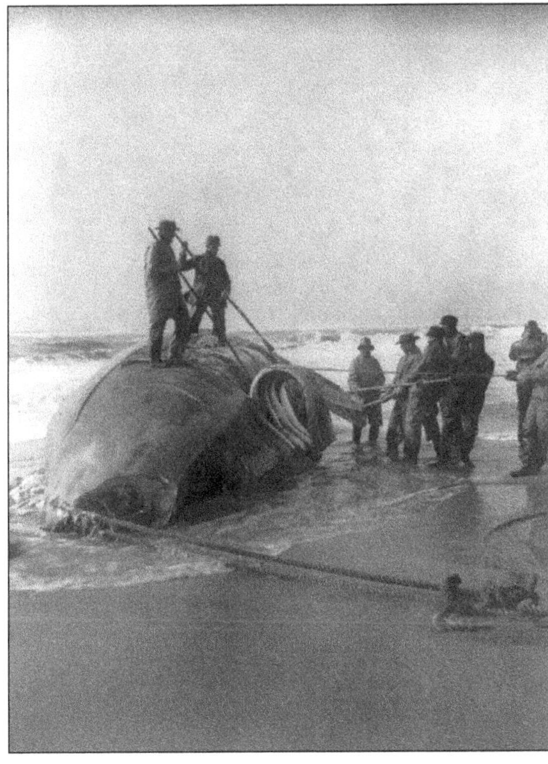

Whaling, while bringing prosperity to Hudson, also brought many undesirable consequences. Seal skins were also brought back to Hudson to be made into shoe leather at Hudson's tanneries. Hudson's glory days in whaling were over by 1844.

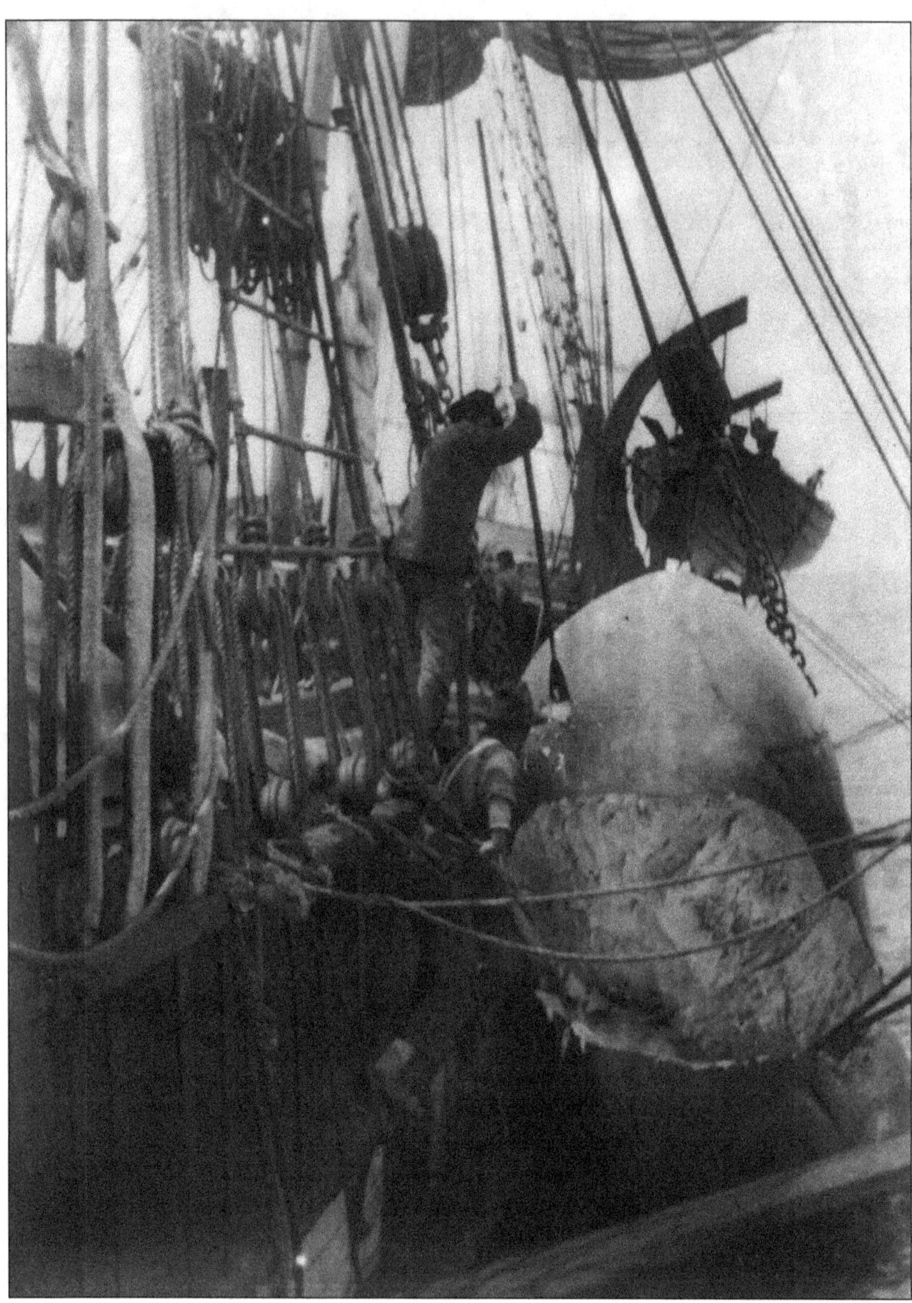

The processing of a sperm whale is seen here. Capt. Robert Waterman was born in Hudson in March 1808. His father was a Nantucket sea captain who died at sea when Waterman was eight years old. Waterman set three sailing records, and his 74-day trip from Hong Kong to New York City has never been beaten by a sail-powered vessel. Known as a bully, Waterman was once convicted of assault against a crew mate. The N.L. & G. Griswold shipping company, seeking a high-quality captain for its new clipper *Challenge*, offered Waterman a $10,000 bonus if he could get the ship to San Francisco within 90 days. When news of his violence on the ship towards many crew members reached the public, one newspaper called for him to be "burned alive," and he narrowly escaped being hanged.

Eight

Greenport

In 1652, Jan Franz van Hoesen purchased the land that is now the city of Hudson, most of Greenport, and part of Stockport. By 1800, Hudson had a population of 4,048, which included 88 slaves. According to Mary Wend, "The city fathers circa 1837 were niggardly calculators absolutely devoid of any expectations or hope whatsoever for the future of Hudson." In 1833, a small piece of Hudson became part of Stockport; in 1837, when Greenport was formed, these gentlemen permitted the city to be reduced to an area of less than three square miles, to be entirely circumscribed by the new town. Greenport was the last town founded in the county. The Rip Van Winkle Bridge, in the south part of town, connects Greenport to the village of Catskill.

The end of whaling and the Bank of Columbia closing in 1829 caused a depression and considerable losses in Hudson. Once prosperous, Hudson was now inert. Hudson became surrounded on three sides by Greenport, named for its beautiful, verdant green color seen from the Hudson River. Many former farms existed on what is now Joslen Boulevard. Hard cider was the favorite drink of early Dutch inhabitants, who, on cold winter nights, would warm the beverage with a red-hot poker from the fire. Dutch was still spoken in Hudson in the early 1900s.

The Peter Hallenbeck murder, perpetrated by his nephews on Christmas Eve 1901, took place in his home, in what was then known as the hamlet of Greendale, within Greenport. The murder was widely written about, including in the *New York Times*. The Van Wormer boys were denied burial in Greenport after their death by electrocution.

In the 1800s, Greenport was a center for the quarrying of limestone, granite, and marble on Becraft Mountain, where Hudson's water supply comes from. Greenport Conservation Area, a 714-acre riverside parcel about two miles outside the city, offers trails unfolding to the Hudson River.

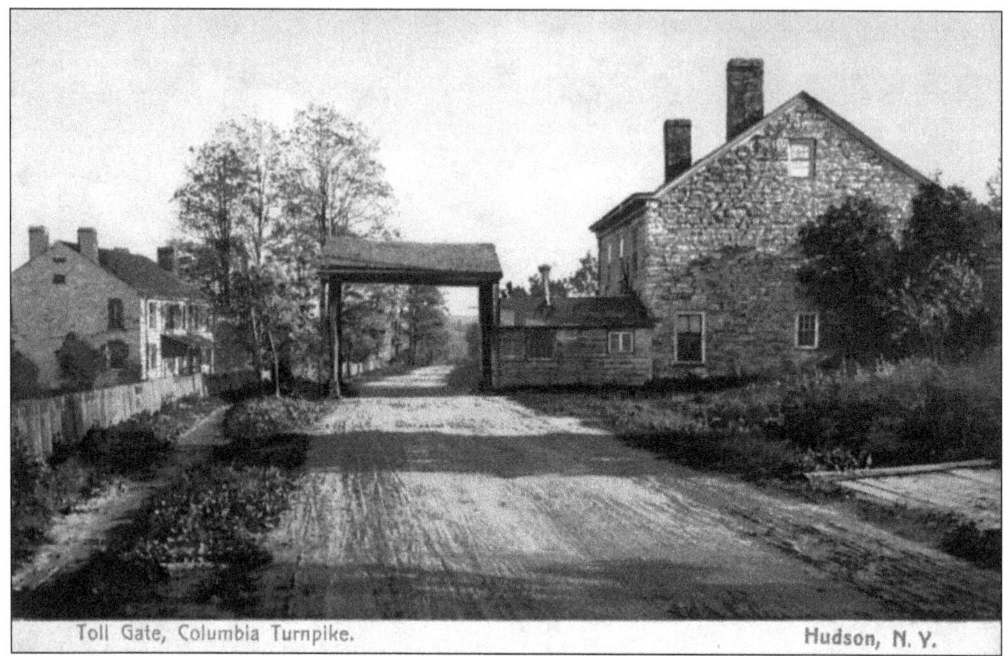

This is an 1860s or 1880s postcard image of the tollgate on the Columbia Turnpike in Greenport, which is now Route 23B. Exempt from tolls were people traveling to or from a funeral or to and from a mill for grinding grain for one's family.

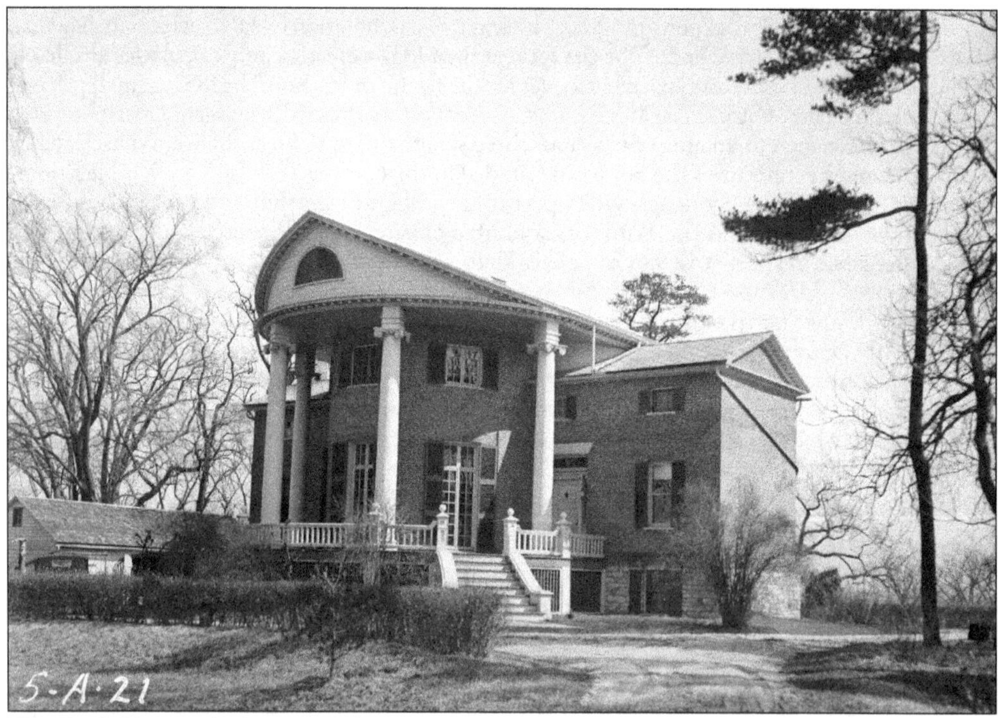

The Turtle House, also known as the Joab House, is on what was formerly Post Road in Greenport Center. The road is now Fabiano Boulevard, and the house, built by sea captain Joab Center, is listed in the National Register of Historic Places.

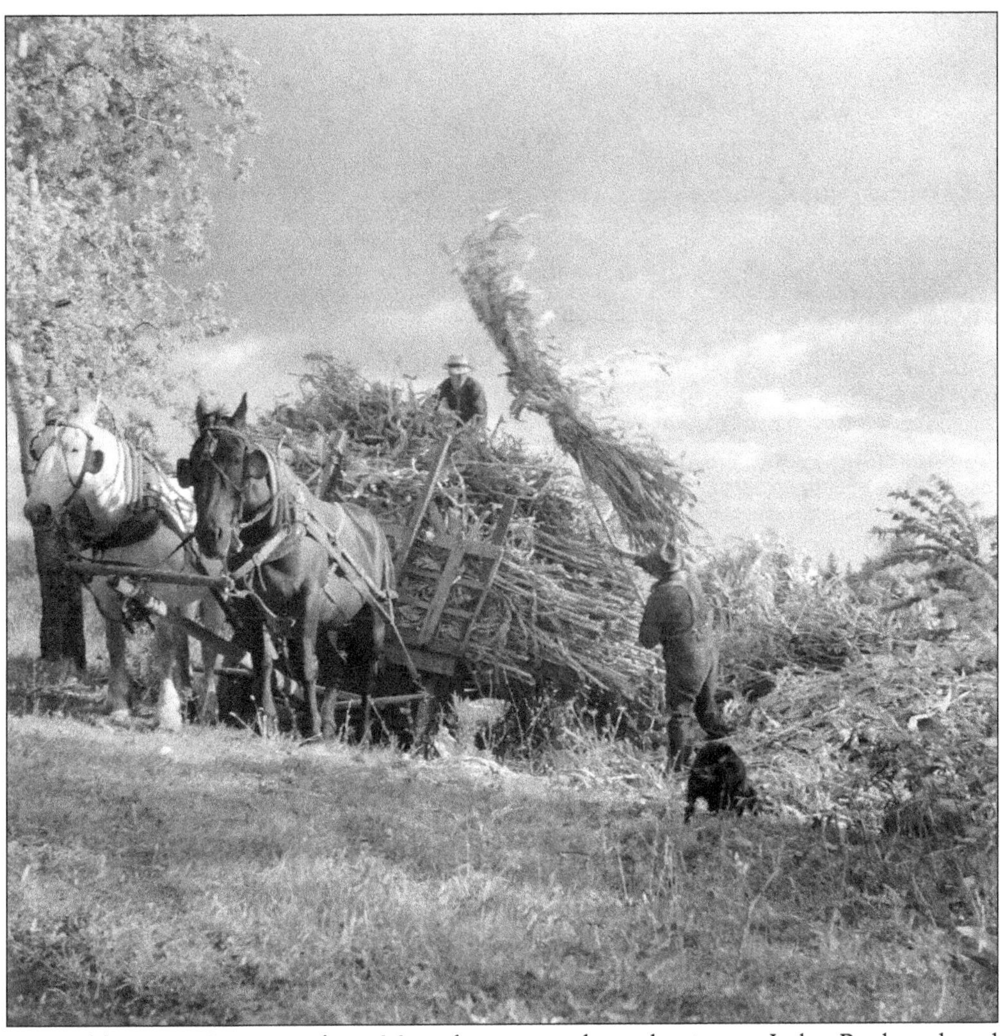

Pictured here is a Greenport farm. Many farms existed on what is now Joslen Boulevard, and flocks of sheep were a common sight in the area.

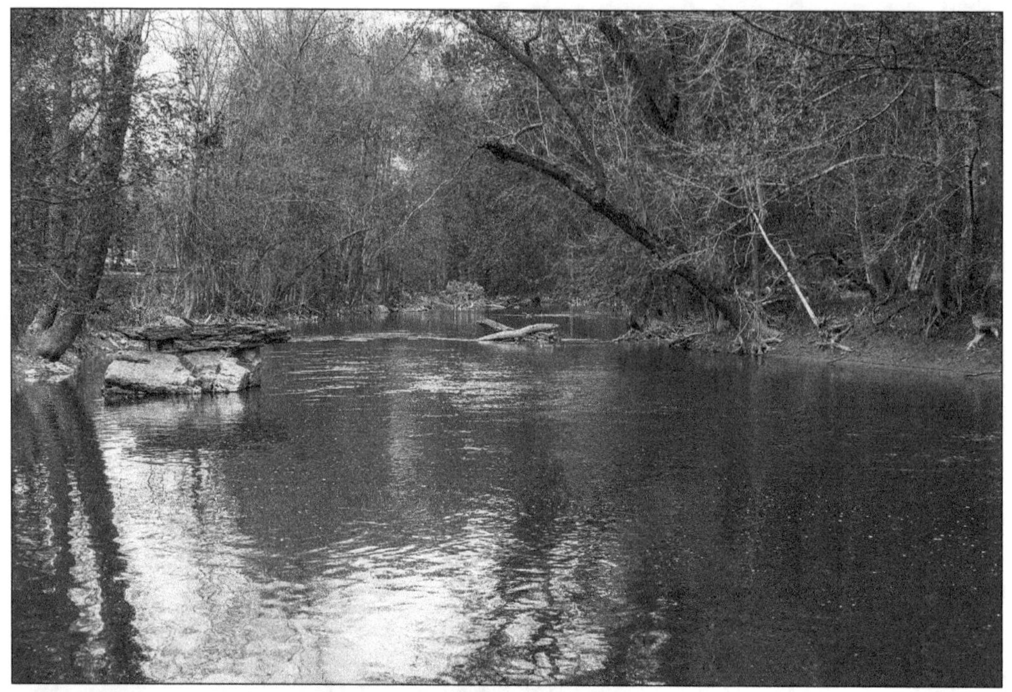

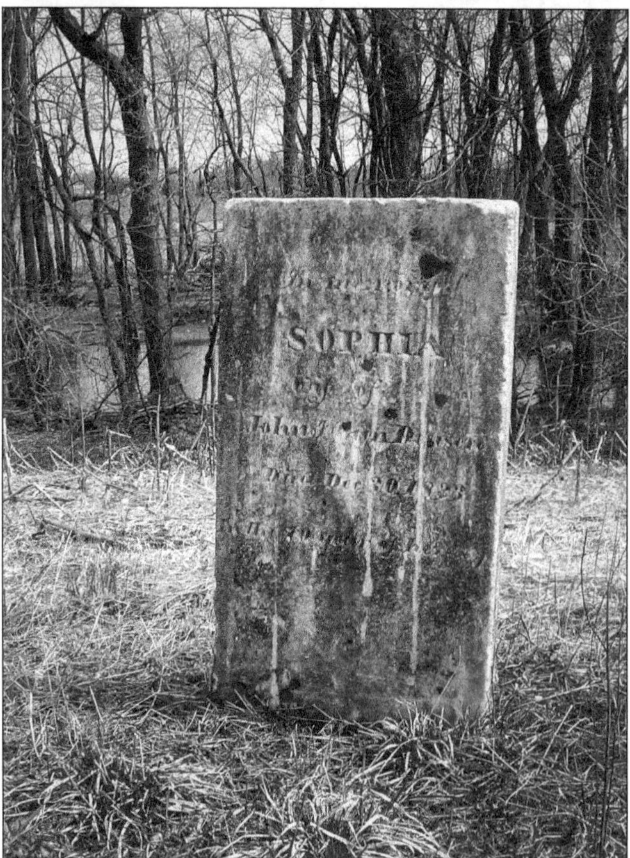

This is a view of Spook Rock Road's legendary rock, the site of Indian legends and ghost stories. (Courtesy Dan Region.)

Stalks and headstones are seen near Spook Rock Road, just outside of Greenport. (Courtesy Dan Region.)

Nine

Architecture

Warren Street, known as the spine of the city and called the "long straight street" by Henry James, has a mixture of Federal, Greek Revival, and Georgian townhouses, Second Empire mansions, and Victorian houses. In Hudson, some 20th-century Craftsman-style bungalows can also be found. Nearby Willard Place and Allen Street are predominantly Victorian, including a house with an Egyptian-style lotus motif on the columns.

The whales on city street signs honor Hudson's whaling times. The *New York Times* has called Warren Street "the best antiques shopping in the Northeast." Downtown Hudson has been named one of the richest dictionaries of architectural history in New York State. In the 1980s, a former field representative for the New York State Historic Preservation Office, Neil Larson, said, "What's unusual about Hudson is that it's so intact. It reflects a Yankee history, a town that really boomed in the 1840s. Hudson maintained the scale and character of an early 19th century city."

In 2003, the city created a historic preservation commission to review applications for new construction in the district or exterior modifications to existing buildings that go beyond routine maintenance. It consists of seven members appointed by the mayor. At least one member must be an architect, one a historian, and one live in the district. All must have an interest in preservation. So much has changed since the 1980s, when Hudson was considered derelict and full of "handyman specials." A buyer's market then, rents in Hudson have since soared, and real estate is at a premium as the city becomes more and more gentrified. Subsidized housing is also becoming more prevalent.

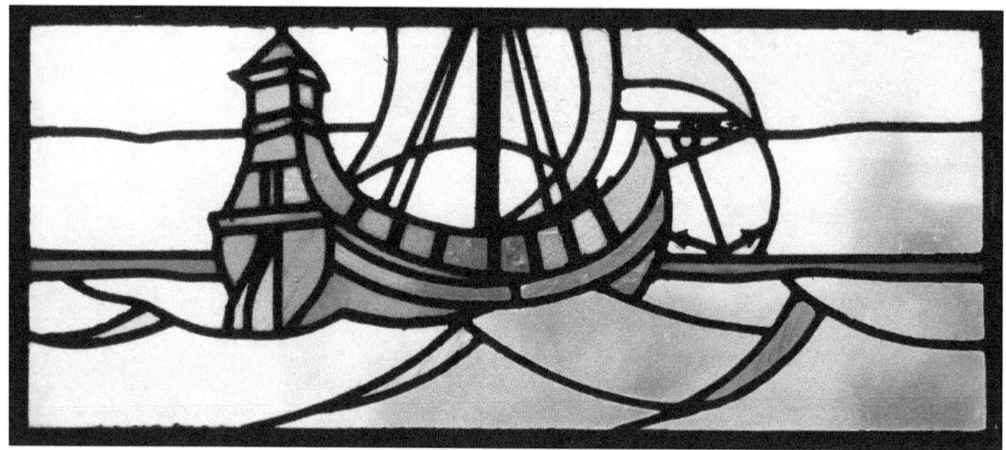

These Heinecke & Bowen leaded-glass windows are at the Morgan Jones house, later known as the Scovill Mansion and now the Inn at Hudson, in the billiards room. One window depicts a stag design, and the other is a replica of Henry Hudson's ship *The Halfmoon*. While no other known examples of these exist, examples from the house's library can be found at the Metropolitan Museum of Art in New York City.

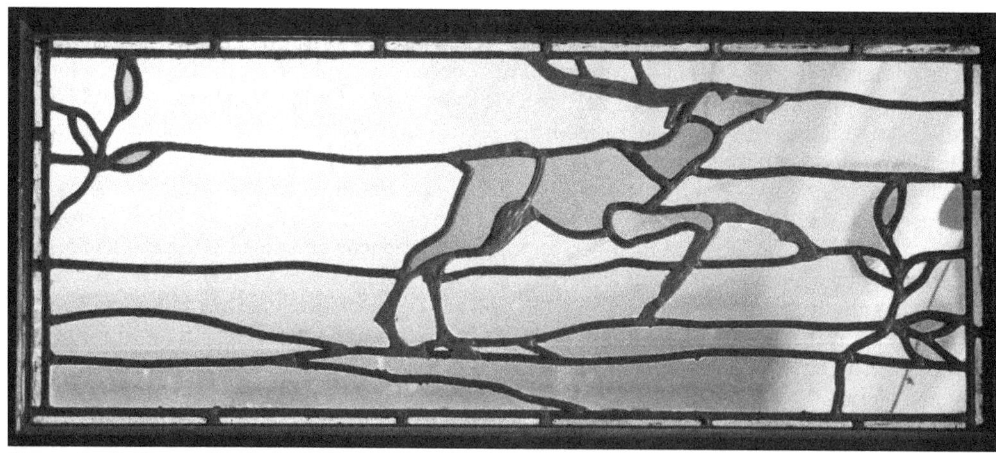

Heinecke & Bowen made significant contributions to American stained glass and was considered prominent in its revival during the 1880s. Bowen was a former associate of Tiffany & Co. Leaded glass has added refractive properties, used as a base in colored glass. Current Hudson Fortnightly Club members recall seeing the brilliant windows of the mansion while attending many holiday and Halloween house parties there as junior high school students at nearby St. Mary's Academy. (Courtesy Windle Davis.)

Seen at right is the gallery porch at Olana, on Route 9G in Hudson. Below is the studio porch. Serving a major role in Olana's preservation was the youngest of Frederic Church's three sons, Louis Palmer Church. After taking ownership in 1900, Louis electrified the house in 1917 by installing a gas-powered generator under the west porch of the studio wing. He wrote, "As I looked from its broad veranda one beautiful sunshiny morning the scene that spread before me filled me with regret that I had the soul of an artist without the power to wield the brush. It seemed the spot of all others to lend inspiration, and it is no wonder that the fame of Mr. Church is so great and lasting to live long after he has gone to his last resting place."

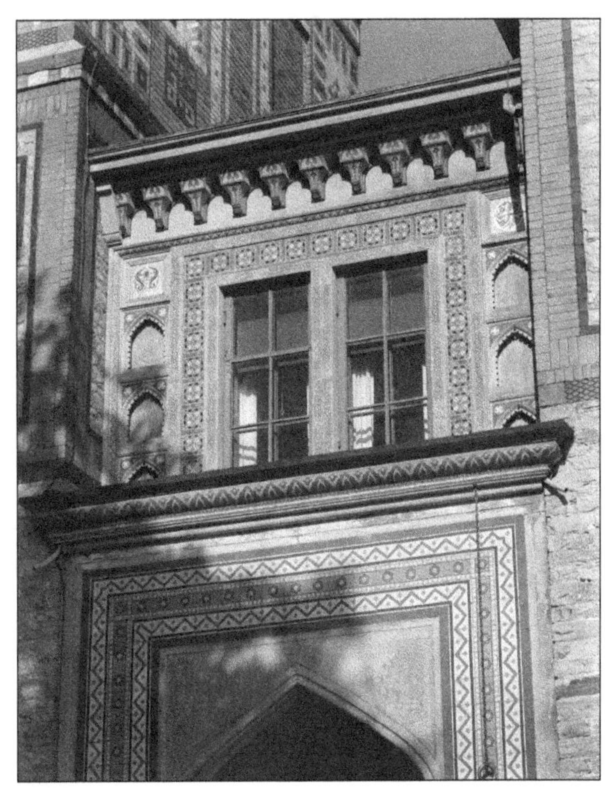

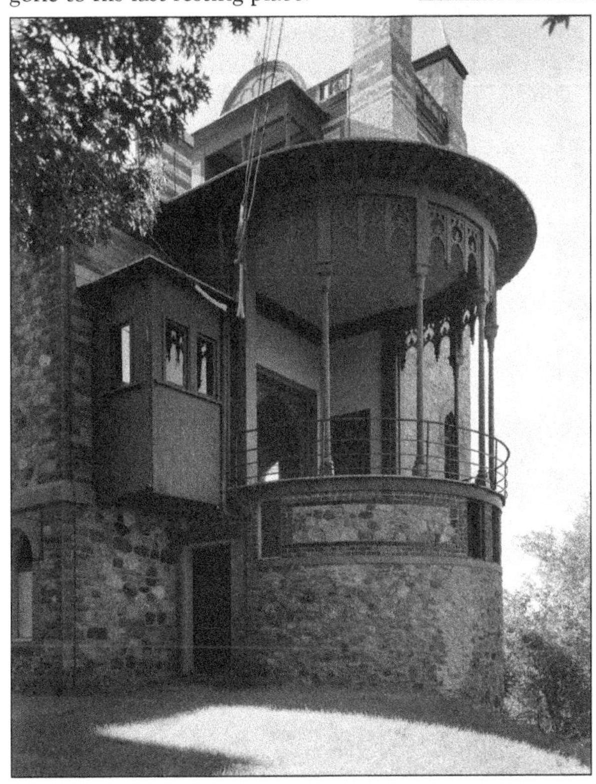

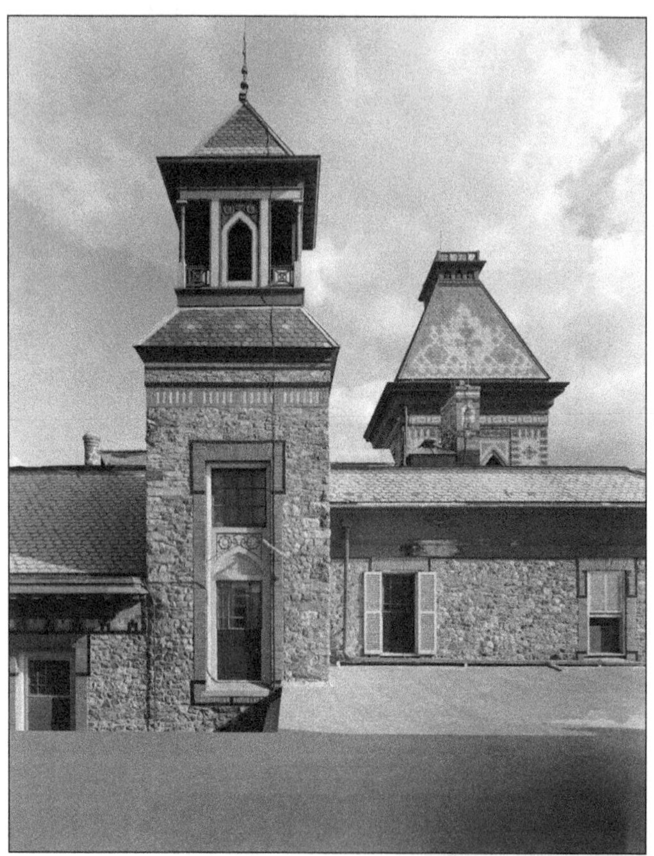

Seen here are the towers at Olana. Frederic Church's Olana is still considered one of the most notable houses in America, "situated in a vast park beautified by the taste of the artist," according to James Anthony Ryan. Church's family lived here with artifacts of human civilization united with nature's elements and much friendship, laughter, art, and worship. Olana is Church's last great masterpiece carried out; a livable artwork of domestic and artistic harmony. Having opened its doors to the public on June 3, 1967, Olana is now a New York State Historic Site operated by the New York State Office of Parks, Recreation and Historic Preservation.

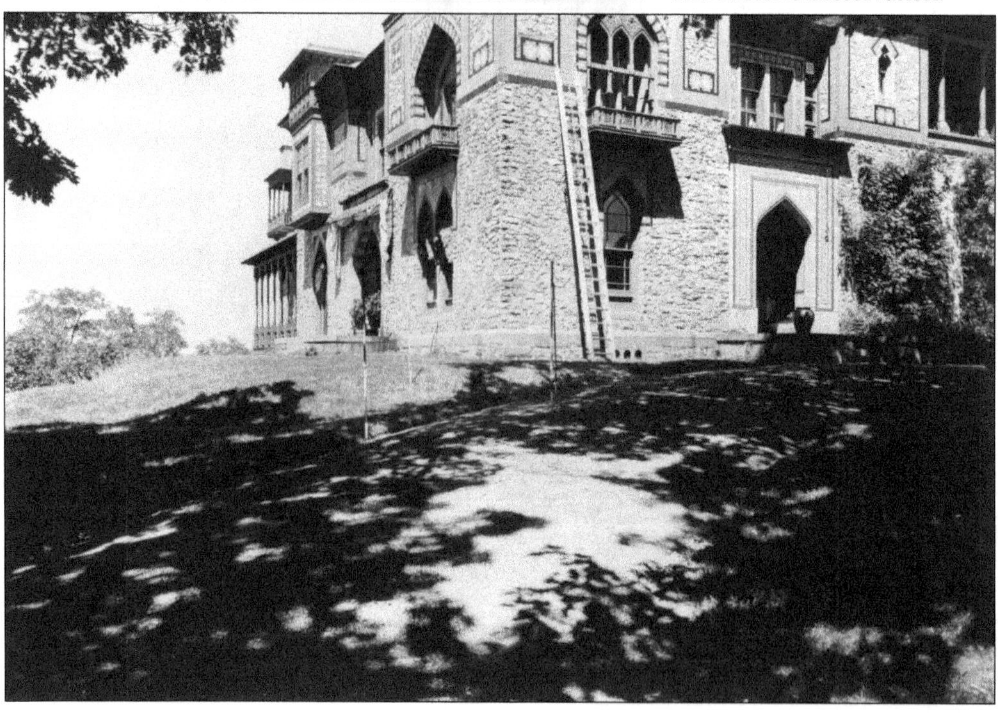

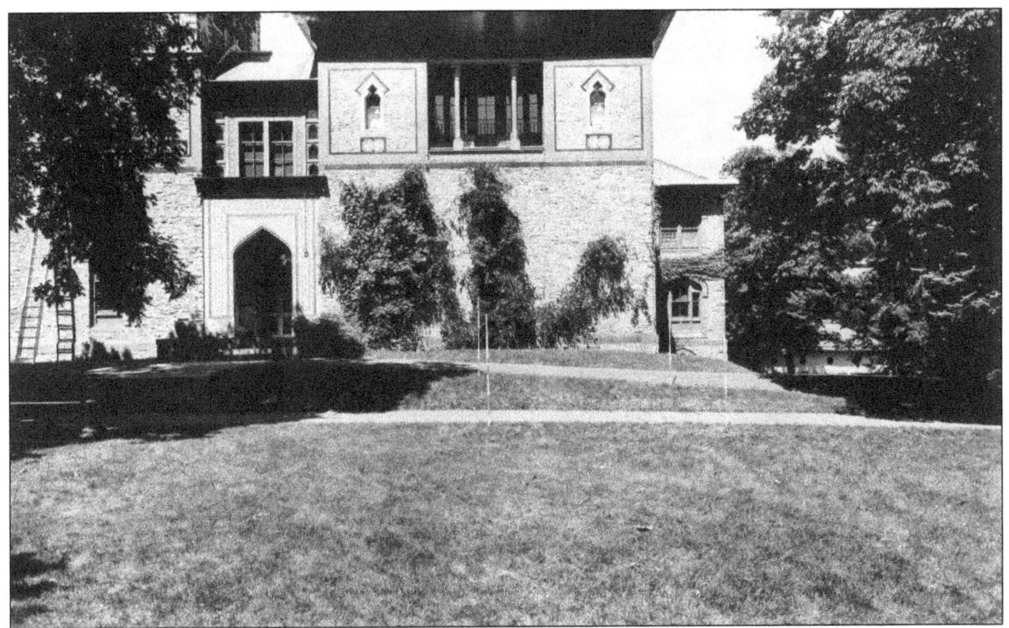

This is the east portion of the south facade at Olana. By 2000, Friends of Olana had 800 members who achieved the purchase of collections and objects for the house, conservation of the art within, and creation of curatorial positions. These are programs of the National Park Service established for the purpose of documenting historic places. Records consist of measured drawings, archival photographs, and written reports.

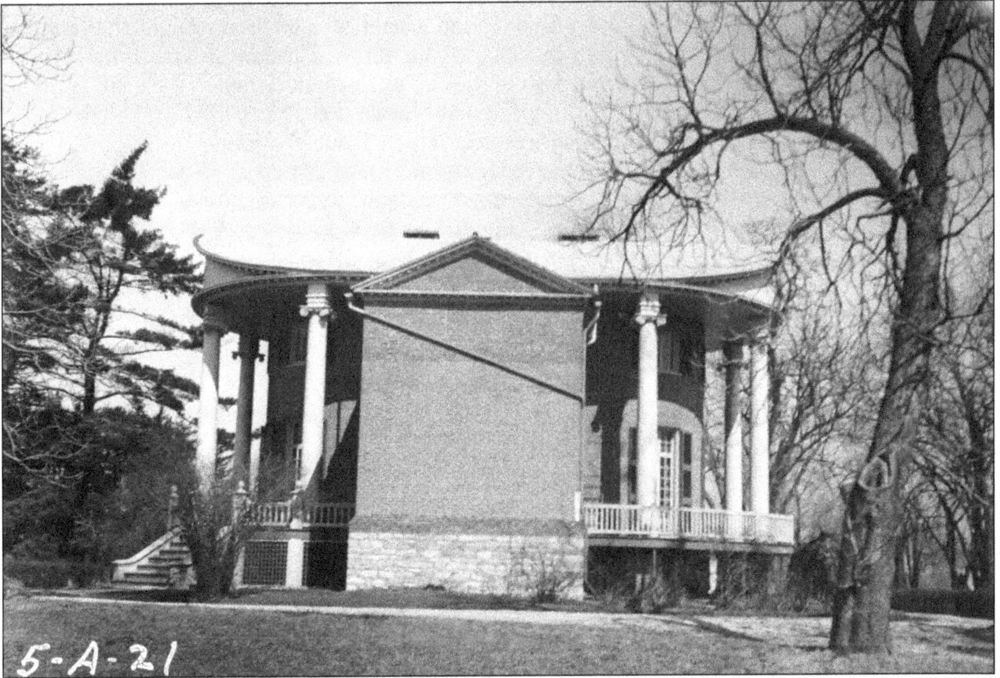

This is a 1937 image of the sea captain Joab Center's Turtle House on Fabiano Boulevard, formerly known as Post Road, in Greenport. The house is on approximately nine acres of land and is listed in the National Register of Historic Places.

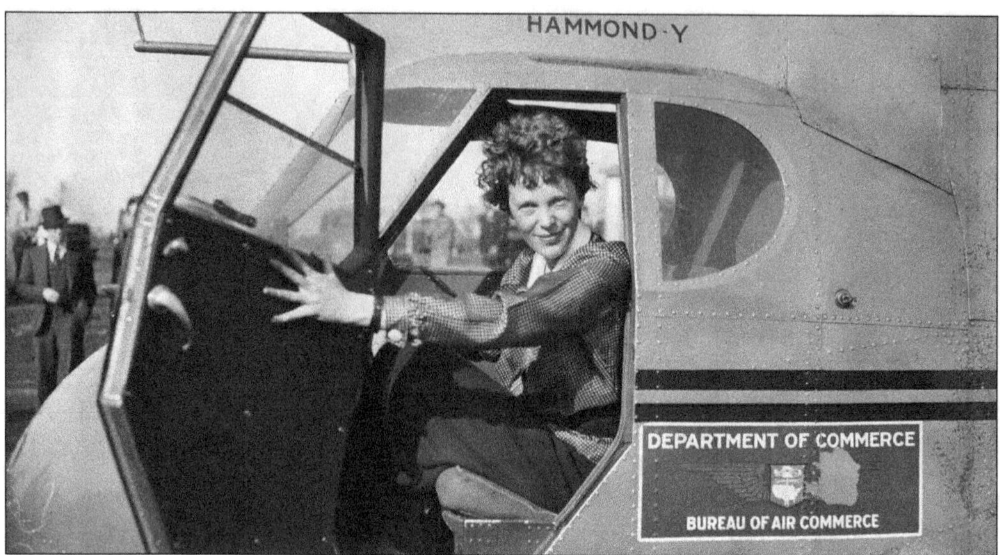

Aviatrix Amelia Earhart is seen above, and the St. Charles Hotel in Hudson seen below. After Earhart and her copilot crash-landed in a Livingston farm field, the farmer invited her to stay at his house. Gracious but preferring not to impose, Earhart stayed at the St. Charles Hotel instead. She was a frequent visitor to upstate New York while campaigning for Pres. Franklin Roosevelt, before her disappearance. Her husband, George Palmer Putnam, who was awaiting her return to a California airport, said, "Technicians familiar with Miss Earhart's plane believe, with its large tanks, it can float almost indefinitely. With retractable landing gear and smooth seas, safe landing (on the sea) should have been practicable." The *Associated Press* reported at the time of her disappearance, July 3 1937, "Coast Guard headquarters was advised tonight that Amelia Earhart was believed to have alighted on the Pacific Ocean near Howland Island shortly after 5 p.m. Eastern daylight time today. A message from the cutter *Itasca*, stationed in the vicinity of the island in the mid-Pacific, said: 'Earhart unreported at Howland at 7 p.m. [E.D.T.]. Believe down shortly after 5 p.m. Am searching probable area and will continue.' " Amelia Earhart is believed to have died around Howland Island, trying to fly around the world solo.

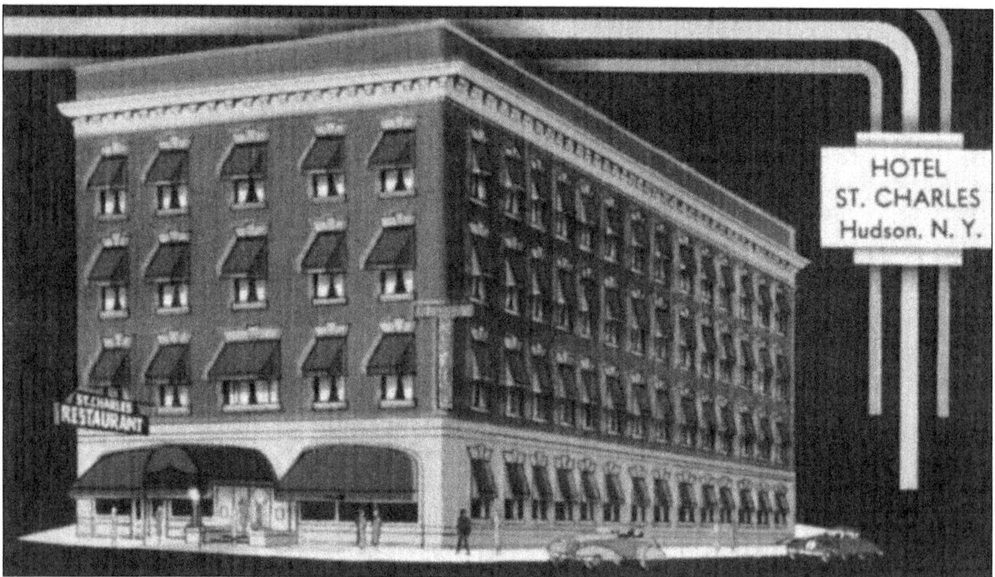

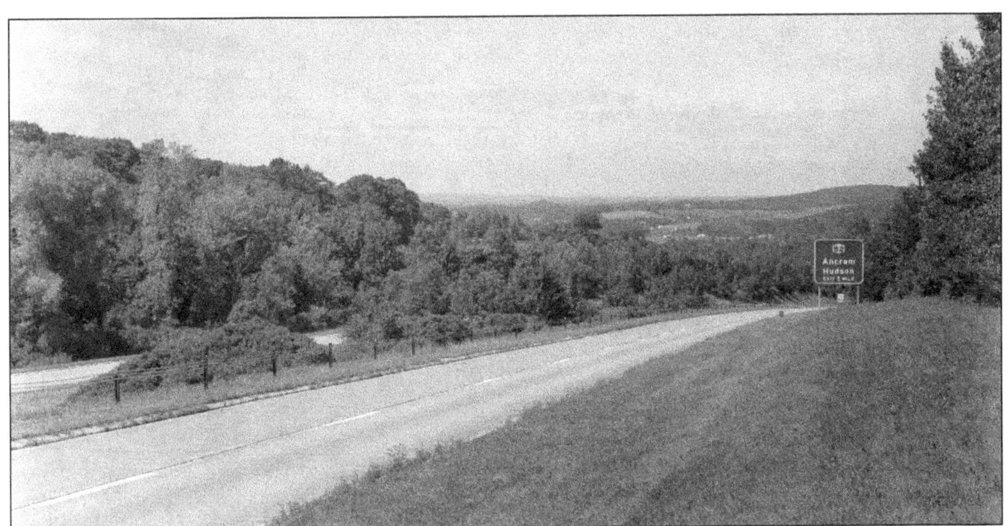

Above is a view of Route 82 mile marker 106.5 on the Taconic State Parkway, near Hudson. Below is a 1940 image of the Taconic State Parkway crossing the Hudson Highlands. Franklin D. Roosevelt was primarily responsible for signing legislation that would take this route through the Hudson Valley scenic region, providing access to state parks. The serpentine, hilly route was designed by architect Gilmore Clarke to showcase views of the Hudson Highlands, the Catskills, and the Taconics. The present route, completed in the 1960s and placed in the National Register of Historic Places, is one of the primary routes to upstate New York from New York City and Long Island. Described as "a consummate work of art, fit to stand on a par with our loftiest creations" by sociologist Lew Mumford, the Taconic and its engineers were praised for avoiding "brutal assaults against the landscape."

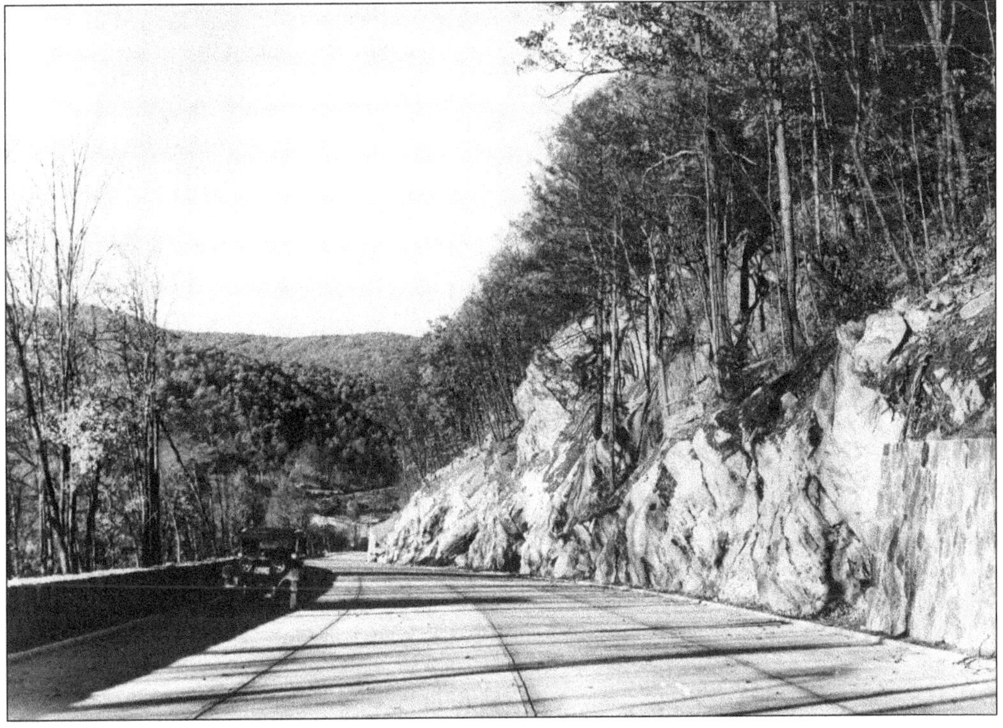

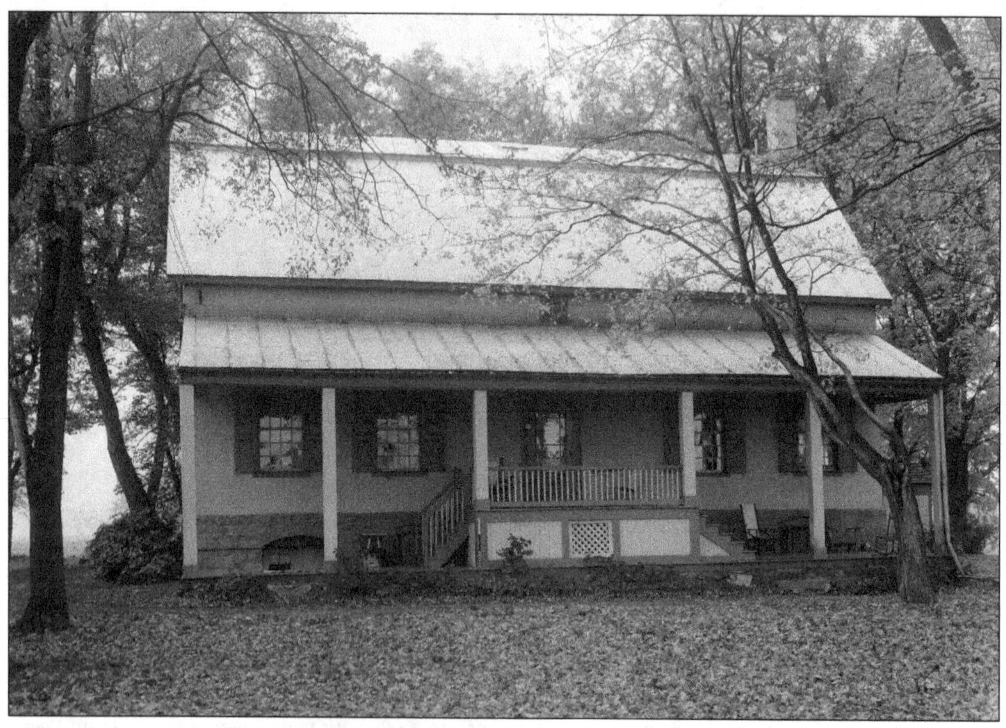

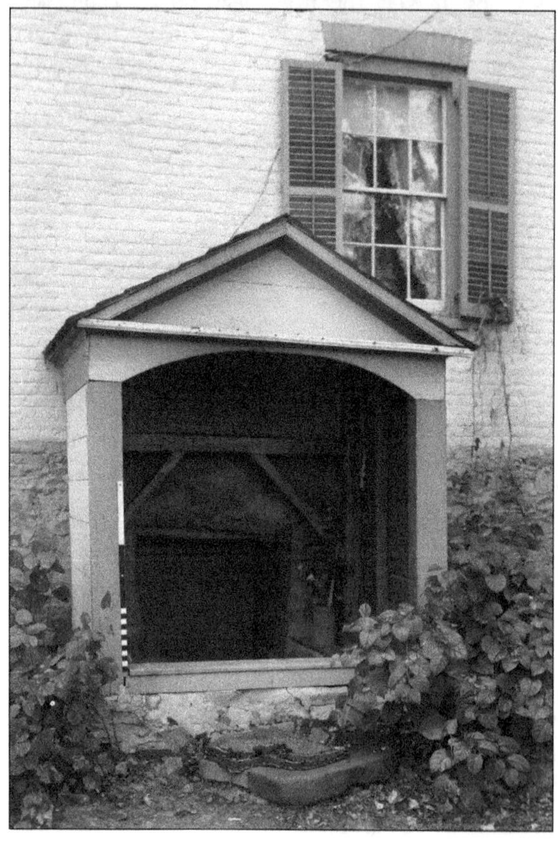

Seen here on September 23, 1937, are details of the rear (west) elevation and the cellar entrance of the Ten Broeck House on Route 82. The 18th-century house is located in an apple orchard, and the earliest known date of its existence is 1734. Its huge, hand-hewn timbers are consistent with early Dutch settlers, and its wide wooden floors and original fieldstone basement are still intact. Built before the American Revolution, the property was later exchanged for the Walter T. Livingston property in Livingston, after 1808. The oldest surviving six-over-six sash window was removed and used as a model for the replacement of all windows. Previously a camp for migrant workers, the house is now owned by two New York City architects.

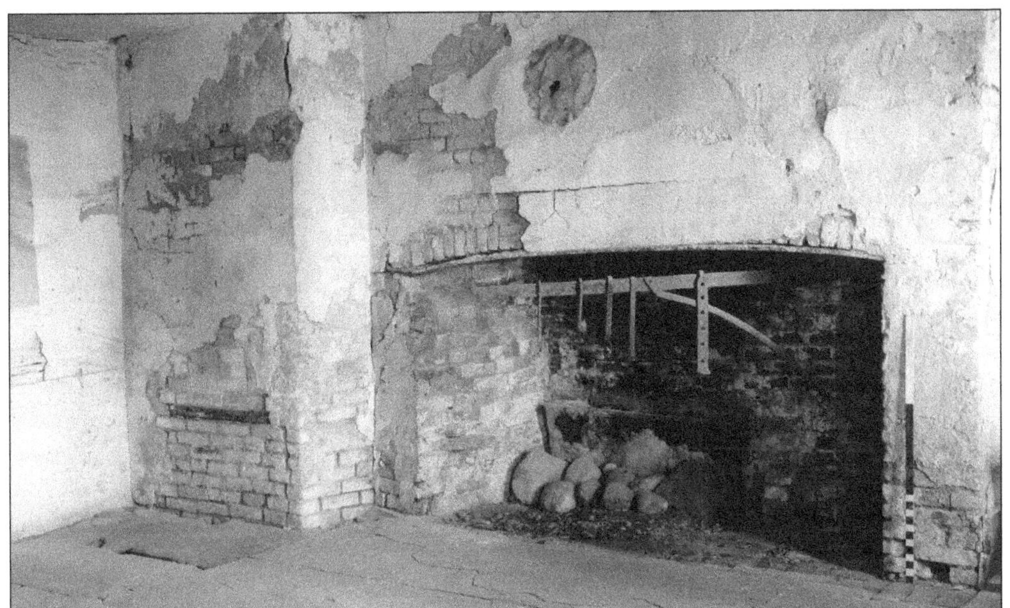

Seen above in 1937 is a Dutch oven in the basement of The Hermitage in Linlithgo. Seen below in 1934 is the Clifford Miller House on Route 23 in Claverack. The Hermitage was started by Peter R. Livingston during the American Revolution but never completed. The 1805 Clifford Miller House, built in the Georgian style with some Regency- and Federal-style details, is also known as the Jacob Rusten Van Rensselaer house and is listed in the National Register of Historic Places. Samuel Livingston married Maria Van Rensselaer and settled in Claverack in 1712, becoming the ancestor of the Ten Broecks of that town. The Livingston family of New York was one of the foremost Colonial families in America. Robert Livingston (1654–1728) acquired a vast land tract in what later became Duchess and Columbia Counties, and in 1686, he received manorial rights for this property by royal charter.

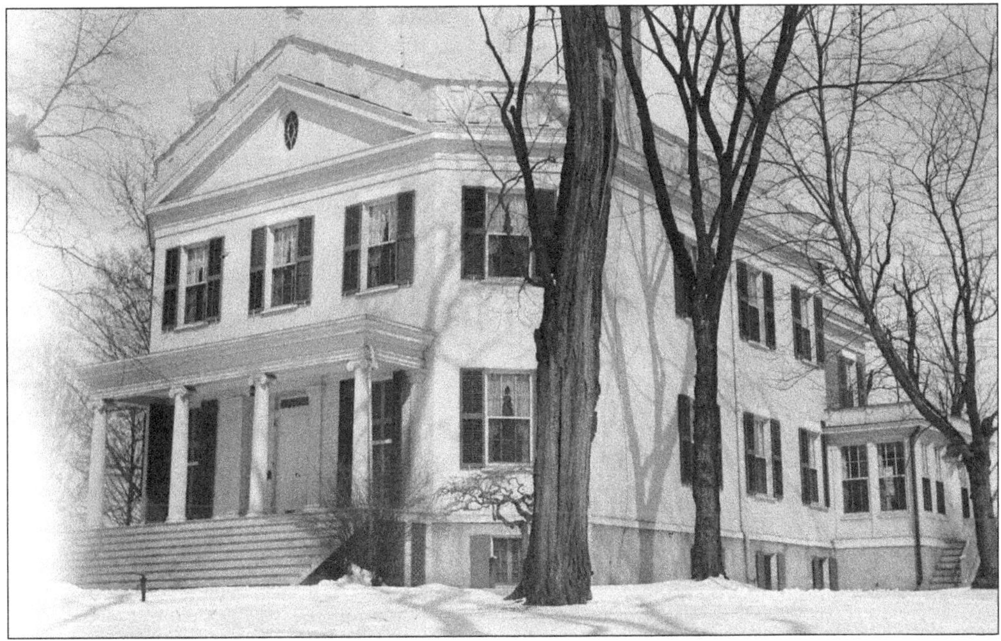

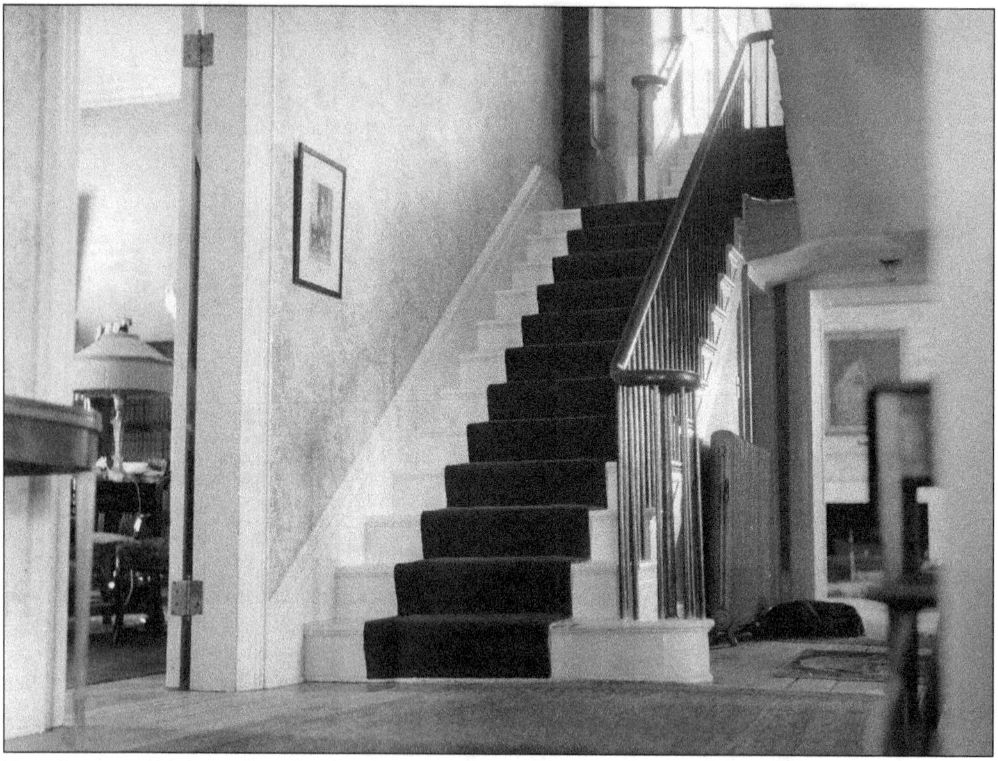

Seen here in 1934 are details of a staircase and a drawing and reception room fireplace in the Clifford Miller House. According to *Chronicles of Wealth, No. 9*, published on December 12, 2002, "Wealthy Astors, Mills and even a Gerry sought to improve their social status by marrying Livingstons. These proved by the exceptional achievements of selected descendants, that they were still able to make a fortune, by participating in the technological and economic revolution, which characterized the Gilded Age. In the 19th century the Livingston fortune waned after being divided many times, but the family kept a social status which was clearly above much wealthier families. Livingstons defined the class, which was considered America's aristocracy in those days." Robert Livingston also sold 6,000 acres of his manor to Queen Anne to be used for the Palatines.

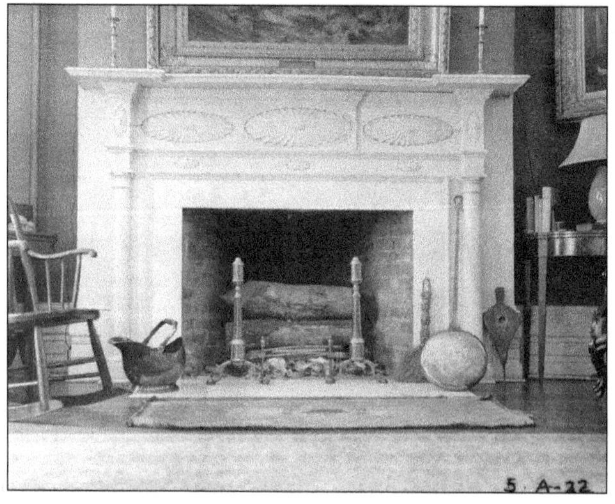

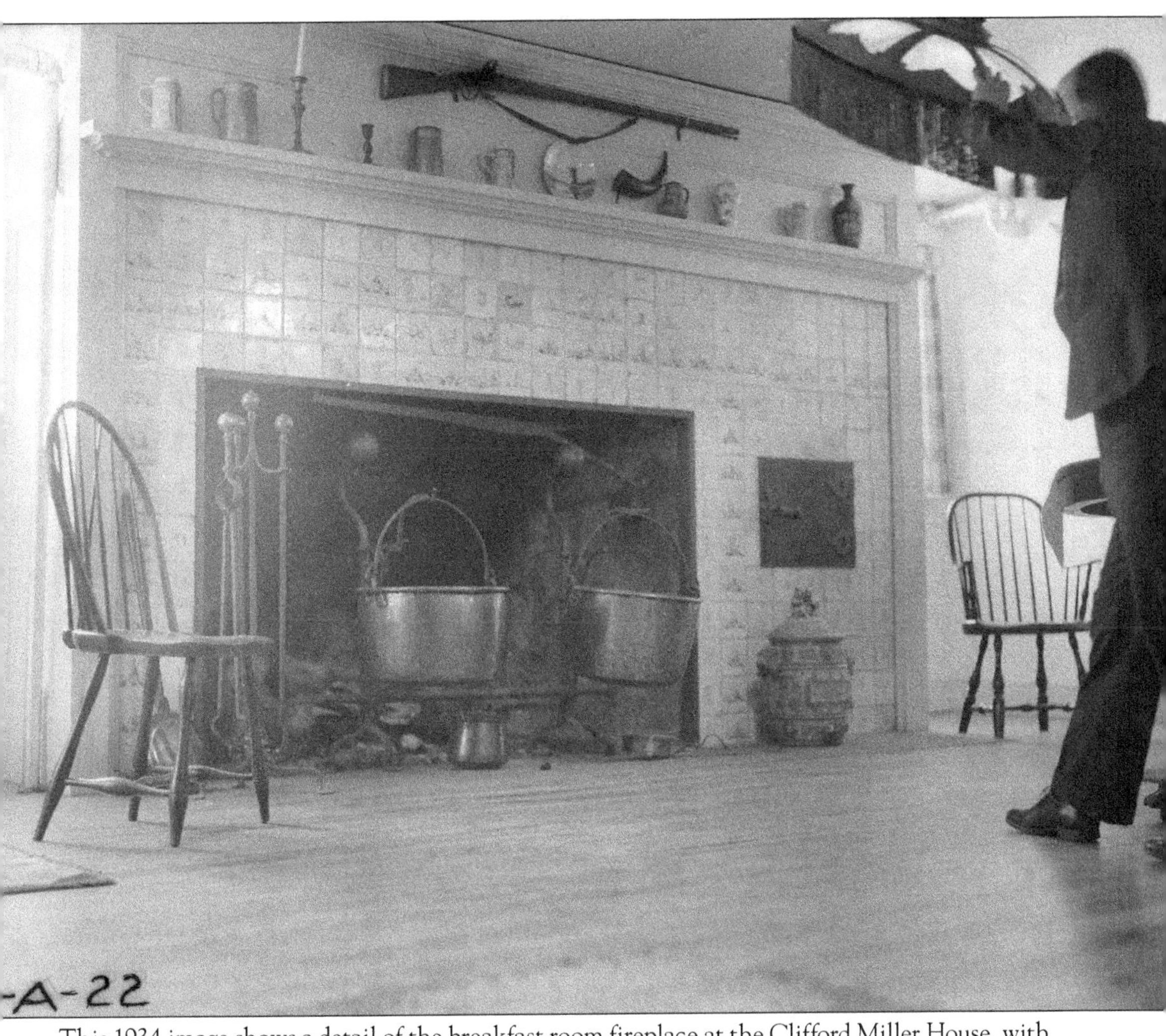

This 1934 image shows a detail of the breakfast room fireplace at the Clifford Miller House, with the Red Mills nearby. In a 1913 issue of *House Beautiful*, Clara Brown Lyman wrote an article titled "How a Businessman Became a Skillful Country Gentleman." In it, she said, "But sentiment alone did not lead Clifford Miller to buy a three hundred acre farm in the heart of the Hudson Valley—he believed he could make it just as profitable an investment as his business in New York. He was looking for a fresh outlet for his capital apart from the city noise and discord which had begun to tell on his health and nerves. Originally all the land East of the Hudson River and as far north to Albany and Troy was part of the Van Rensselaer Manor."

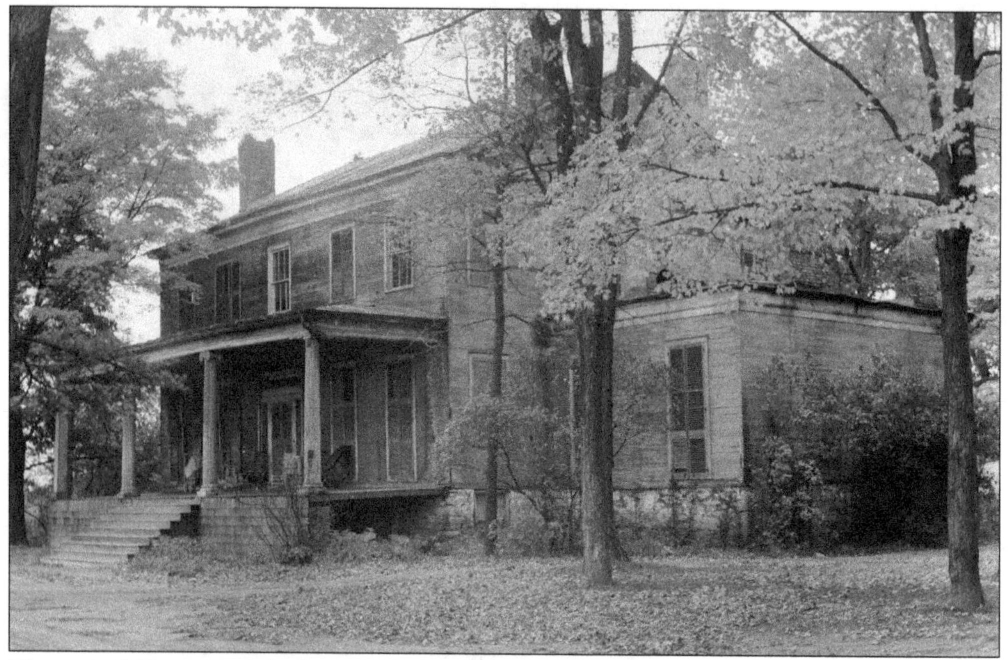

This is a 1937 image of the Proper House, also known as the Livingston House, built in 1800. The Livingstons migrated from Ancram, Scotland, and were descended from William, Fourth Lord of Livingston. Descendants of the Livingstons include two presidents of the United States, George H.W. Bush and George W. Bush, as well as First Lady Eleanor Roosevelt.

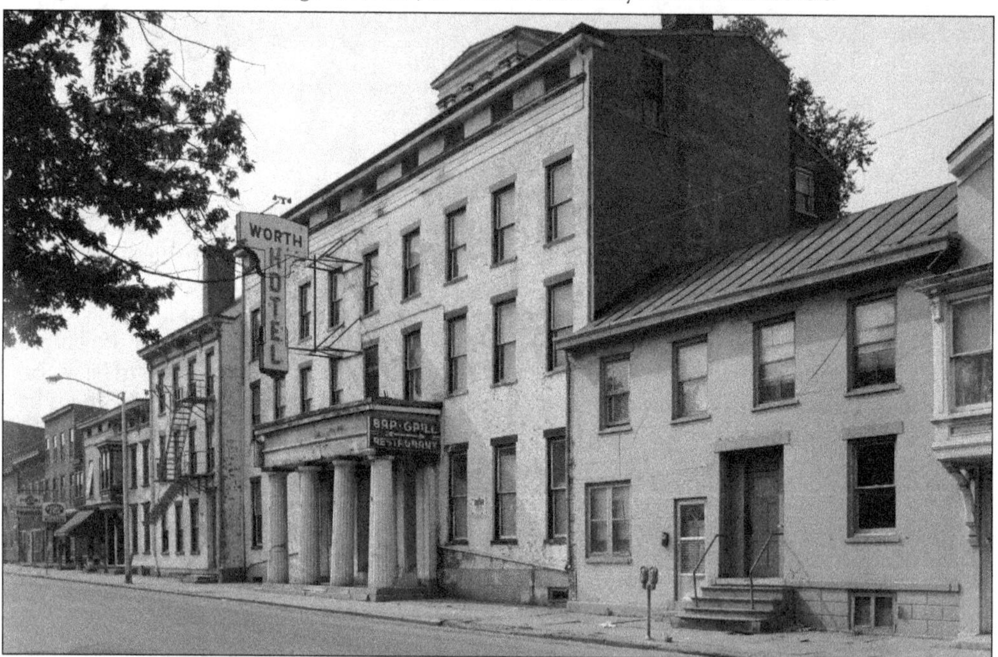

This is a general view from the northeast of the former General Worth Hotel at 213–215 Main Street (now Warren Street) in Hudson. Demolished in 1970, it was among the many taverns that existed in Hudson from 1786 to 1946, which were the scenes of parties, secret trysts, balls, and meetings.

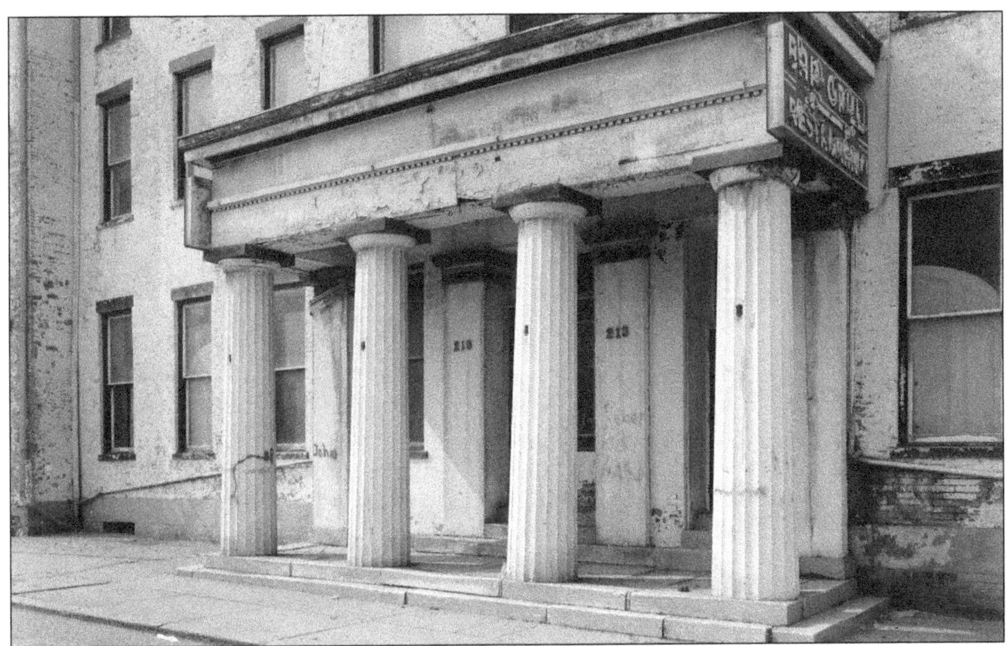

Seen above is a detail of the main entrance portico at the General Worth Hotel, and below is the main staircase from the first floor to second floor, seen from the south. It was named for Gen. William Jenkins Worth, who became a national military hero and an officer during the War of 1812, among many other wars and battles. Worth's father, Thomas, was a Hudson shopkeeper in the 1790s and later became a captain of a whaling ship. His mutinous crew slayed him with an ax. Gen. William Worth's boyhood home in Hudson still stands in the locally designated historic district. Worth Avenue and the hotel are not the only places named for him; Worthville, Pennsylvania; Worth, Illinois; Worth County, Georgia; the Lake Worth Lagoon and the city of Lake Worth in Florida; and Fort Worth and Lake Worth in Texas were also named in his honor. He was a legend in his time.

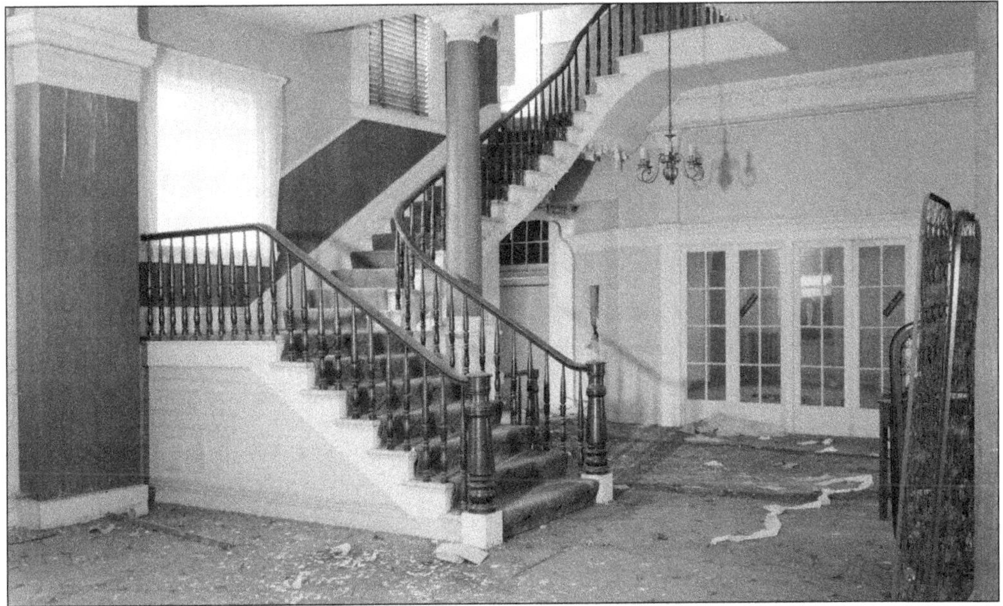

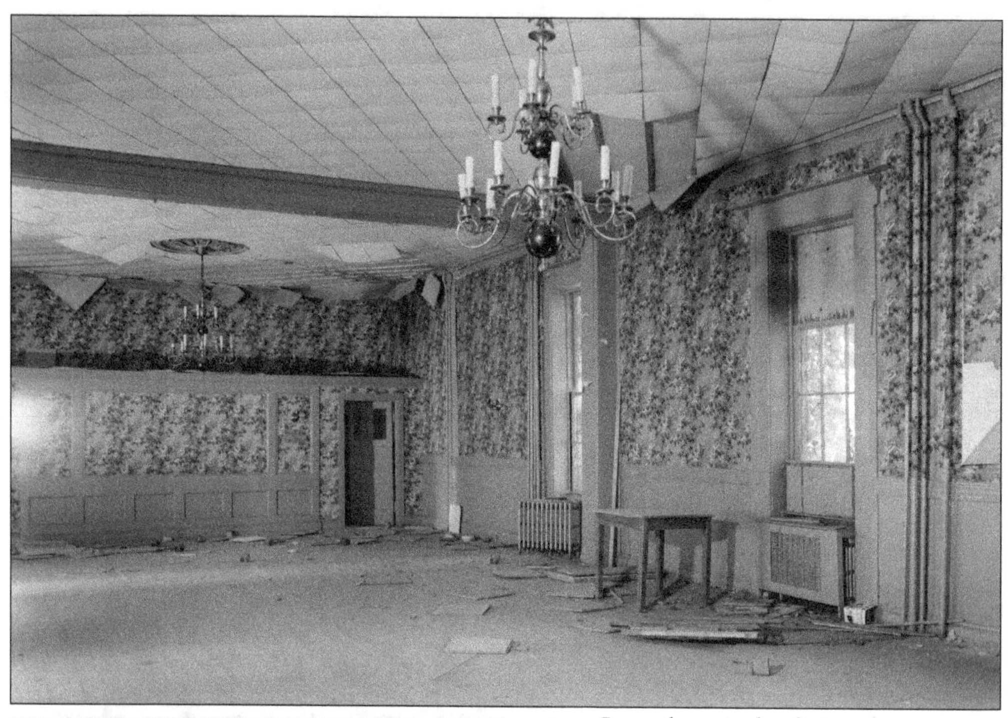

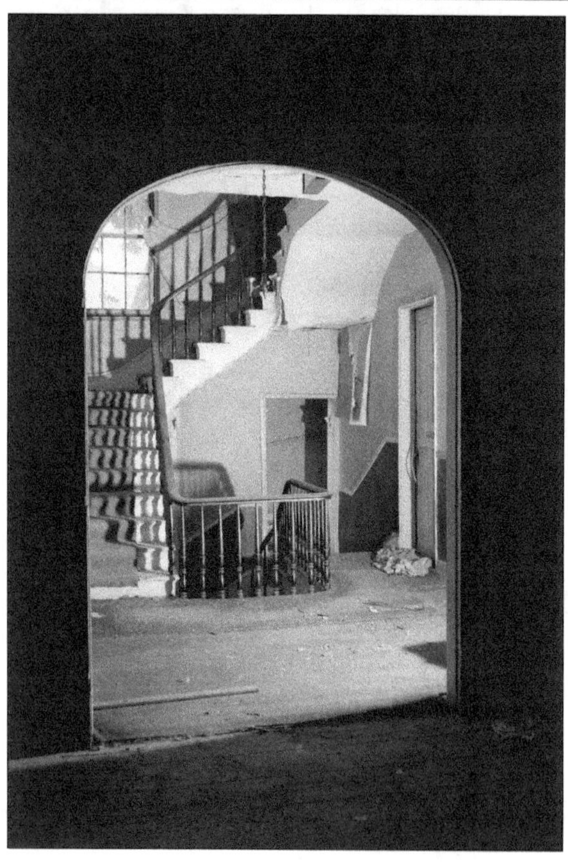

Seen above is the dining room on the first floor at the General Worth Hotel. At left is the stair hall and staircase on the second floor, from the east. On November 12, 1860, the *Hudson Star* reported, "Having taken possession of the Badgley Hotel (formerly the Hudson House) it will be hereafter called the Worth House." There hung in the ballroom a portrait of Worth by Chatham Center artist Hugh McKay, showing Worth in full uniform. In 1934, the Potts Memorial Hospital in Livingston acquired the property, changing the name from Worth House to the General Worth Hotel. One of the most important celebrations at the Worth Hotel was in 1935 when the Rip Van Winkle Bridge was dedicated. That evening, after the bridge was formally opened, a banquet there was attended by 236 happy attendees, including the mayor of Albany.

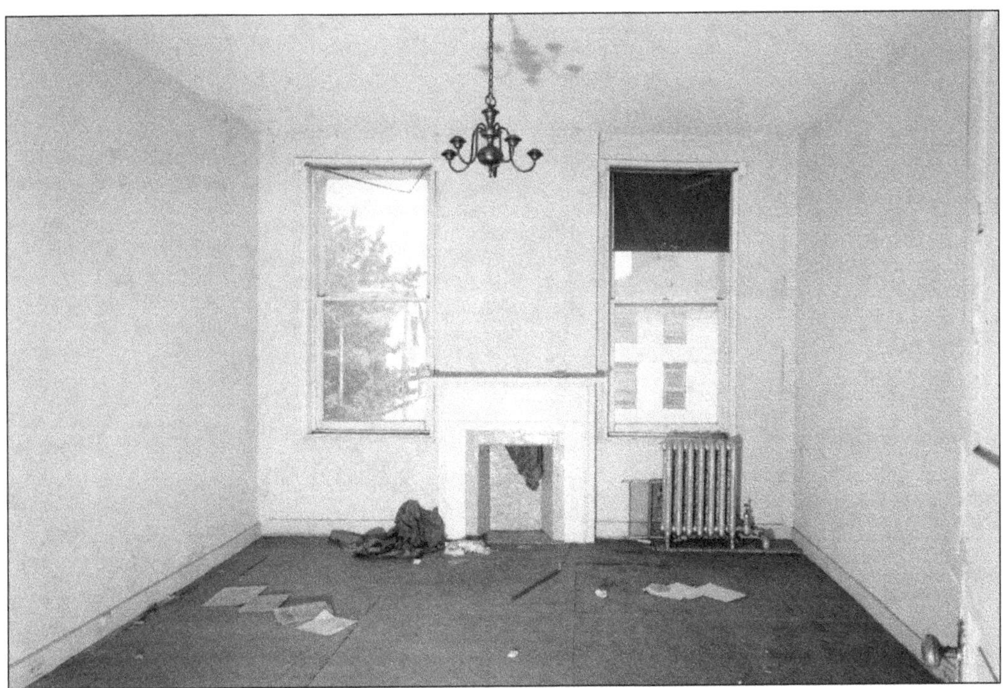

Above is a typical bedroom in the central area of the second floor of the General Worth Hotel. Bvt. Maj. William Jenkins Worth said, "But an officer on duty knows no one—to be partial is to dishonor both himself and the object of his ill-advised favor. What will be thought of him who exacts of his friends that which disgraces him? Look at him who winks at and overlooks offences in one, which he causes to be punished in another, and contrast him with the inflexible soldier who does his duty faithfully, notwithstanding it occasionally wars with his private feelings. The conduct of one will be venerated and emulated, the other detested as a satire upon soldiership and honor."

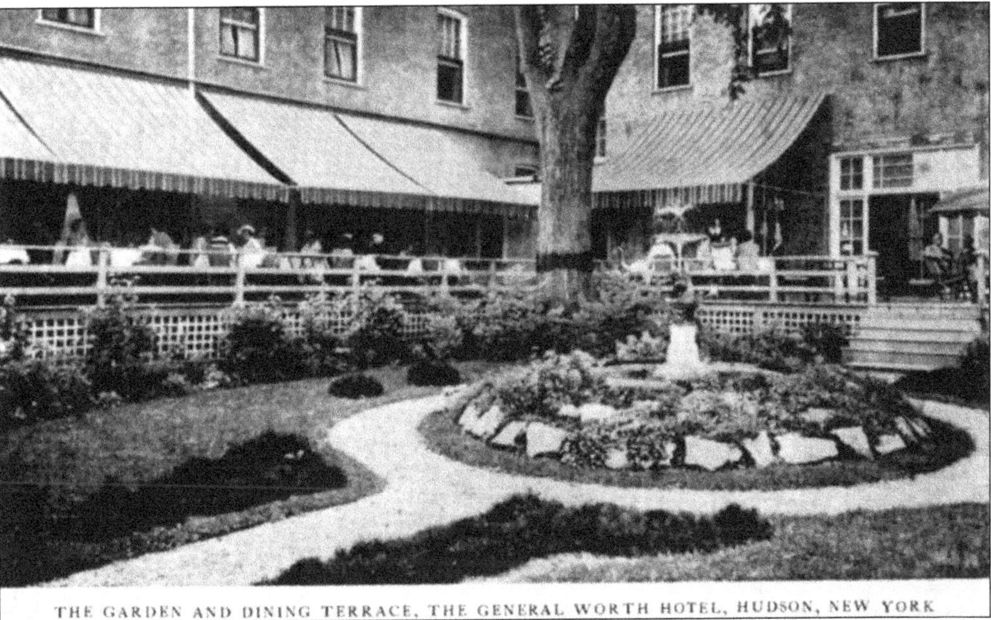

THE GARDEN AND DINING TERRACE, THE GENERAL WORTH HOTEL, HUDSON, NEW YORK

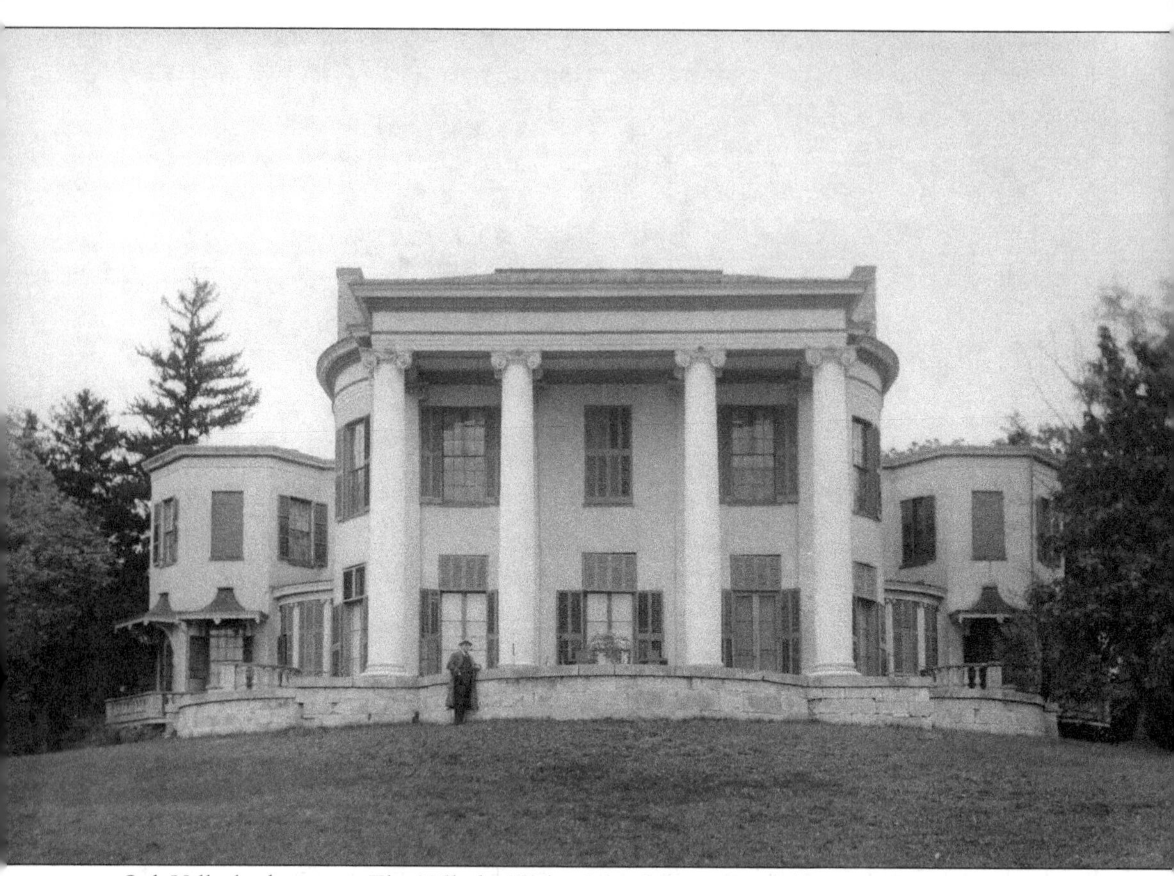

Oak Hill, also known as The Hill, the Widow Mary's House, and the Mary Livingston House, was built in 1790 in Hudson. A view of the oval parlor exists in *Historic Houses of the Hudson Valley*, published in 1942. John Livingston climbed the highest oak tree in determining where to build his house for the best views. There existed an intimacy between this house and Talavera, a house in Claverack, as both houses were visible to one another due to being so high. A semaphore code system of communicating was effective between the two households before the invention of the telephone. According to Capt. Franklin Ellis in 1878, "A grandson, Henry W., living south of Johnstown, is the only member of this branch of the family left in the town. He is also a maternal descendant of Count de Grace, the companion of Lafayette, and equally distinguished for his service in the American cause in the Revolution."

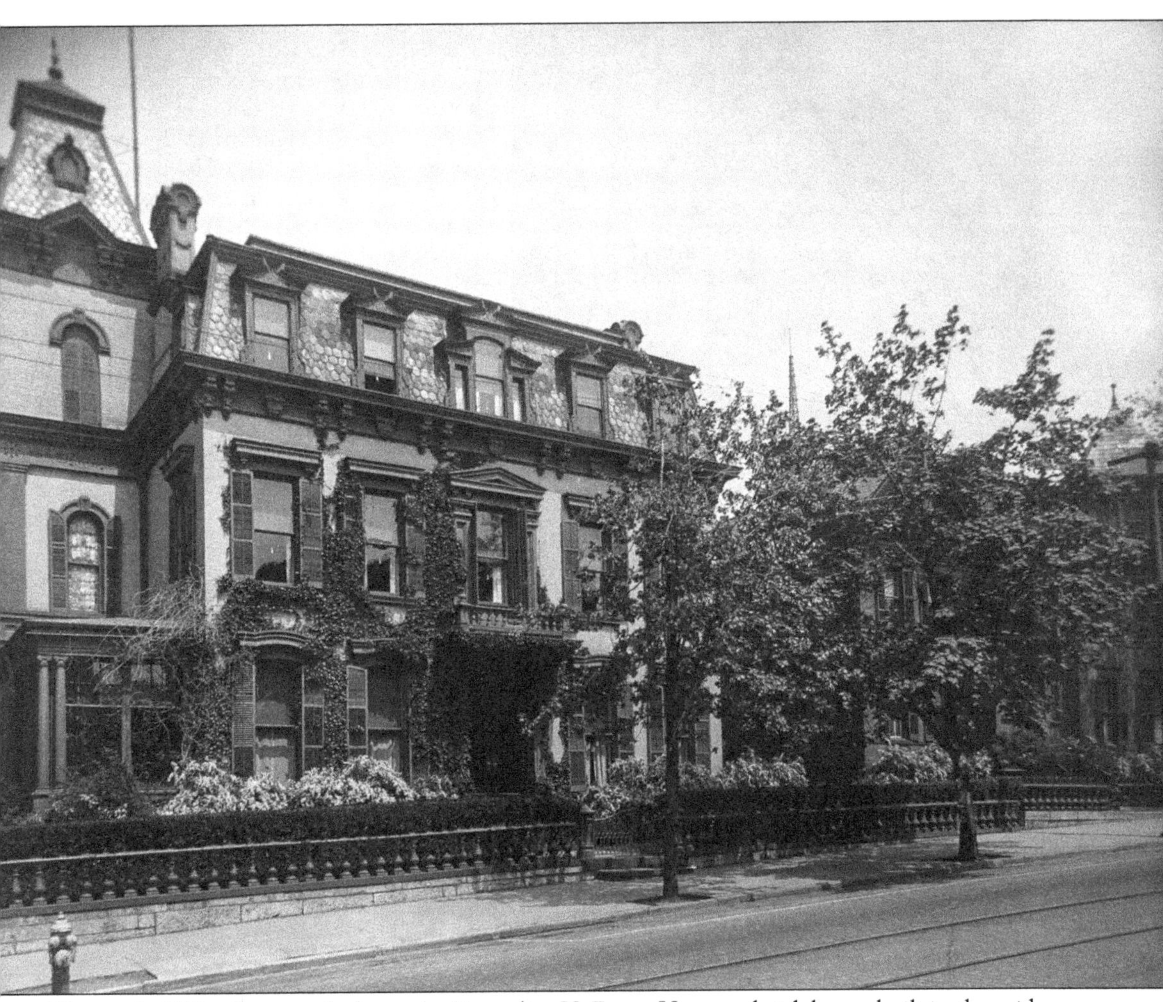

This early-1920s photograph shows the Cornelius H. Evans House, a brick house built in the mid-19th century on Warren Street in Hudson. Evans was a brewer and served two terms as Hudson mayor. His father had purchased a brewery in 1796. The house demonstrated the family's prosperity. The brewery closed in 1920 with Prohibition. In the 1940s, the house was sold to Congregation Anshe Emeth, a local synagogue, and then, in the 1970s, it was sold back into residential use. In 1974, the house was listed in the National Register of Historic Places. The house has a mansard roof with dormer windows shingled in fish-scale slate, climbing ivy, a parking area behind the house, a hallway with original wainscoting, and the original staircase. The molded woodwork, white marble mantels, stained glass, brass doorknobs, and interior shutters are all original. (Courtesy Dan Region.)

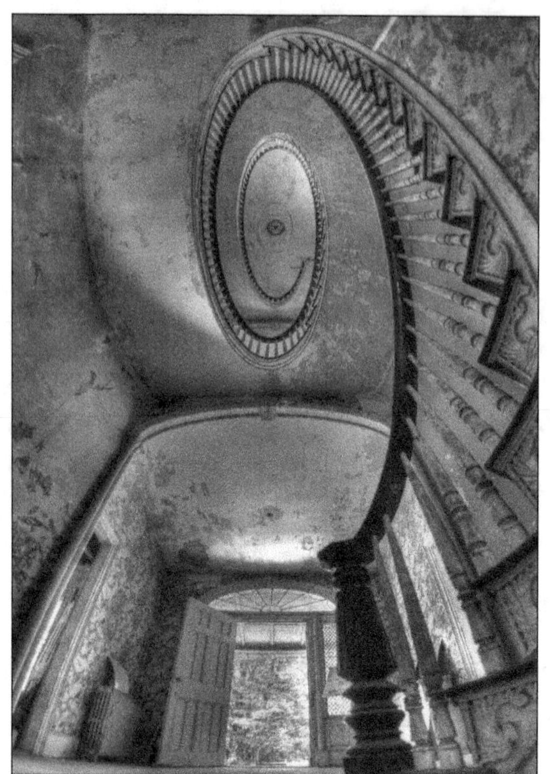

The elliptical staircase at the Dr. Oliver Bronson House is seen here. It was a Federal-style house originally built for Samuel Plumb in 1812. The house was later reinvented by the premier architect of his day, Alexander Jackson Davis (1803–1892). The superintendent of the nearby New York State Training School for Girls lived in the Plumb-Bronson house until the 1970s. For additional information about the Dr. Oliver Bronson House and its ongoing restoration, please visit www.dobhdaybook.wordpress.com. (Courtesy Michael Fredericks.)

These officers' quarters at the United States Military Academy at West Point are another example from architect Alexander Jackson Davis. Davis also worked on a few state capitols, including Indiana and North Carolina, for which he created the basement floor plan and the reflected ceiling plan.

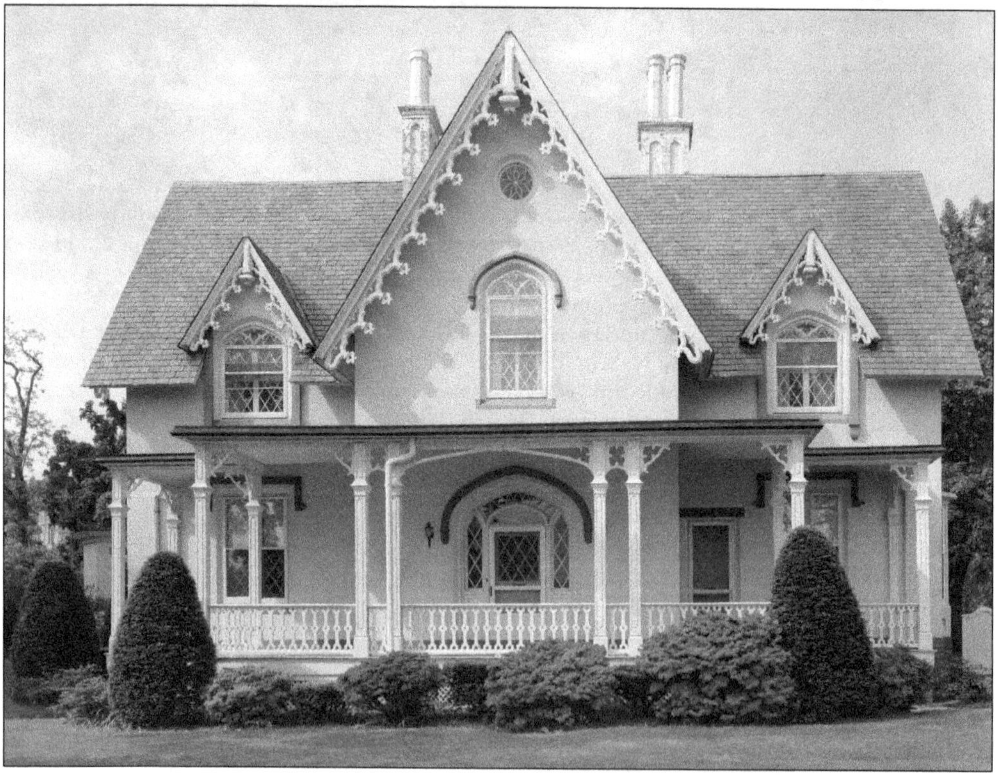

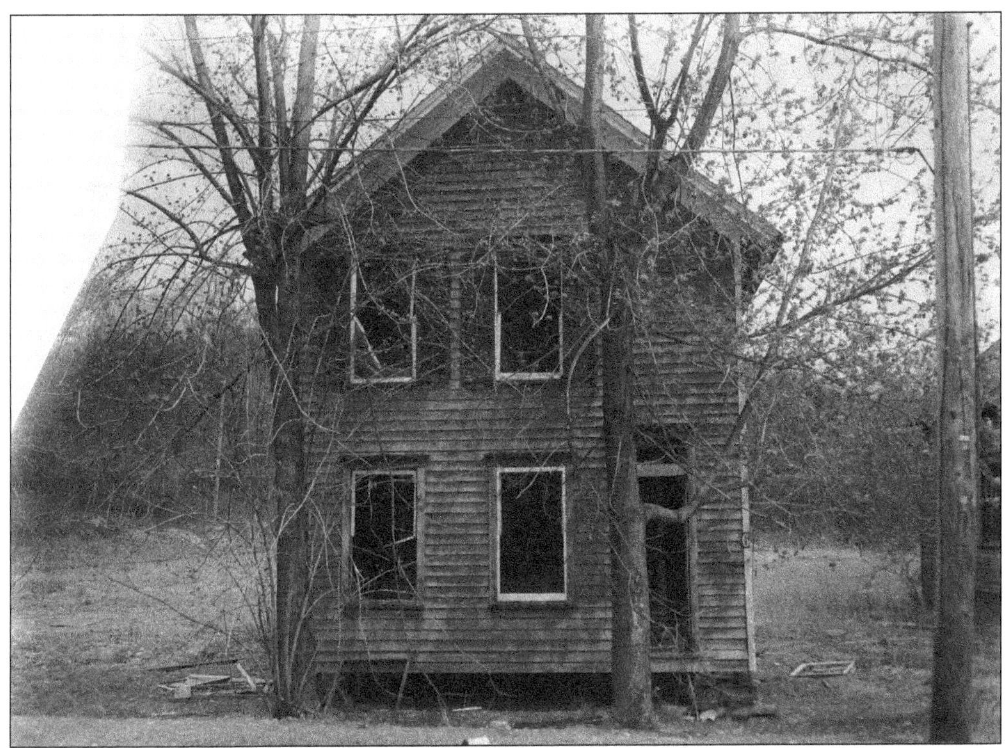

Seen here is the south (front) elevation at 6 Power Avenue in Simpsonville, a neighborhood in Hudson with houses built in the 1850s, on the site of the former home of Joel T. Simpson. This neighborhood featured a unique Chinese-Gothic residence, making it one of the most outstanding architectural studies in the entire Hudson Valley region. Briefly, the State of New York considered buying the property for the nearby training school. A high number of Simpsons owned the property through the years. The property changed hands many times in the 1880s, with one buyer doubling his investment in five days after reselling. The buildings did not contain heating systems and were prone to flooding. While the walls were substantial, wooden elements rotted over time.

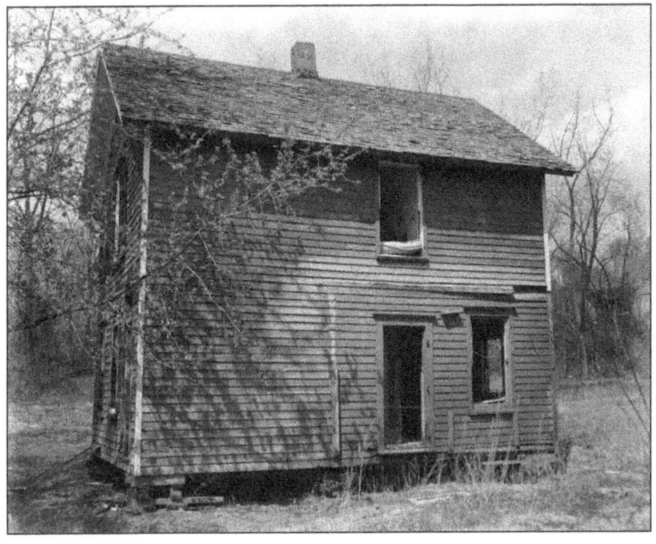

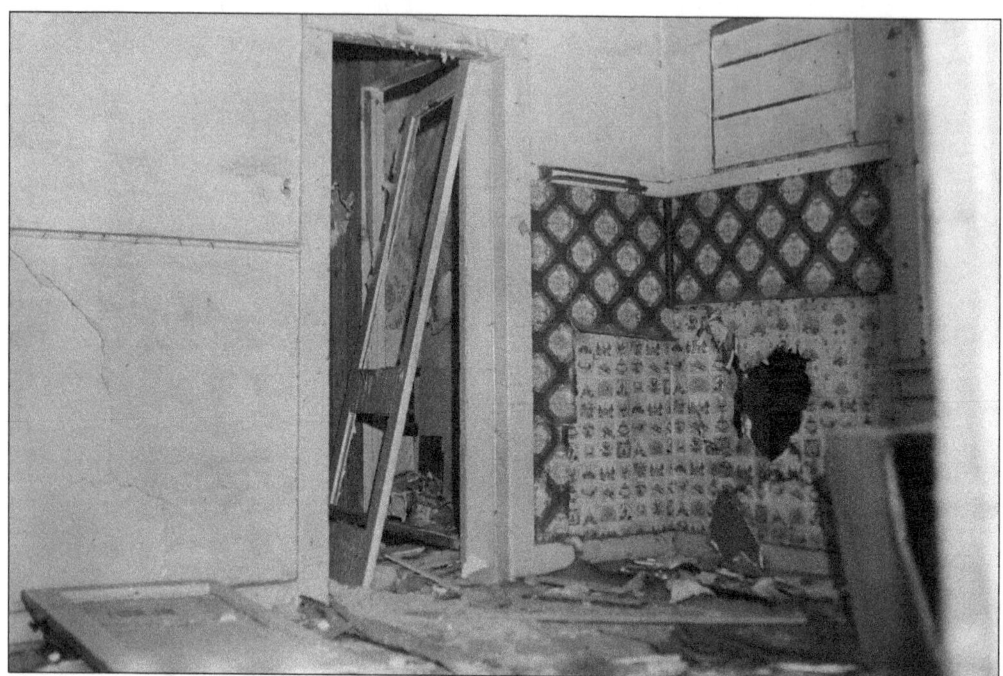

This is another view of 6 Power Avenue in the Simpsonville neighborhood in Hudson. The houses were overgrown with weeds and vines throughout the neighborhood. Because of substantial deterioration of most of the structures, it had been recommended they be demolished for safety and public health reasons. In 1906, the parents of a Mrs. Ensign and a Miss Stackpole purchased the property, along with the land where Gifford Wood Company stood.

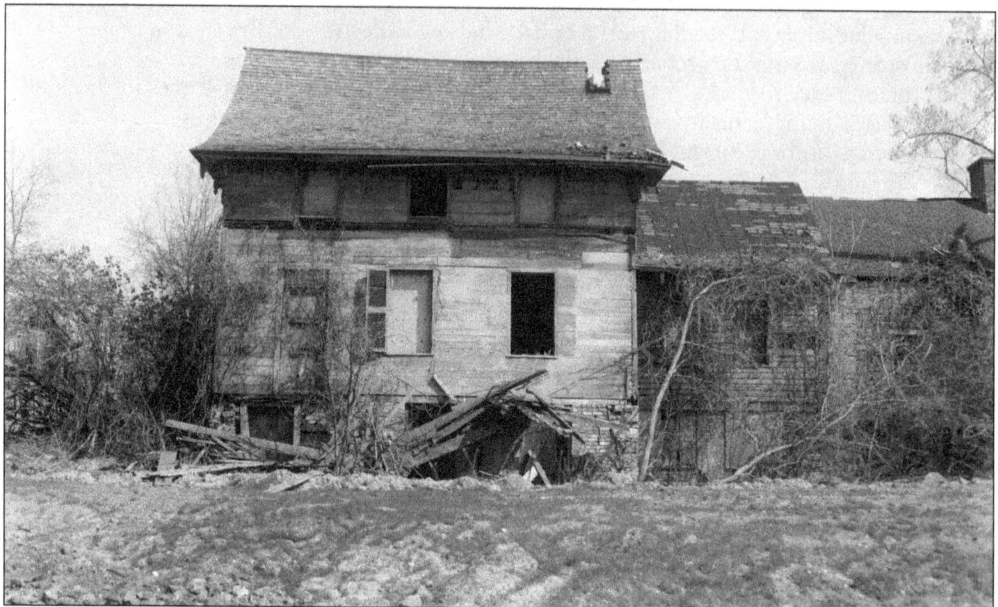

This view shows the southwest elevation at 7 Power Avenue. Considered the most significant of the houses in the neighborhood, 7 Power Avenue was beyond saving, and its interesting architectural elements had been destroyed by vandals and the elements. William Stackpole, an owner of Simpsonville, was a contractor and horse trader who had worked on the armory foundation.

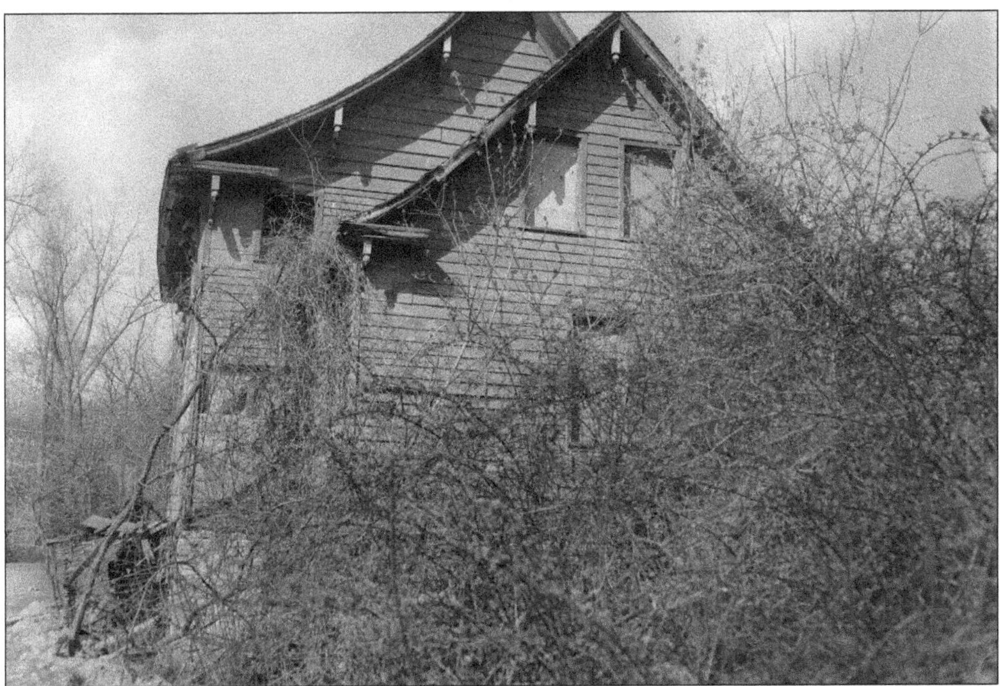

This view shows the southeast elevation of 7 Power Avenue. Many historians and locals are at a loss in recalling this neighborhood; its stories are lost to time. The houses were on land bordering a giant swamp extending back from the Hudson River under the towering Mount Merino.

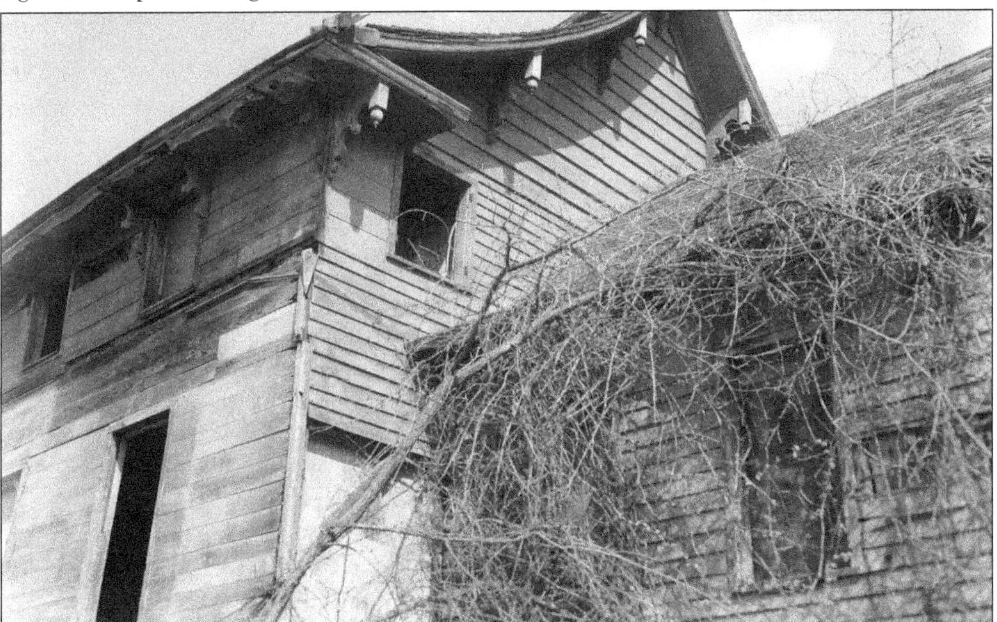

This view shows the bracketed cornice and pendant detail at 7 Power Avenue. There is speculation that some of the seafaring men of the whaling times, along with their families, lived here, but this has not been confirmed. Because of its proximity to Hudson's waterfront and the Hudson River, it is possible that many of the workers in the shipbuilding and whaling industries could have settled here.

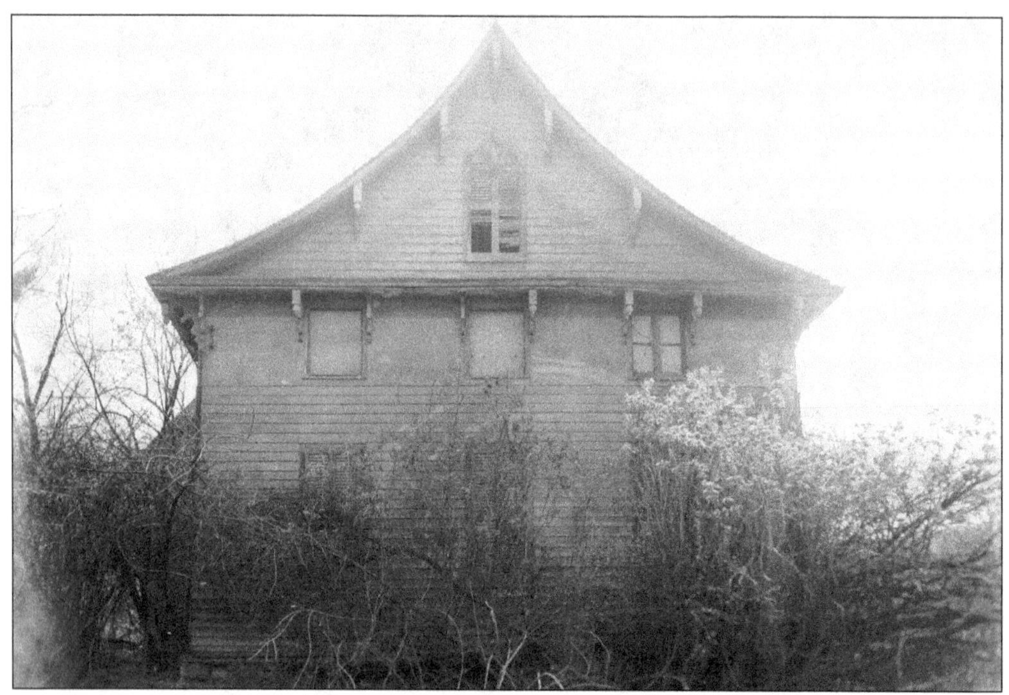

This view shows the northwest elevation of 7 Power Avenue. Behind the Oriental-styled structure was a small stone building with a matching concave roof and an interior brick oven, which may have been a bakery. Not much is known about this small building.

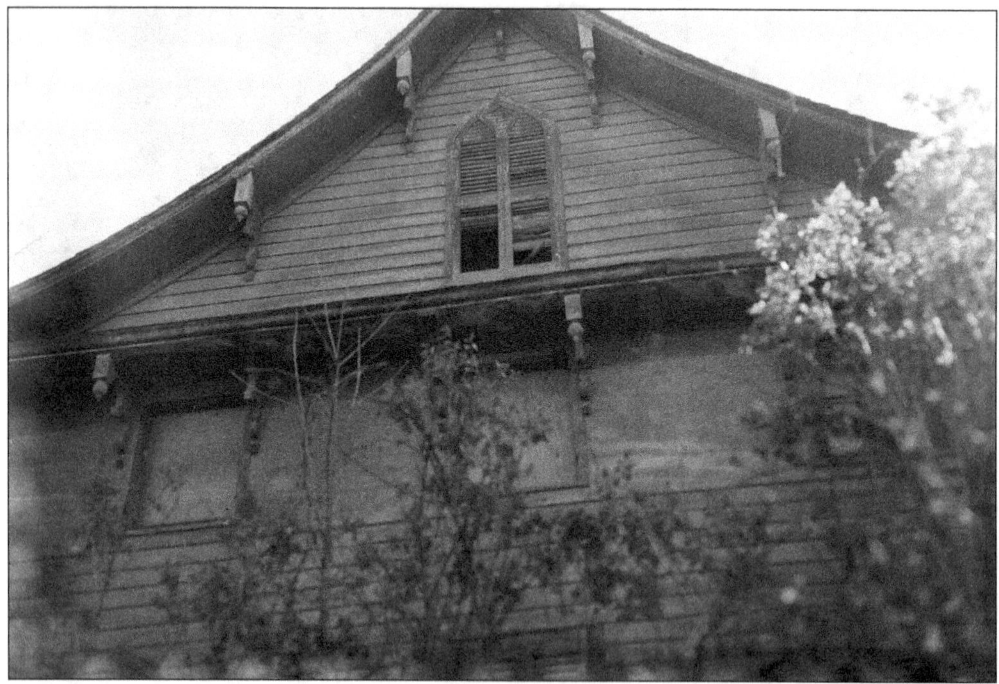

This view shows a shuttered attic window at 7 Power Avenue. Anna R. Bradbury's *History of the City of Hudson* described Joel T. Simpson as a retired Southerner who "for a long period of time, dispensed both a cordial hospitality and beneficent charity from his home."

Seen here is the foundation detail at 7 Power Avenue. The Gothic and gingerbread influences indicate that it was built in the mid-19th century, but it could have been added at a date later than the original construction. Several old, dead trees threatened the structure. There was also an unusual privy accessory to this house with a matching concave roof.

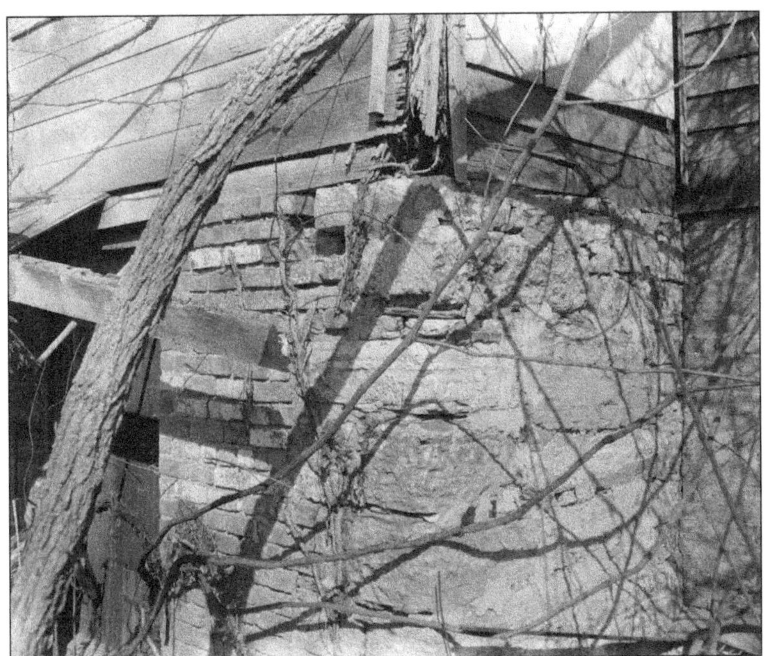

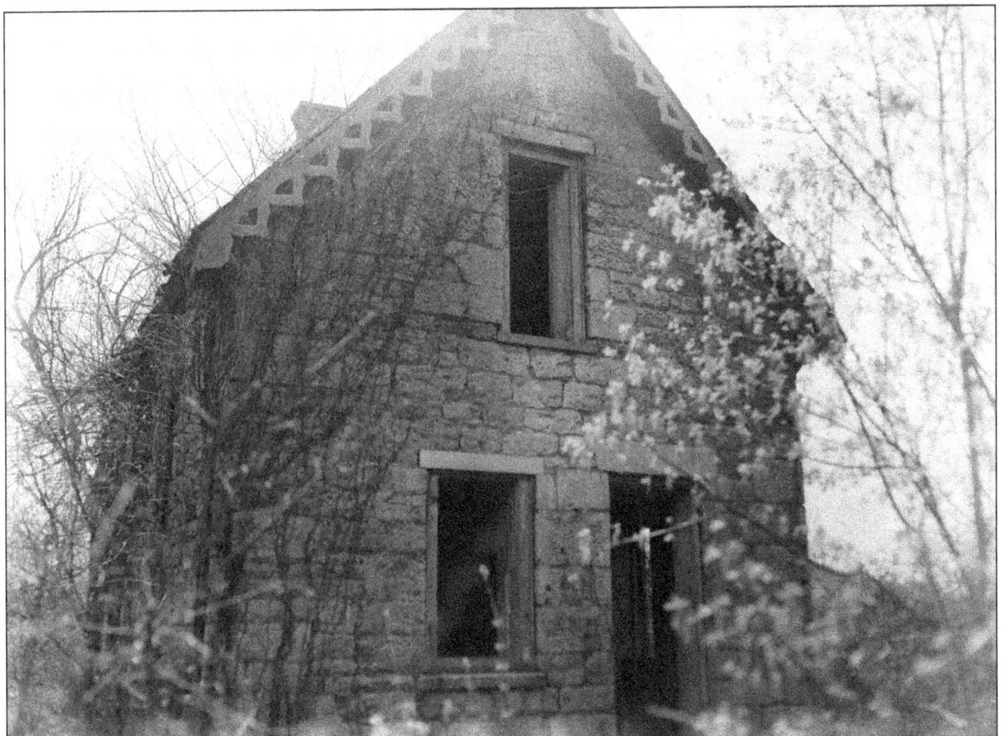

The view shows the northwest (front) elevation at 8 Power Avenue in Simpsonville. This building was the least threatened by flooding due to its higher elevation, and it had been marked for salvation. Only the elevation of a portion of Power Avenue and the access driveway above flood level would have insured all-weather access. Plumbing would have necessitated a tie-in to the sewer that ran along that side of Power Avenue.

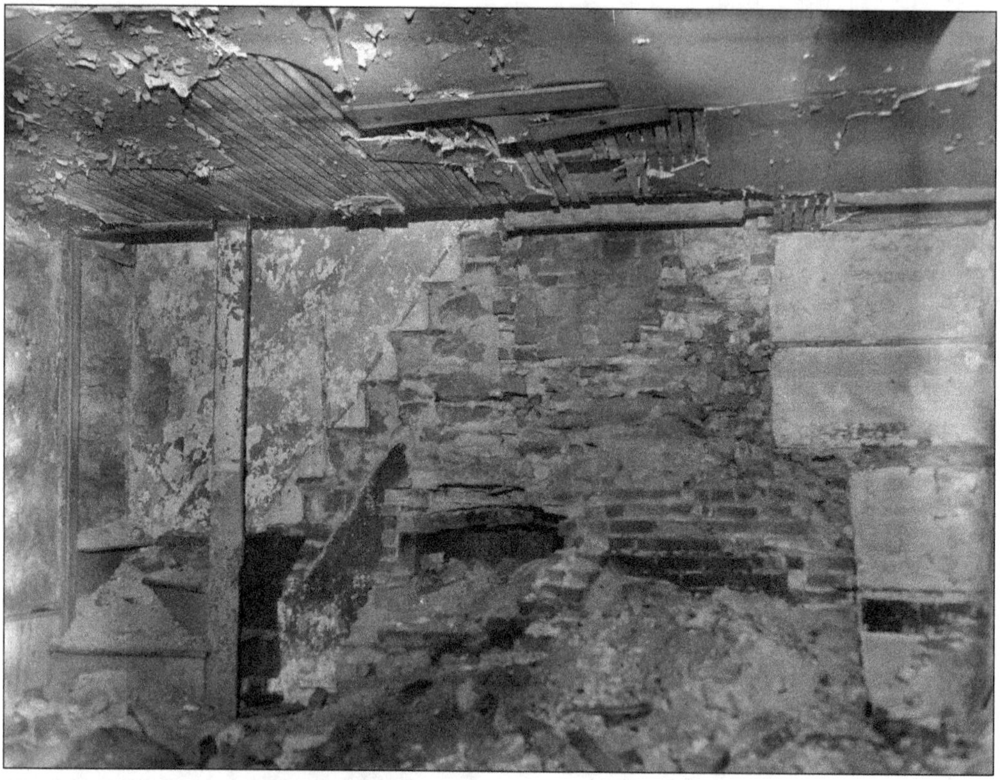

This is an interior view of 8 Power Avenue. It is important to remember that none of the houses had indoor plumbing, but they still survived until the 1970s. Former Hudson mayor Paul Colwell recalled playing with friends in Simpsonville in his youth. "It was a lovely spot, except it was filled with mosquitoes," he says. He also remembers an elderly woman telling stories of years ago when sailing ships came so close to Simpsonville that their great bowsprits towered over the buildings.

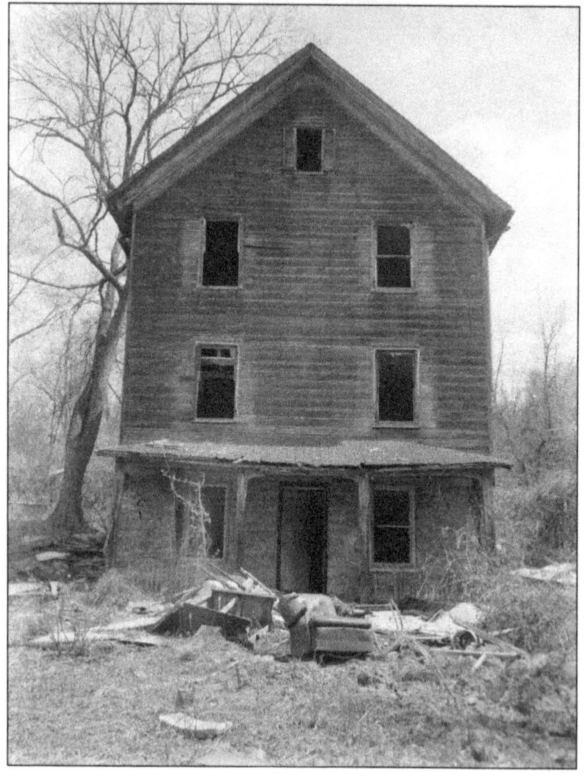

This view shows the west (rear) elevation of 10 Power Avenue. While some people remember, it seems as if many locals have never even heard of Simpsonville, and some even claim it never existed. Power Avenue was named for George H. Power, once the proprietor of the Hudson & New York Steam Transportation Line and also a former mayor of the city.

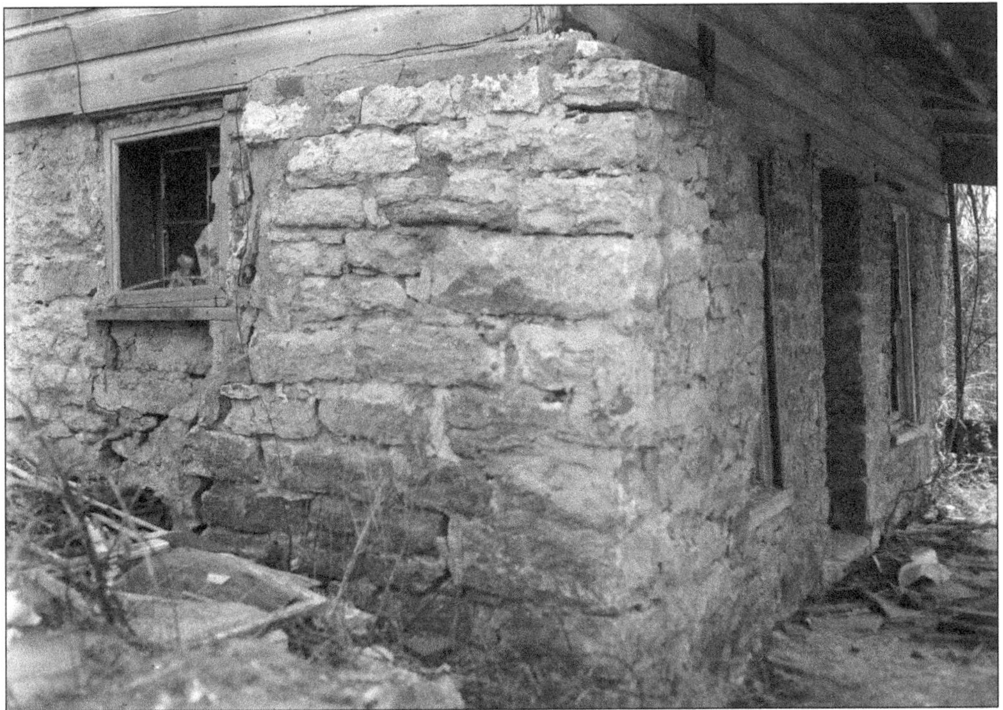

This view looking southeast shows the foundation detail of 10 Power Avenue. The late Henry M. James, a Hudson historian, suggested that Simpson built all the houses on Power Avenue making up Simpsonville. It was a 98-acre tract of land, and Simpsonville residents kept gardens, cows, pigs, and chickens. Reportedly, they paid just $11 monthly for rent.

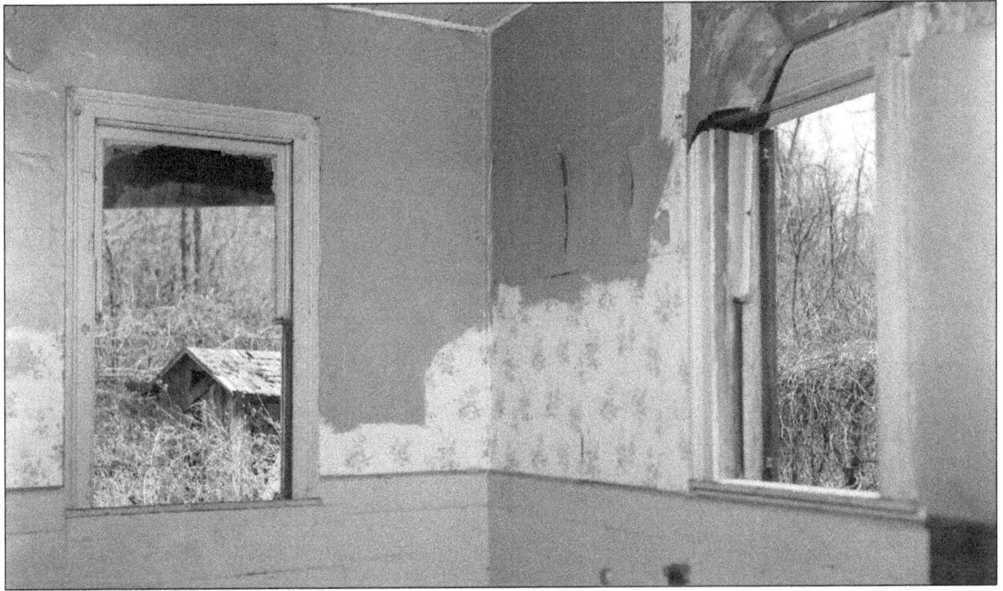

This is an interior view of 10 Power Avenue. Most of the houses were razed in 1981 during an urban renewal program that was making way for an industrial park. The neighborhood included Power Avenue and East Court Street. A neighborhood with many Germans, Simpsonville included the Ressler, Koglman, Lagithe, Kluceritse, Hafner, Gaschel, and Hardy families.

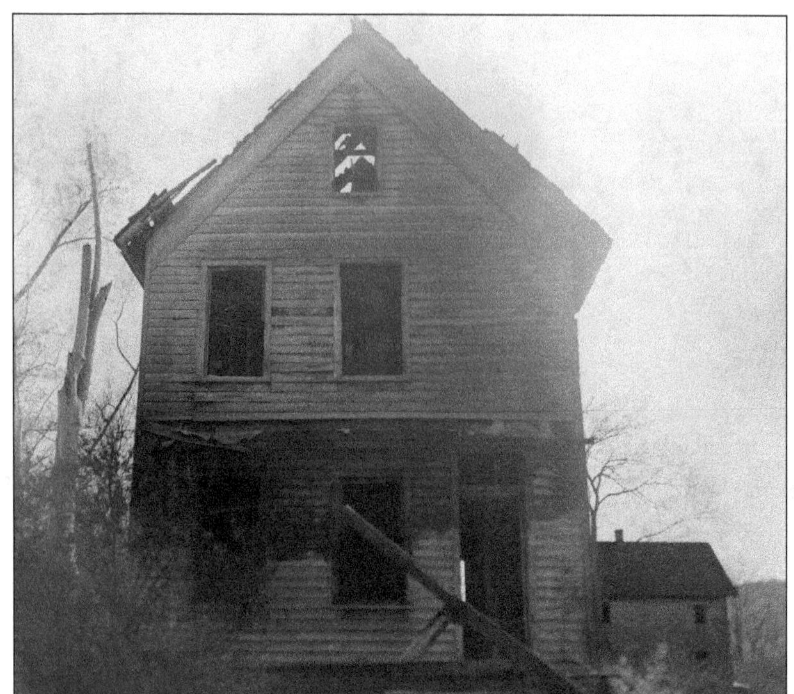

This view shows the north (front) elevation of 11 Power Avenue. The girls from the nearby training school used to climb fences to get away from the school, making allies of Simpsonville grandmothers, who would feed them. "They'd have a ride waiting for them down the dirt road," said former mayor Paul Colwell.

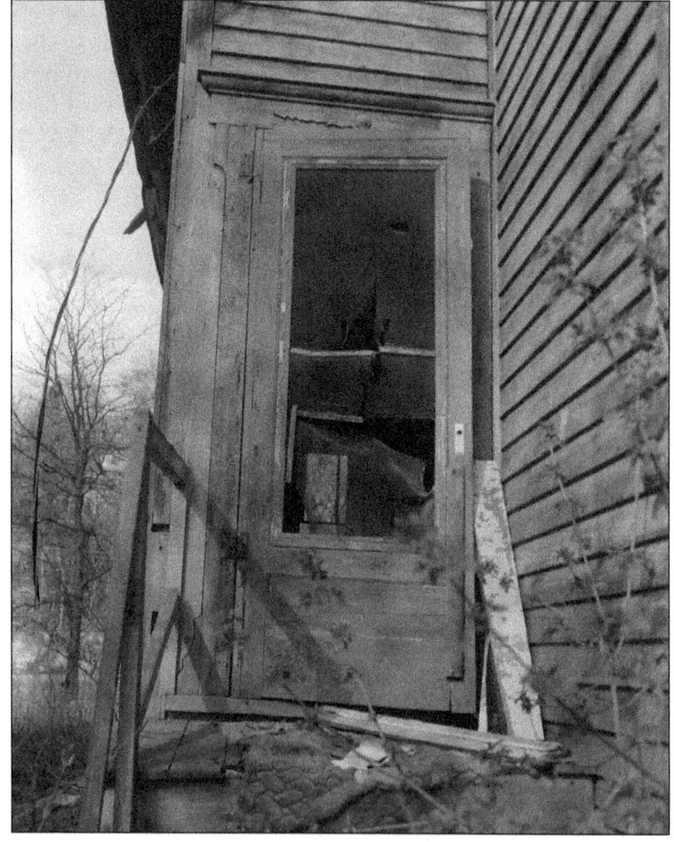

This north view shows the side-door detail of 12 Power Avenue. Residents here worked at the Universal Match plant, Foster's Refrigeration, and the pocketbook factory in the 1940s and 1950s. Since the Stackpole family never worked on the houses, they all fell into disrepair and decay.

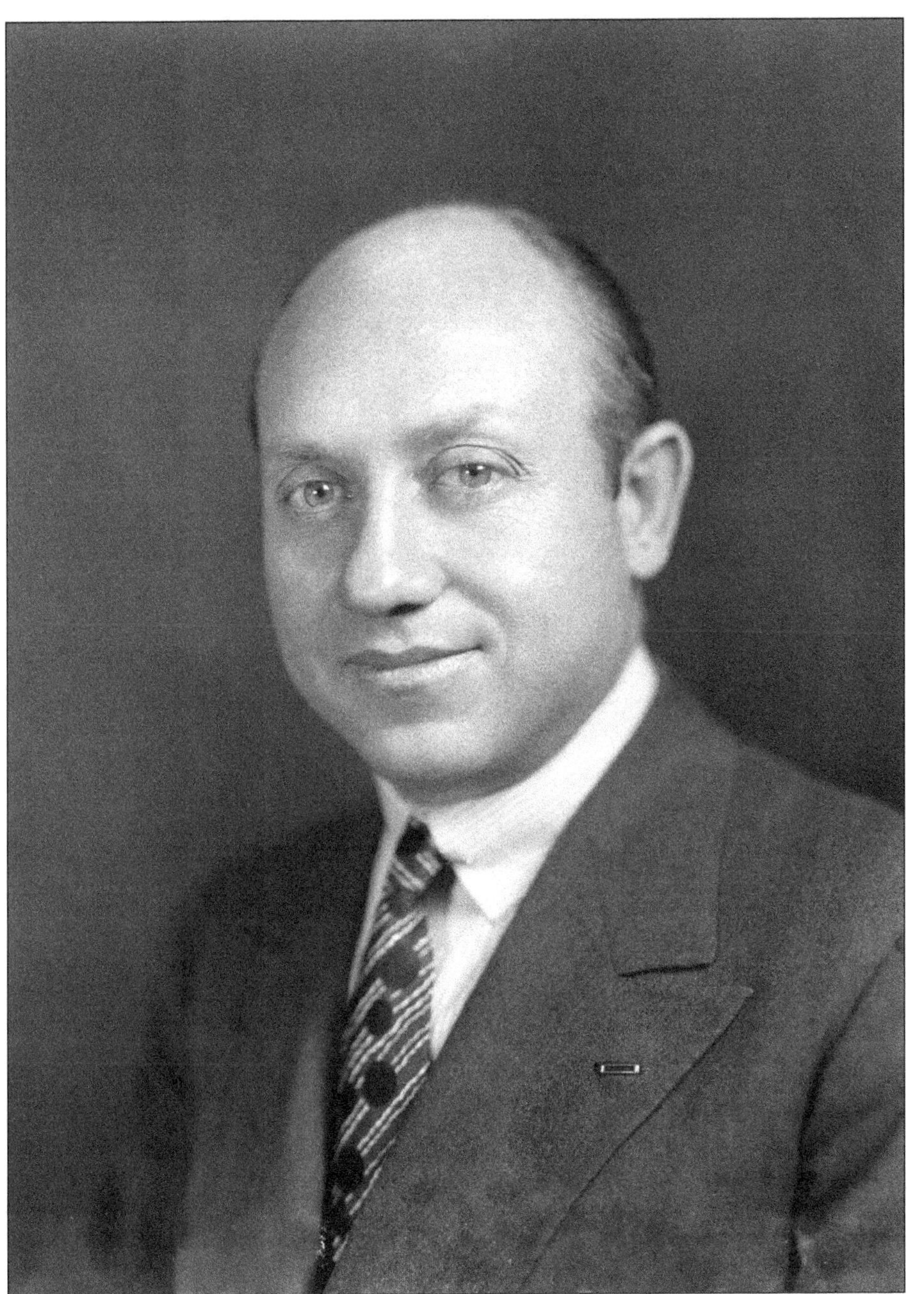

State senator Jacob K. Javits is seen here. Javits, along with state senator Daniel P. Moynihan and Congressman Gerald Soloman, met with Mayor Paul Colwell, who asked for their assistance with the National Advisory Council on Historic Preservation so Simpsonville improvements could go forward. "We decided to go to Washington to see what we could do on the national level," recalls Colwell. The city was to restore the Chinese-Gothic Simpsonville structure as well as the nearby stone house, which was possibly a bakery or milk house. Sadly, that did not occur, and it is unclear what happened to the structures. Mayor Colwell had said there was a fight with preservationists over the property. Former common council president Tom Quigley was instrumental in relocating Simpsonville residents prior to its demolition in 1981.

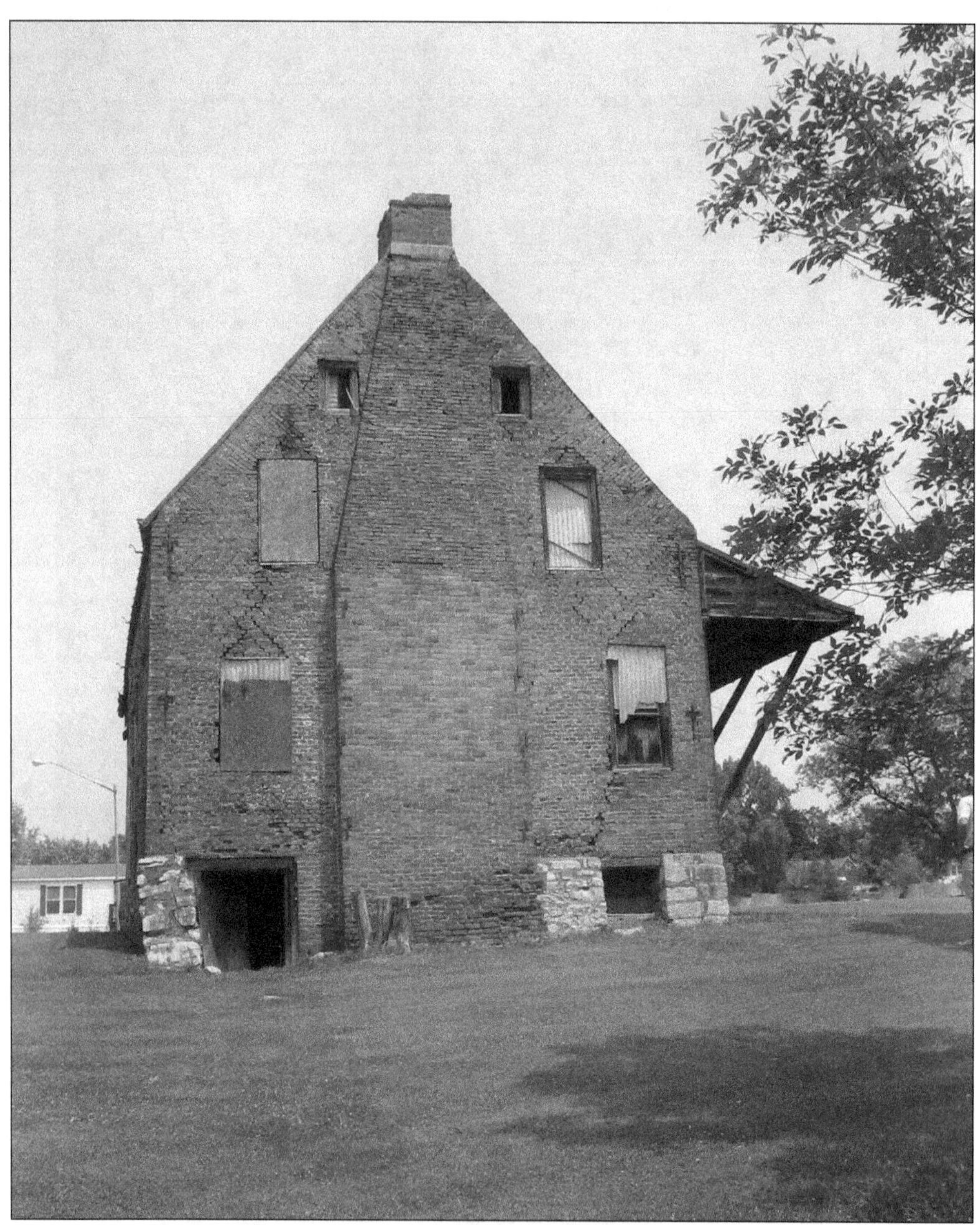

The Jan Van Hoesen House, constructed around 1720, still stands on a tract of land purchased from the Mohicans by Jan Fransen van Hoesen, the grandfather of its builder. The initials of the first occupants of the house were worked into the brick masonry in black clinker headers, believed to be the only surviving regional example of this type of monogramming from the 1715–1750 period. According to Ruth Piwonka, "The van Hoesen house reflects significant aspects of social and cultural history of the upper Hudson Valley. A history of the van Hoesen family and their community at Claverack affords a balancing view of Hudson Valley colonial history which usually emphasizes manor lords and tenants at the expense of successful freeholers who established themselves in prosperous agricultural and mercantile activities." (Courtesy William E. Krattinger, New York State Division for Historic Preservation.)

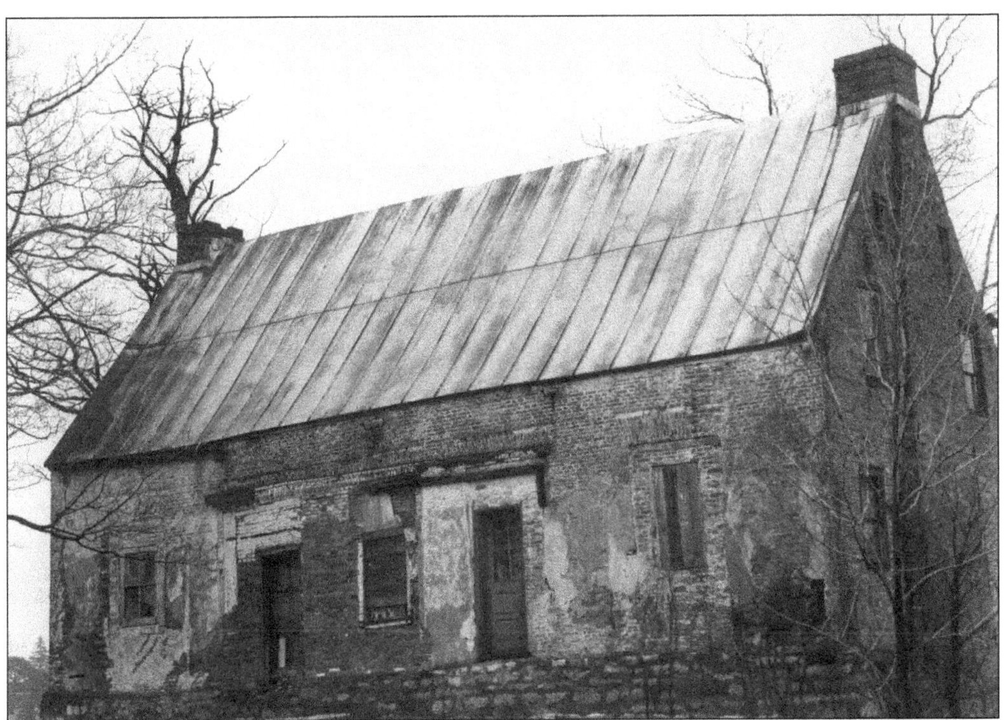

The Van Hoesen House is located on the first elevation of land rising 20 feet above a principal flat on the east side of Claverack Creek and Route 66. In older times, the approach to the house was from the southwest and northeast on a local road that led to Claverack Landing (what is now Hudson) on the Hudson River. What is now the backside of the house was originally meant to be the facade of the home. The architectural style of the house originated in 16th- and 17th-century Dutch and northern European vernacular dwellings that were descendants of the medieval longhouse. (Both, courtesy William E. Krattinger, New York State Division for Historic Preservation.)

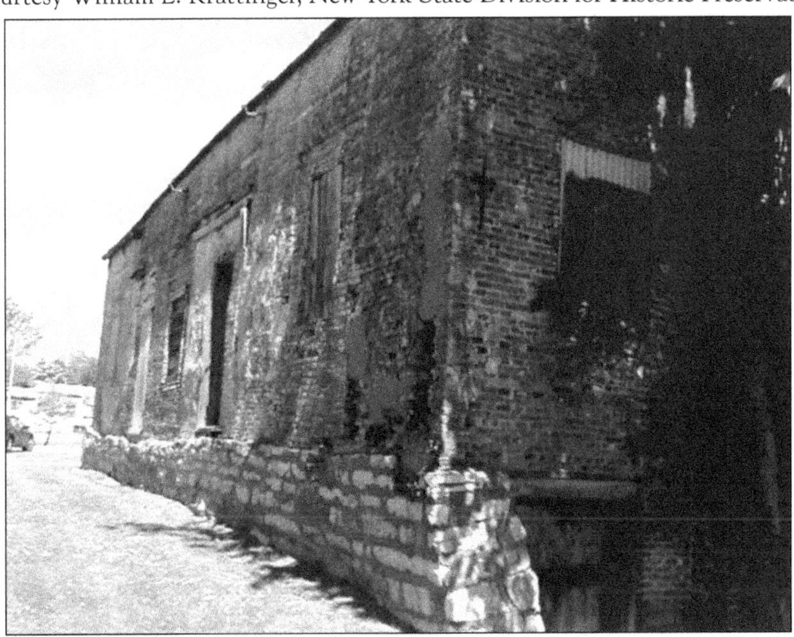

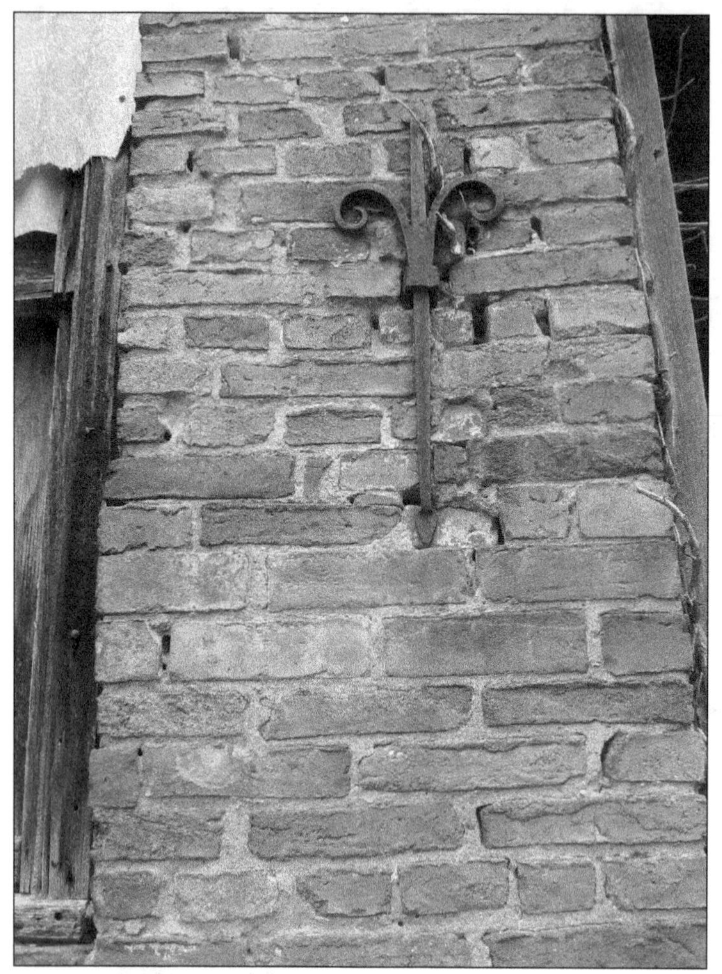

Fleur-de-lis and wrought-iron beam anchors are on both gables of the Van Hoesen House. In 1679, Maria Van Rensselaer petitioned to have a house built near the shore for farmers' convenience, as they needed accommodations after long wagon journeys. The present front is covered with stucco. The tin roof most likely was a later replacement of the original shingle or, possibly, tile roof. The house conforms to a rural pattern by having its main entries in the side walls and its chimneys in the gables. (Both, courtesy William E. Krattinger, New York State Division for Historic Preservation.)

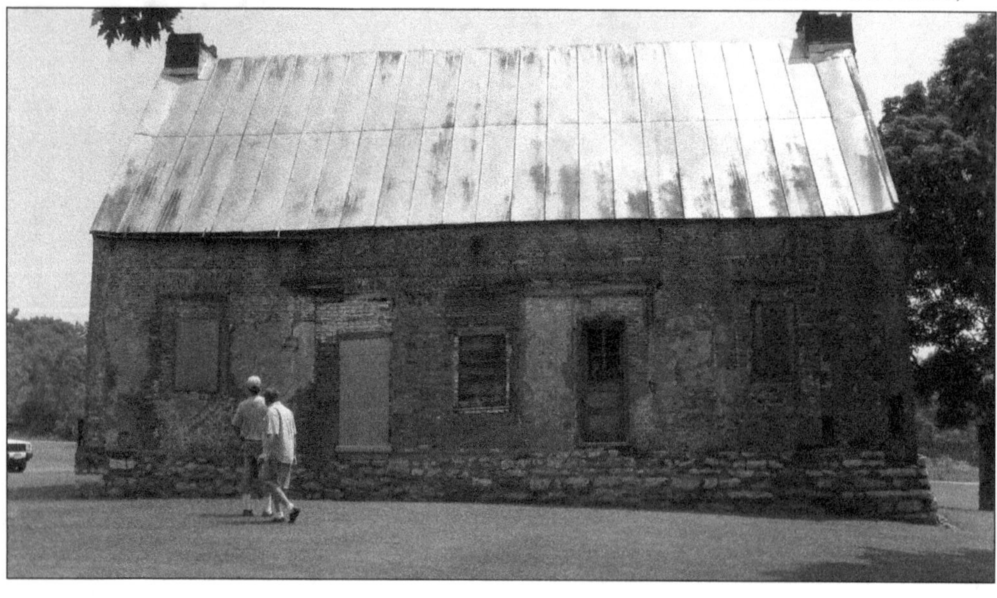

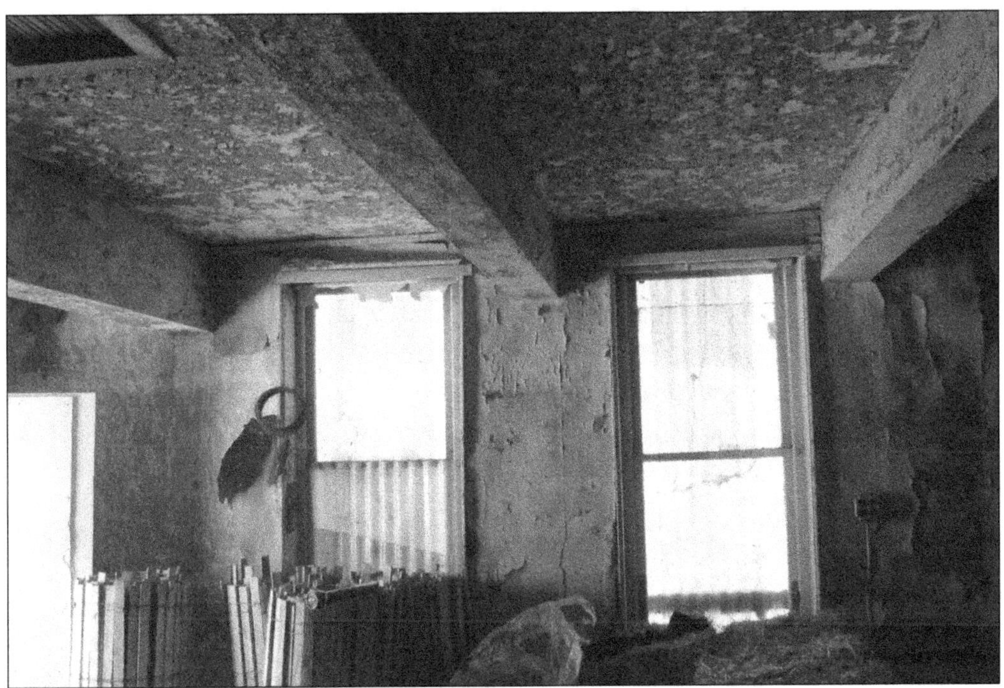

The interior of the Van Hoesen House, seen above, dates from the Federal period. It features a central hall, a passageway with exits at each end that are not centered, and unheated entryways, similar to houses in Albany County. Jan Van Hoesen and his wife had 11 children, and he served as the deacon of the Lutheran church in Athens, New York. The view below shows the back of the Van Hoesen House, facing Route 66. The Dutch word *dak* is defined as "roof, to give shelter to." Looking out from the windows, one can envision times in the 1700s when another person looked out the same windows and saw wilderness, wild animals, and, possibly, visitors approaching, such as the Mohicans. (Both, courtesy William E. Krattinger, New York State Division for Historic Preservation.)

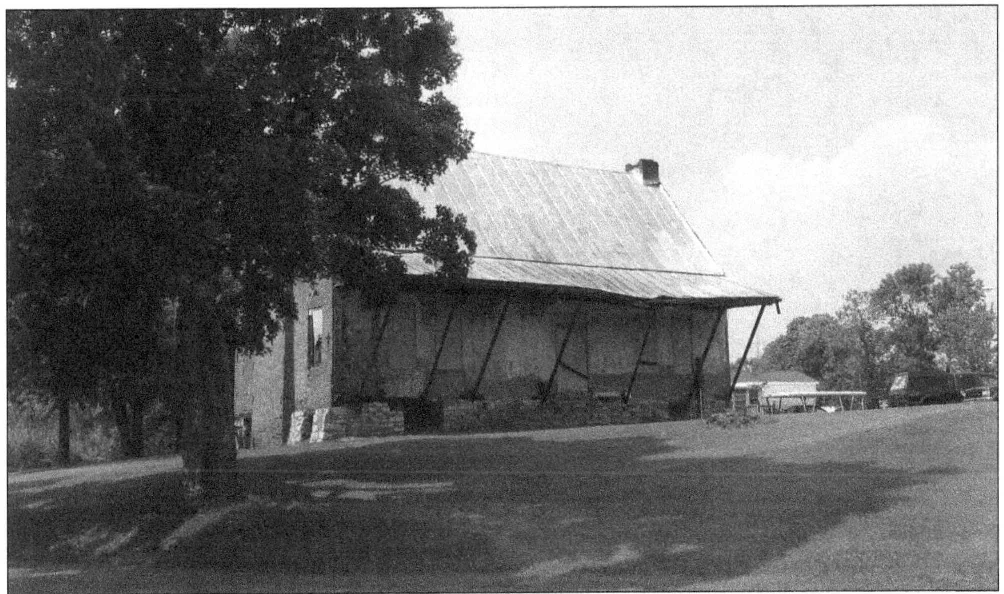

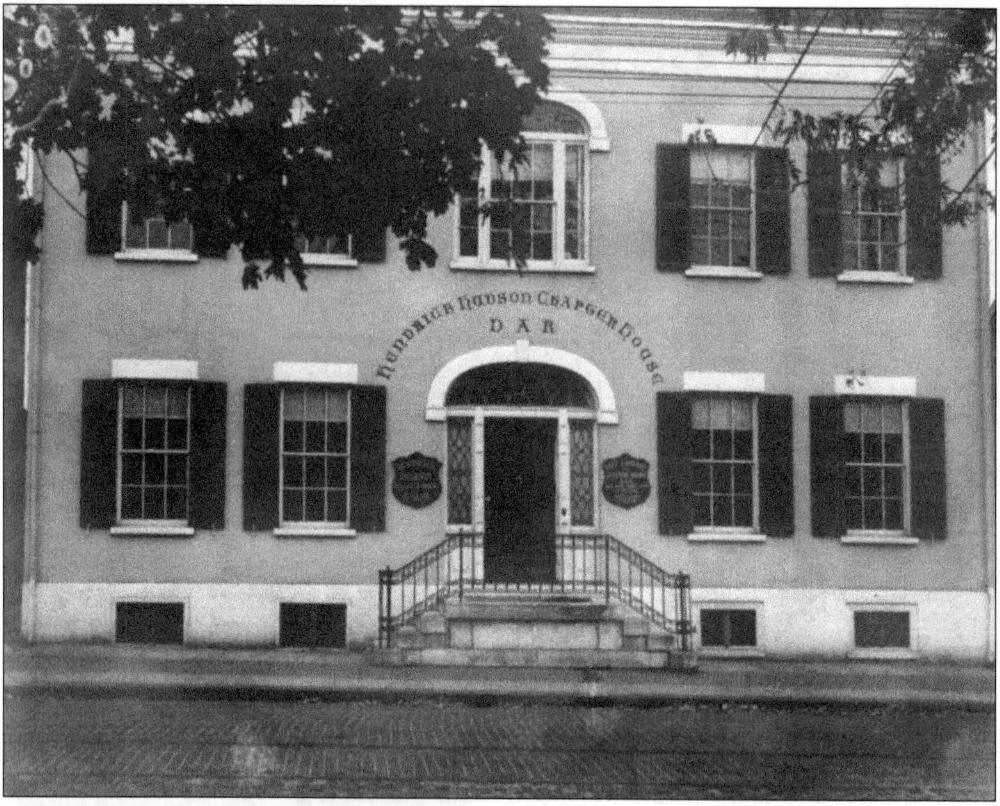

The Robert Jenkins House Museum and Library is owned and operated by the Hendrick Hudson Chapter of the Daughters of the American Revolution (DAR). At 113 Warren Street, it is seen in this photograph, which also shows trolley tracks. The museum has exhibits on the Civil War and whaling artifacts, including Col. David S. Cowles's boots. The archives of the Hudson Fortnightly Club, established in 1888, and the Greenport Historical Society are also housed here. The building designer was master carpenter Barnabas Waterman, whom many of the fine local Federal-period houses are attributed to. The site is open on Saturdays in August, September, and October. (Courtesy Mary Howell, Columbia County Historian.)

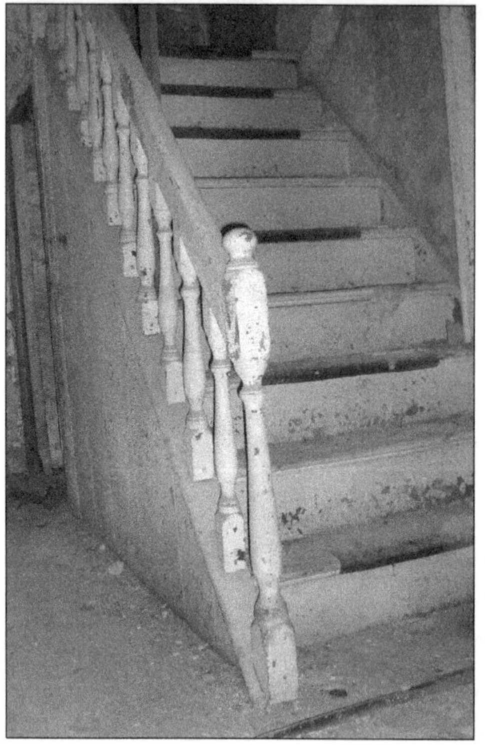

Seen here is an interior staircase in the Van Hoesen House on Route 66 in Greenport. The house is unoccupied and being restored through the efforts of the Greenport Historical Society and the Van Hoesen House Organization. These groups actively seek new members interested in history and preservation.

Ten

A Mosaic of Hudson

In the time and space provided in this book, one hopes to capture what Hudson was and is. Hudson's imagery is important, and photographs were, at times, hard to track down. History is often scattered about, and it is through the efforts of many volunteers that Hudson's history is being preserved, hopefully in a cohesive fashion among many entities. Hudson Praxis is a group of individuals hoping to create a museum in Hudson near the Amtrak station devoted to showcasing Hudson's history and relics to both locals and visiting tourists. The Marina Abramovich Art Center will undoubtedly change the landscape of Hudson forever with an influx of visitors and celebrities.

To some, Hudson will always be a rough diamond, a reference to its scarlet past. What if the Mohicans had been unfriendly? What if they had not welcomed Henry Hudson ashore? What if the Mohicans had said no? Where would Hudson be without them?

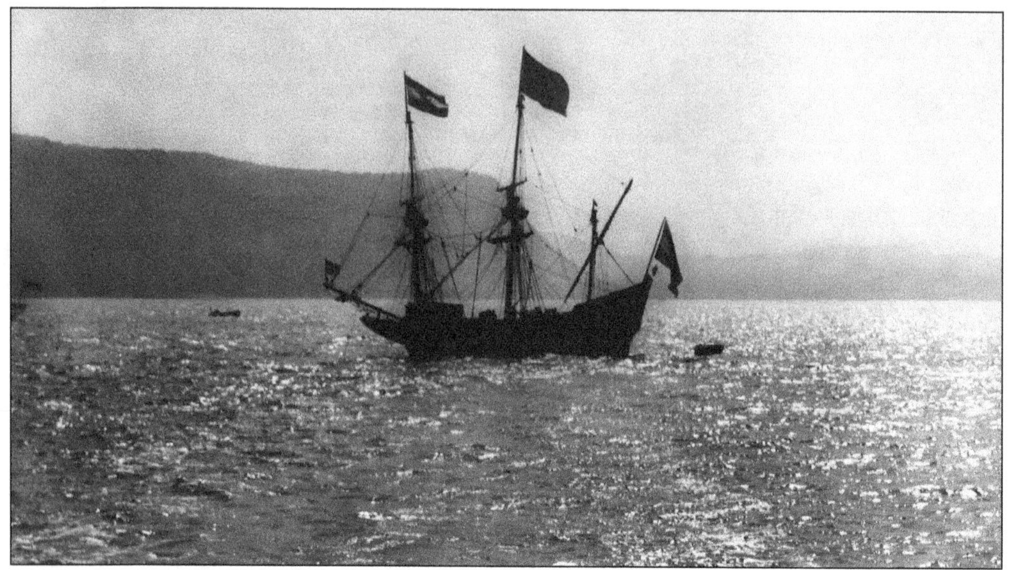

This is a 1909 image of a replica of Henry Hudson's ship *The Half Moon*, reconstructed for the Hudson-Fulton Celebration, which took place from September 25 to October 9, 1909, in New York and New Jersey. The replica was a gift of the State Historical Society of Colorado in 1949. Celebrations marked the 300-year anniversary of his discovery of the river and the 100th anniversary of Robert Fulton's first steamship.

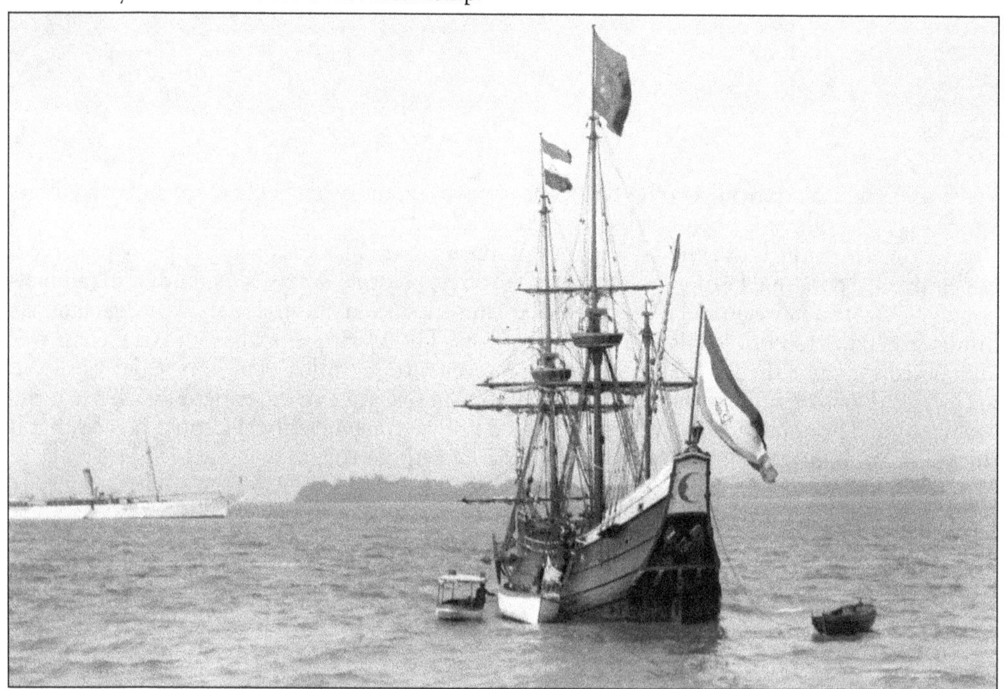

Anna R. Bradbury's 1908 book, *History of the City of Hudson*, claimed that Henry Hudson came ashore on or around September 11 or 16, 1609, stayed for two days, and was in the vicinity of Hudson or Stockport Creek, where an Indian village resided. Interpretations are based on a shipmate's journals. This is a 1909 photograph of *The Half Moon* reentering the Hudson River. (Author's collection.)

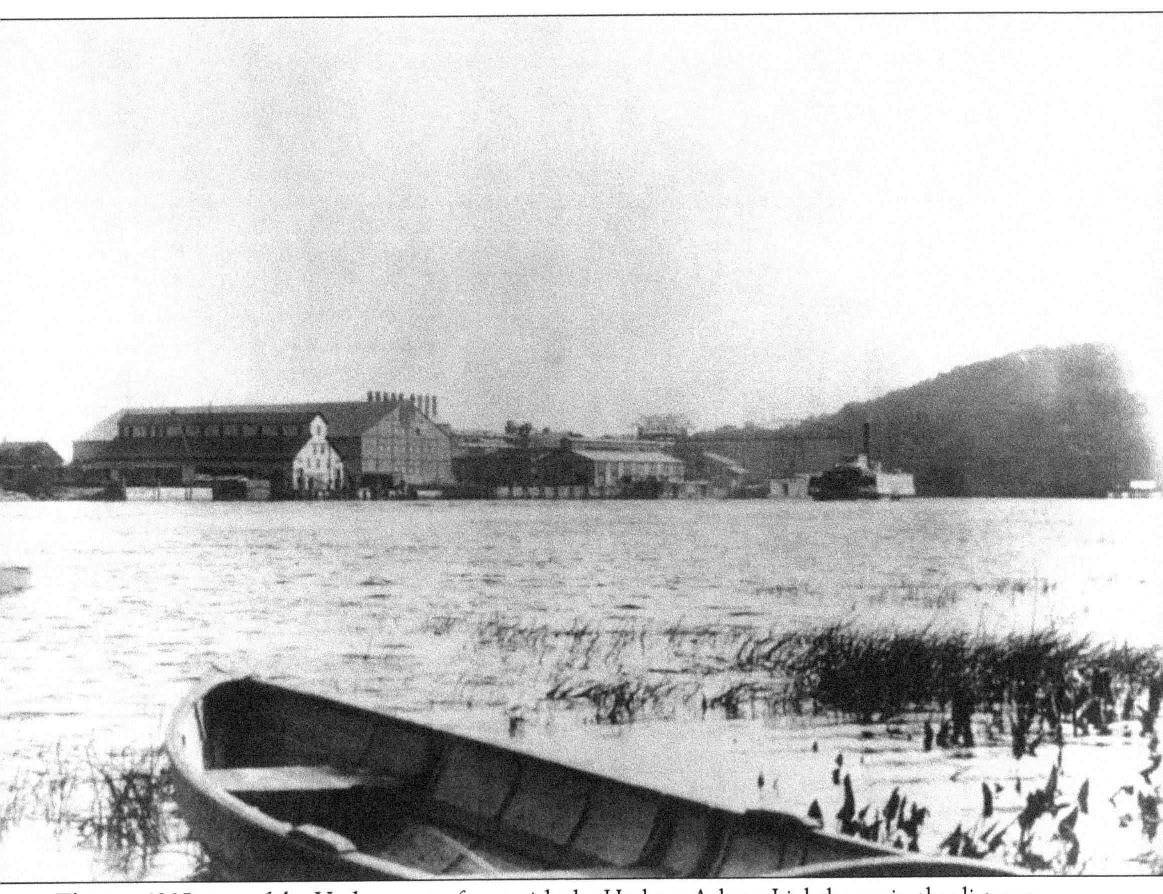

This is a 1905 view of the Hudson waterfront with the Hudson-Athens Lighthouse in the distance. Without the Hudson River and this waterfront, Hudson would never have gotten its start as a city enjoying prosperity from whaling.

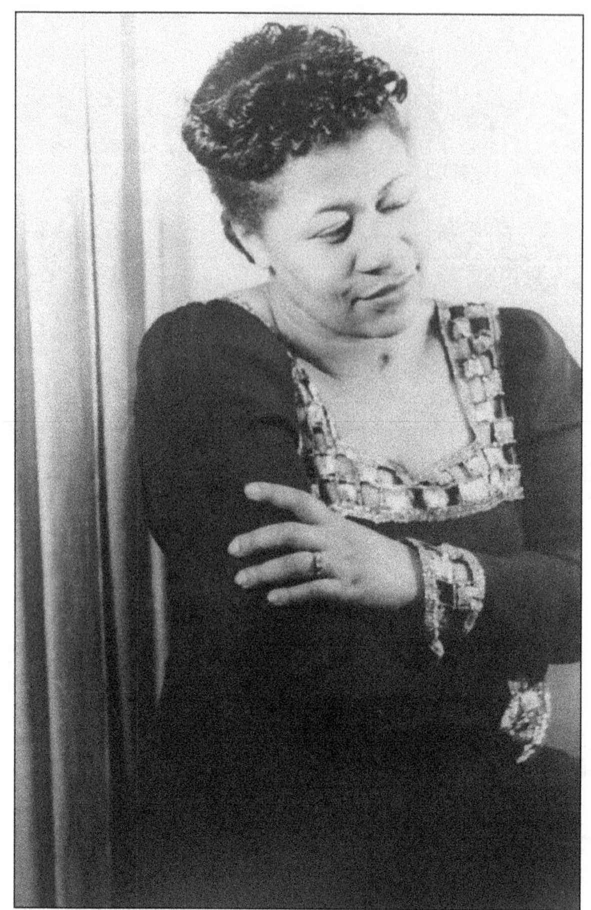

On April 10, 1933, a Westchester County judge sentenced 15-year-old Ella Fitzgerald to the New York State Training School for Girls in Hudson because she was "ungovernable and will not obey the just and lawful commands of her mother." Girls were taught all branches of housekeeping and the nursery, along with nursing and other industries. The school was located within a suburb of Hudson and opened on April 15, 1887. In hopes that more encouraging results could be obtained from younger girls of a more impressionable age, the school was reorganized and reopened as a "Training School for Girls" on June 1, 1904, with age limits from 10 to 16 years of age. Discipline included beatings and solitary confinement. Ella ran away. Within a year, she was singing and recording with Chick Webb, on her way to becoming "America's First Lady of Jazz."

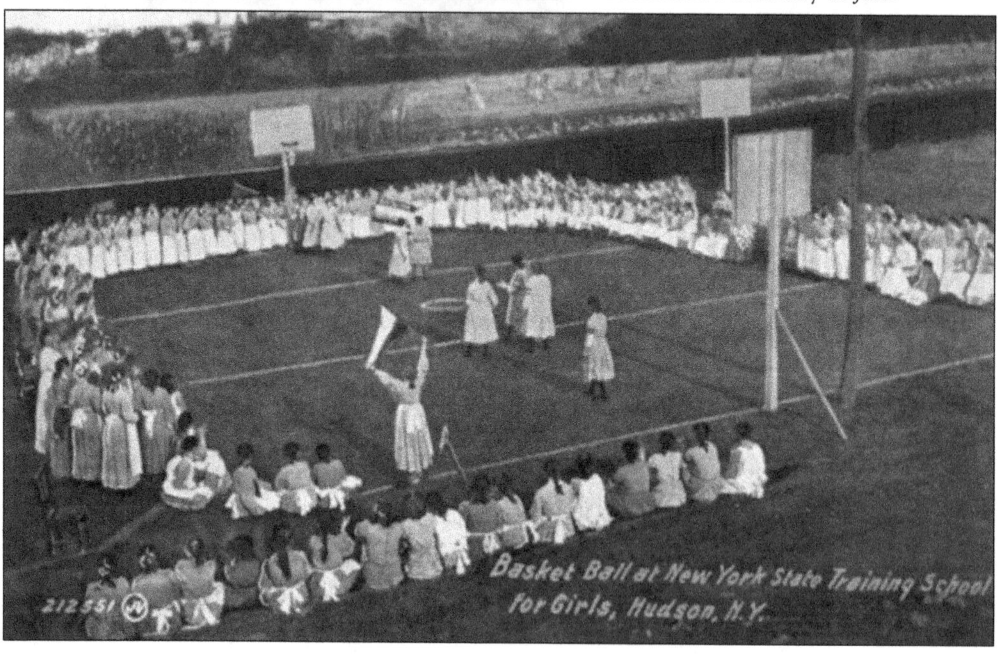

Henry James visited Hudson in September 1905 to gather material for his "American Notes," published in serial form for *The Atlantic Monthly* and *North American Review* and later published in book form. Arriving with two ladies and a French poodle in an automobile requiring repairs, the group went to The Worth for dinner, requesting to bring the dog. Not being allowed to bring the dog in the dining room, they instead found dinner nearby at a "cook shop." James's style of writing was compared to Impressionist painting, and he was known for literary realism. He lived in America and Europe, becoming a British subject later in life. A prolific writer, he published books on travel, biographies, and an autobiography, and he also produced plays. He wrote colorfully and extravagantly to his many friends. His portrait was done in charcoal by John Singer Sargent in 1912.

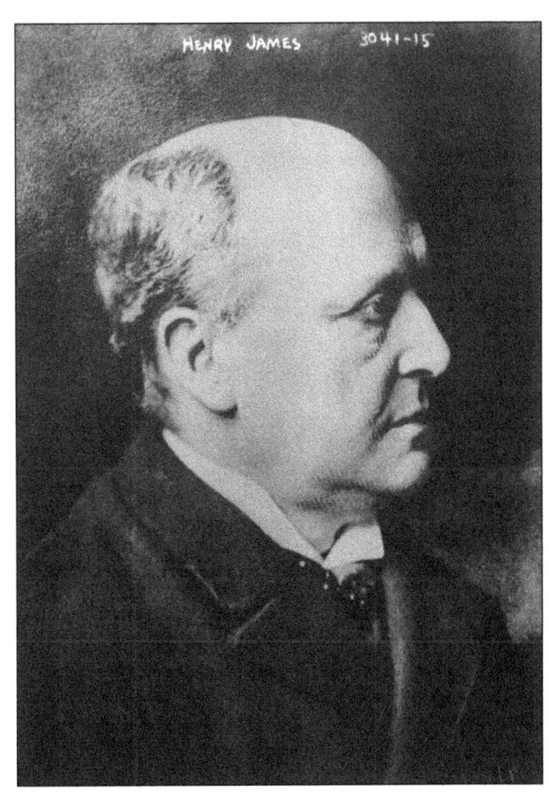

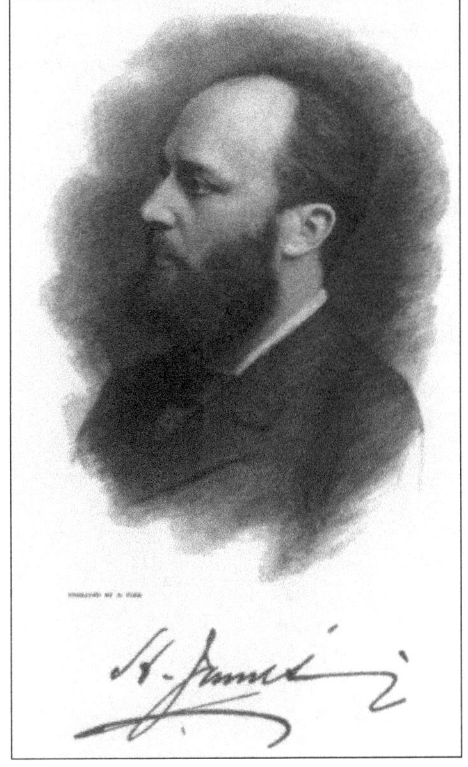

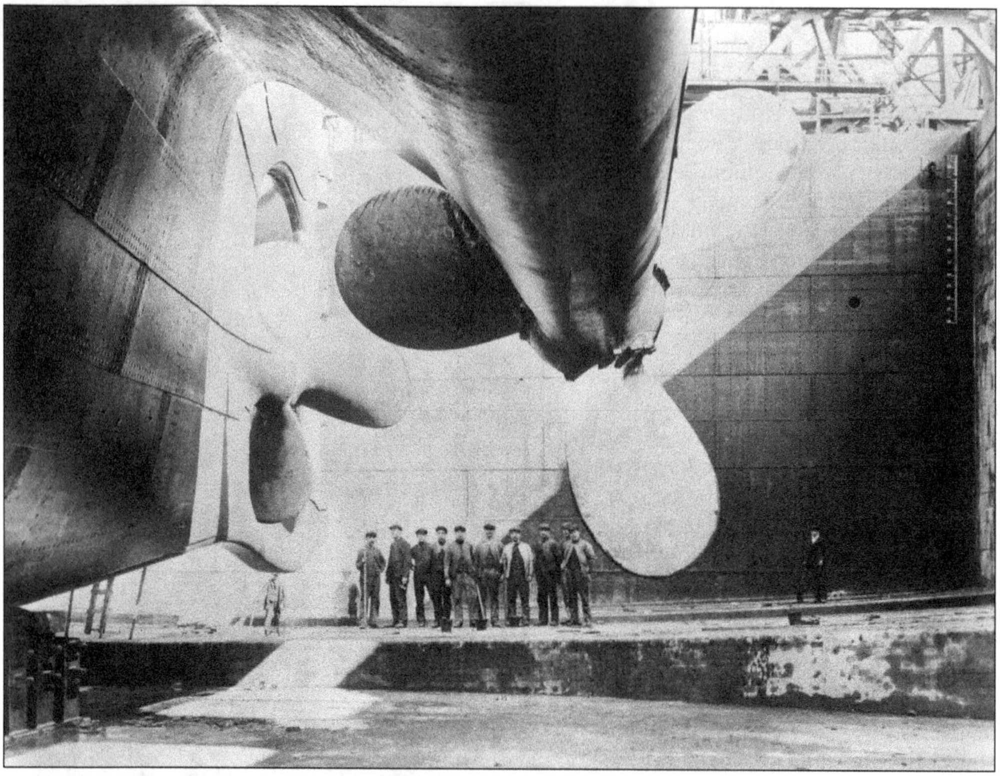

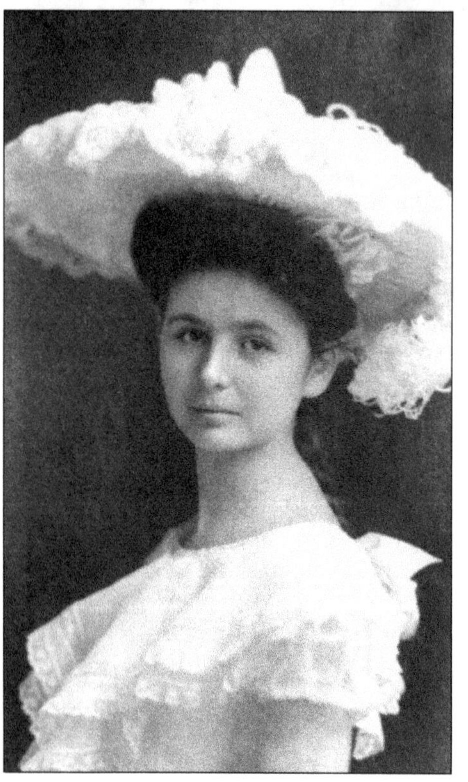

Seen here is the *Titanic* before its launch and a photograph of Hudson *Titanic* survivor Gretchen Fiske Longley, who would frequently vacation on Copake Lake. Longley's daughter later became friends with Hudson resident Kevin Novak, and she explained to him that *Titanic* survivors were considered bad luck and shunned by many superstitious people. Considered the most beautiful woman aboard the *Titanic*, the band played "O You Beautiful Doll" upon Longley's entering the room. The "Unsinkable Molly Brown" helped to raise money for *Titanic* workers whose pay abruptly stopped with the *Titanic* sinking. (Above, courtesy Library of Congress; left, courtesy Kevin Novak.)

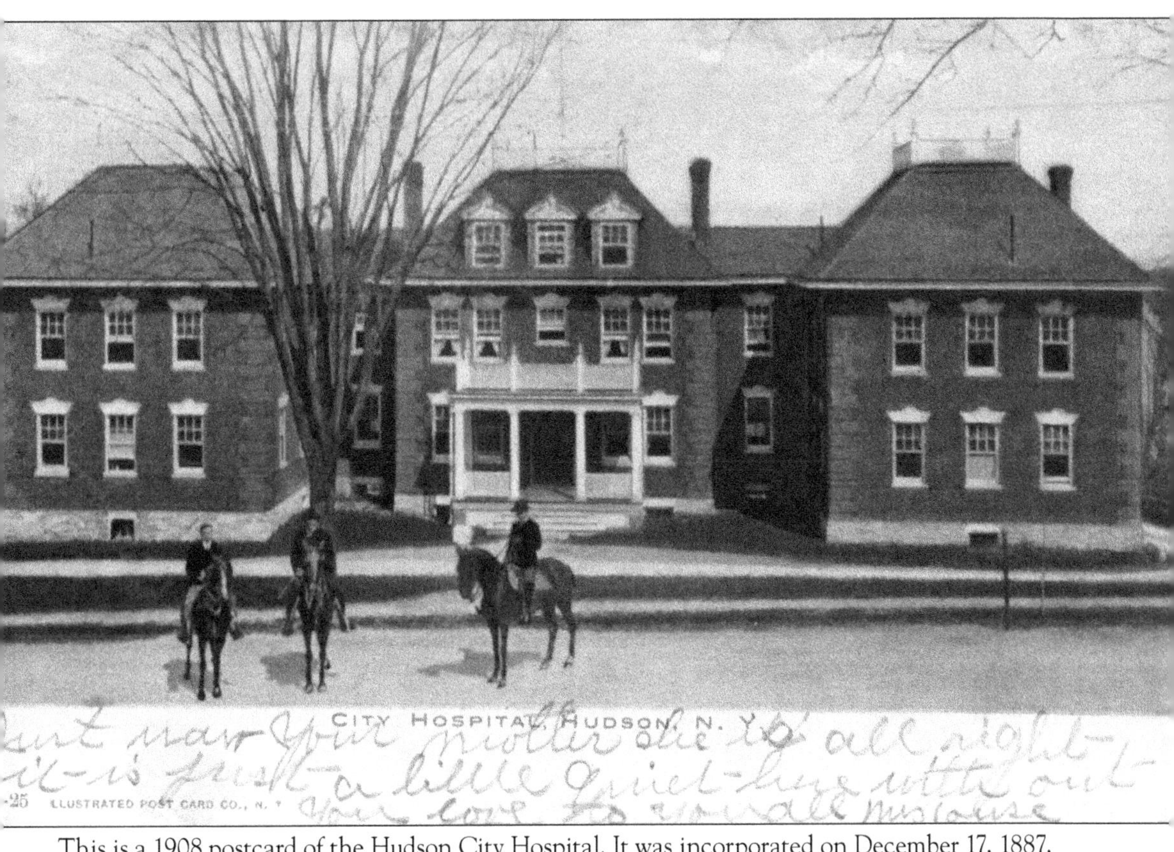

This is a 1908 postcard of the Hudson City Hospital. It was incorporated on December 17, 1887, at the request of Alfred Van Deusen, who wished for the institution to be located in the city and who left a legacy of $5,000. In 1893, the original site was the northeast corner of Washington and Fifth Streets in a rented building that was used as the hospital until July 1897. A nurses' training school was created in connection with the hospital, and the Crawford E. Fritts Memorial Home was provided for the nurses. An ambulance was the contribution of the ladies of the city, and a hospital auxiliary was also created. The hospital was once supported in part by a tax on foreign insurance companies doing business in New York State. The hospital relocated to Prospect Avenue in 1900. Dr. Fritts donated his home, which was located in the rear of the 1900 hospital building. The nurses' residence building was located on the corner of Columbia Street and McKinstry Place. The first cataract operation in New York State was at the Fifth Street location. (Author's collection.)

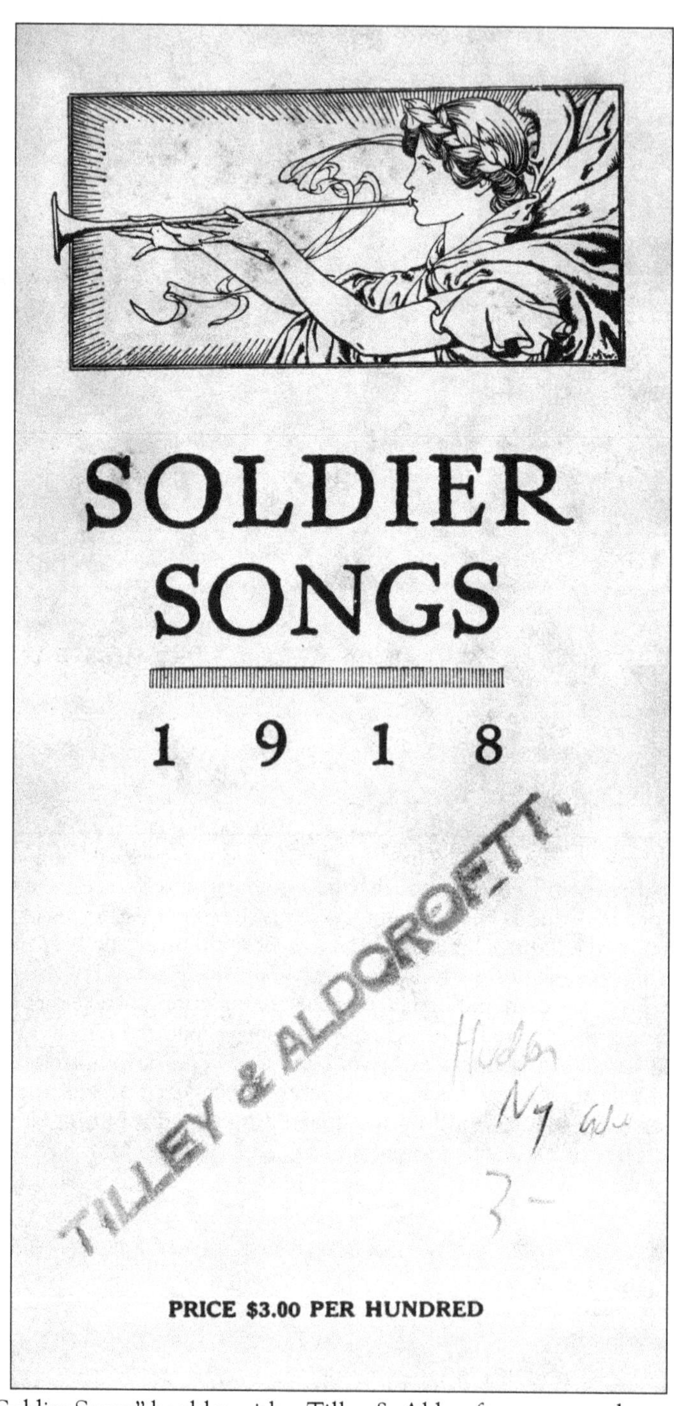

This is a 1918 "Soldier Songs" booklet with a Tilley & Aldcroftt stamp on the cover and printed copyright permissions on each page. Tilley & Aldcroftt, whose building was constructed in 1856 where Face Stockholm stands now at Warren and Fourth Streets, were merchant tailors and clothiers, employing 20 men in their house and producing top-quality merchandise. Richard D. Aldcroftt (1830–1916) was born in Sweden. His January 6, 1916, obituary was printed in the *Hudson Evening Register.* (Author's collection.)

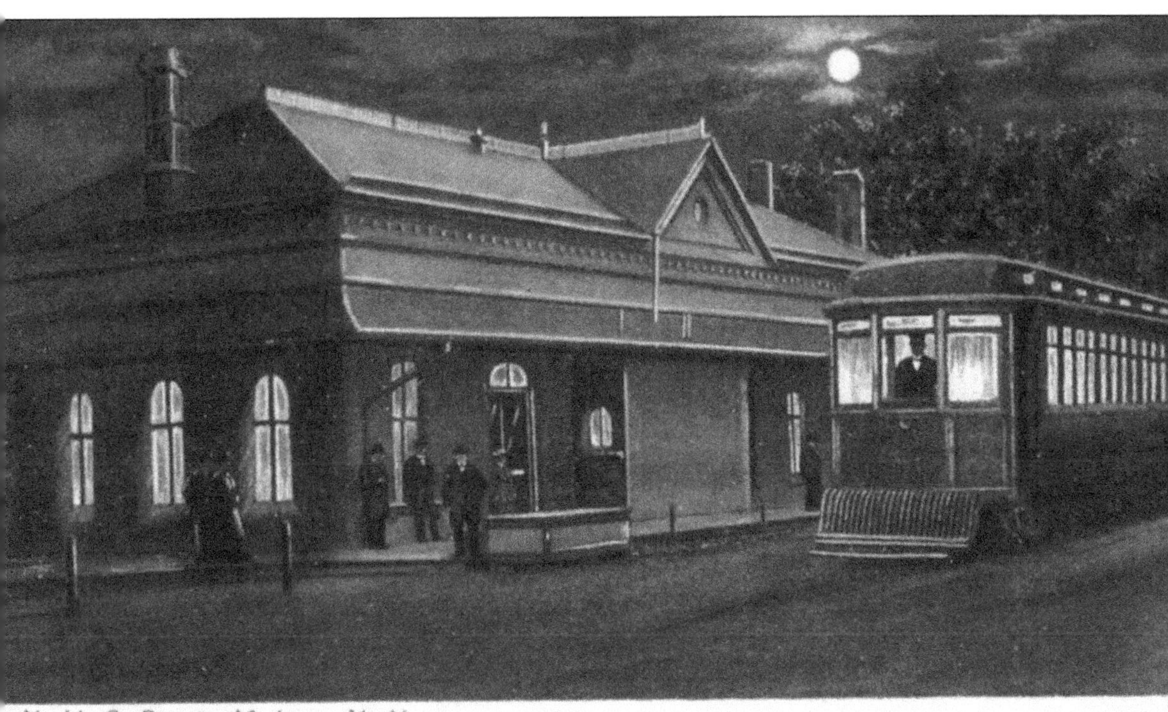

The Amtrak depot was originally built for the New York Central Railroad in 1874, and it is New York State's oldest continually operated station. This mode of transport makes Hudson an easy commute from the stresses of big-city life in New York City. (Courtesy Jon Meredith.)

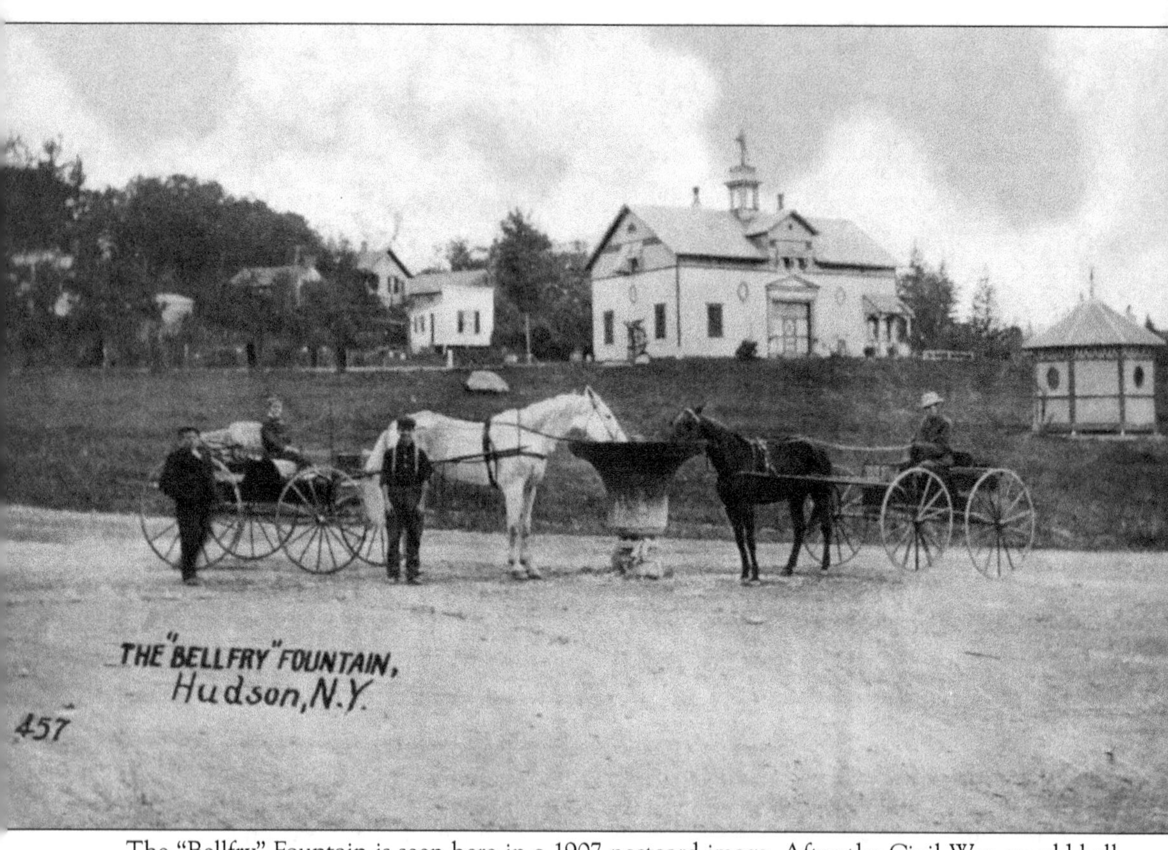

The "Bellfry" Fountain is seen here in a 1907 postcard image. After the Civil War, an old bell watering trough for horses stood at the corner of what are now Green Street and Fairview Avenue. Due to a demand for troops, a call for volunteers was issued in 1862, resulting in Company A being filled within a few days. Becoming part of the 128th Regiment, drills and training for the company were held on the fairgrounds (Camp Kelly). Training was witnessed daily by large crowds. The company was led out of town on September 5, 1862, by Colonel Cowles, who was described as "tall, handsome, soldierly," according to Columbia County historian Mary Howell. He would never see Hudson again. Colonel Cowles's body was returned to Hudson, where he was buried with honors in Cedar Park Cemetery with Masons from 11 towns present. The bell was later returned to its owner. The building behind the bell was a dairy milking parlor. (Author's collection.)

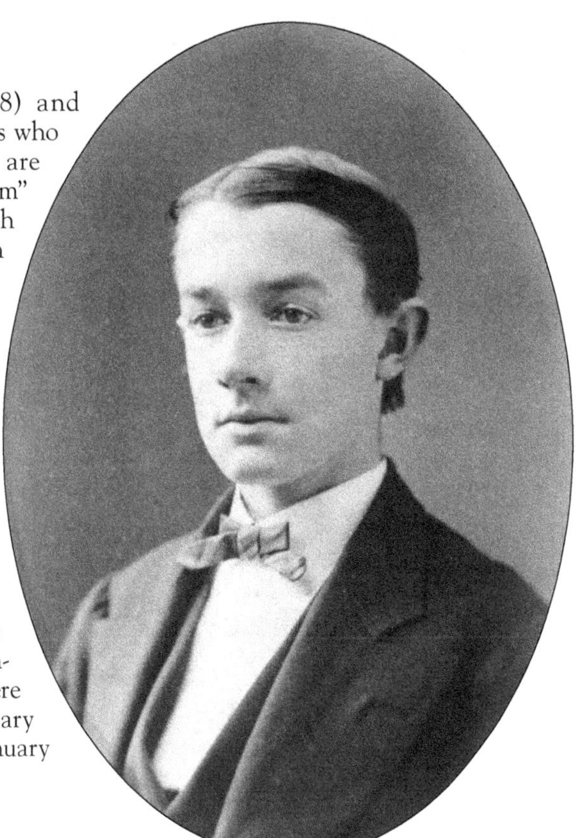

Henry Griffith Lapham (1822–1888) and Samantha Lapham were second cousins who were married to one another. These are Forshew Studio photographs with "Lapham" handwritten in pencil on the back of each portrait. Forshew images were taken during the 1860s, 1870s, and 1880s in Hudson. Henry Lapham was educated in Rutland and at Columbia Friends School in Chatham. The Laphams made a fortune as leather merchants and by consolidating smaller leather-tanning businesses into a few larger businesses, including the United States Leather Co., one of the greatest corporations in America. Buckley & Lapham was the name of their tannery in Sullivan County. Their son Lewis Henry Lapham was one of the founders of the Texaco Oil Company. Henry Lapham's million-dollar pedigree, successes, and failures were followed by trade presses, and his obituary appeared in the *New York Times* on January 30, 1888. (Both, author's collection.)

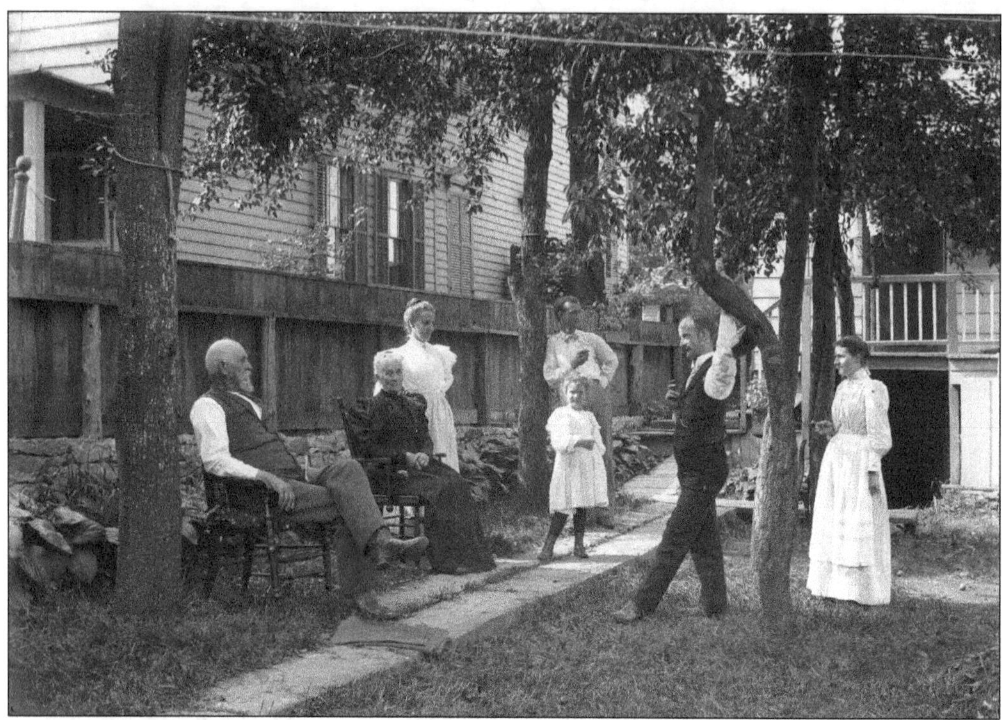

This 1897 image shows a family in Hudson. Photographer Michael Fredericks said, "I found this box one day in my old darkroom that came from who knows where. The only info I have is the date, because there was a calendar in the background of people having Thanksgiving dinner." (Courtesy Michael Fredericks.)

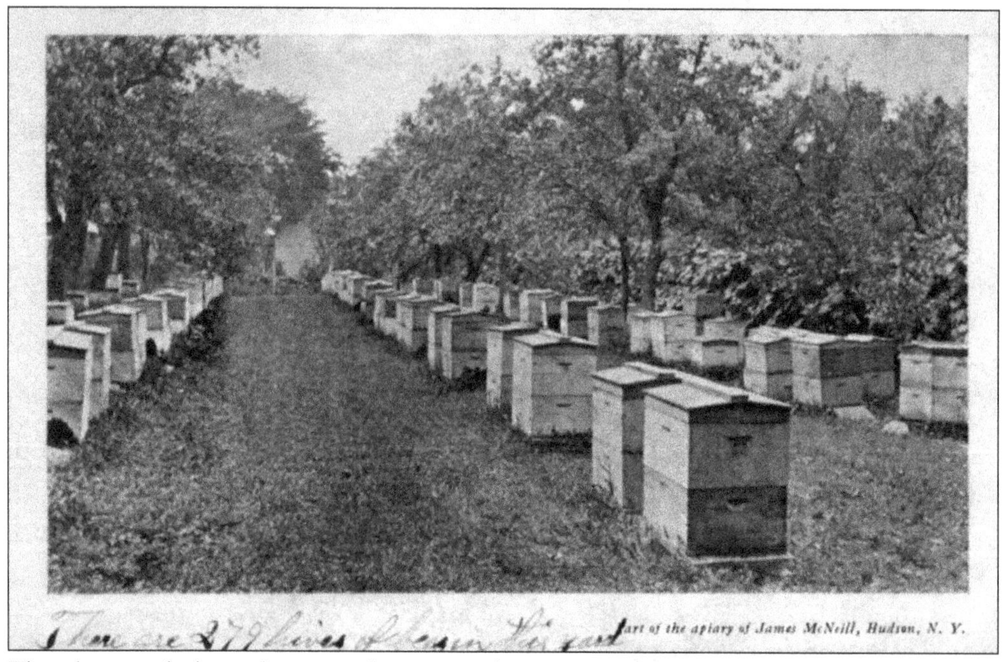

This photograph shows the apiary that was on the property of James McNeill in Hudson. "There are 279 hives of bees in this yard" is handwritten under the image. (Courtesy Jon Meredith.)

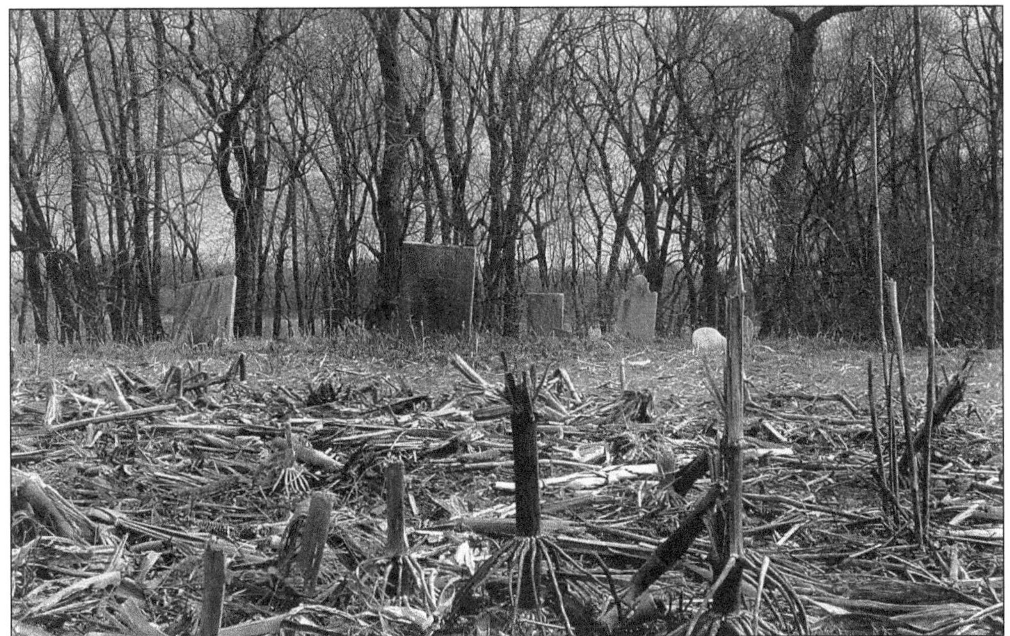

Stalks and headstones are seen here near Spook Rock Road. Kenneth Mynter, a professor at the University of Rochester, completed an excavation of an Indian shelter in the area. There was evidence that it was used 5,000 years ago. Carbon tests proved that cooking fires were used there as far back as 3000 BC. Remnants of meals such as mussel shells and animal bones were found. (Courtesy Dan Region.)

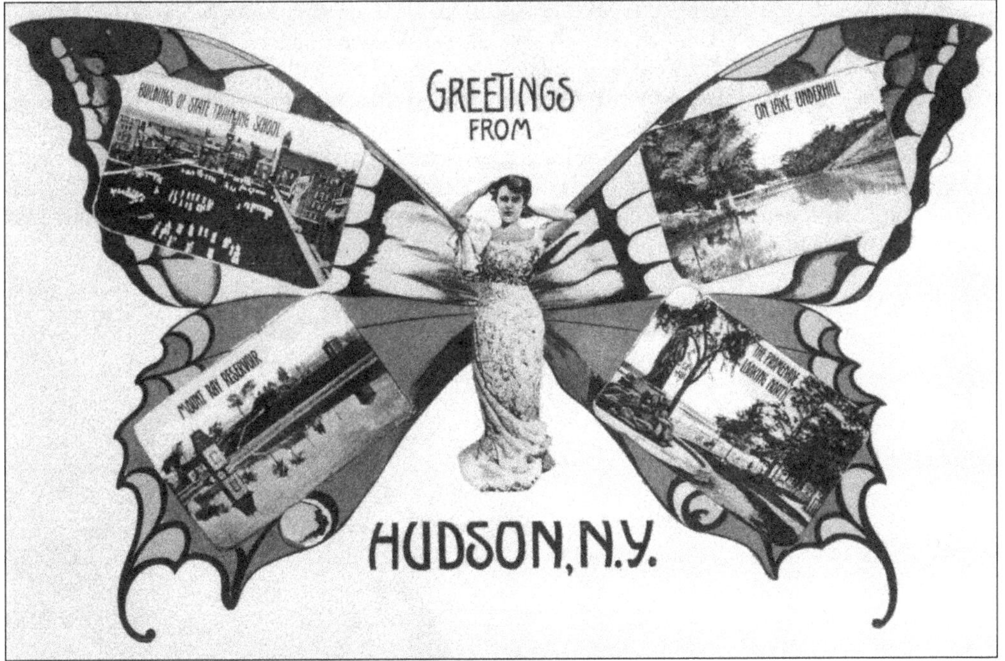

"Greetings from Hudson NY" declares this postcard, which shows scenes of the New York State Training School for Girls, Mount Ray Reservoir, Lake Underhill, and the Promenade looking north, with the St. Winifred statue and the Hudson River visible. (Courtesy Jon Meredith.)

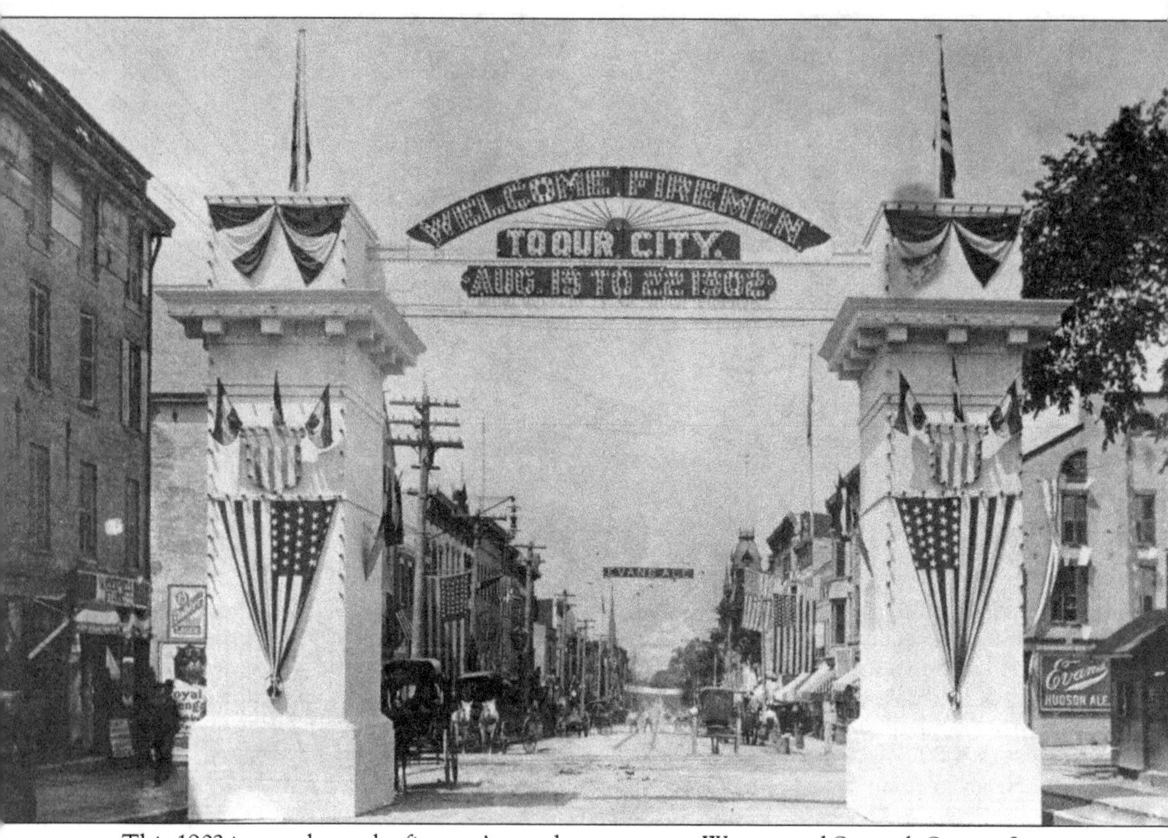

This 1902 image shows the firemen's parade entrance at Warren and Seventh Streets. It was one of the first times electric lights were used in Hudson, as seen here with lights adorning the arches of the entryway. The two oldest volunteer fire companies in the state originated in Hudson in the 1700s. The Fireman's Convention is one of the largest organizations in New York State, originating in the mid-1800s. Hudson is home to the Fireman's Association of the State of New York (FASNY) Museum of Firefighting, which holds the largest collection of firefighting artifacts in the world. Its location is on the grounds of the FASNY Fireman's Home, the first old-age nursing home for firemen in the country. (Courtesy Mary Howell, Columbia County Historian.)

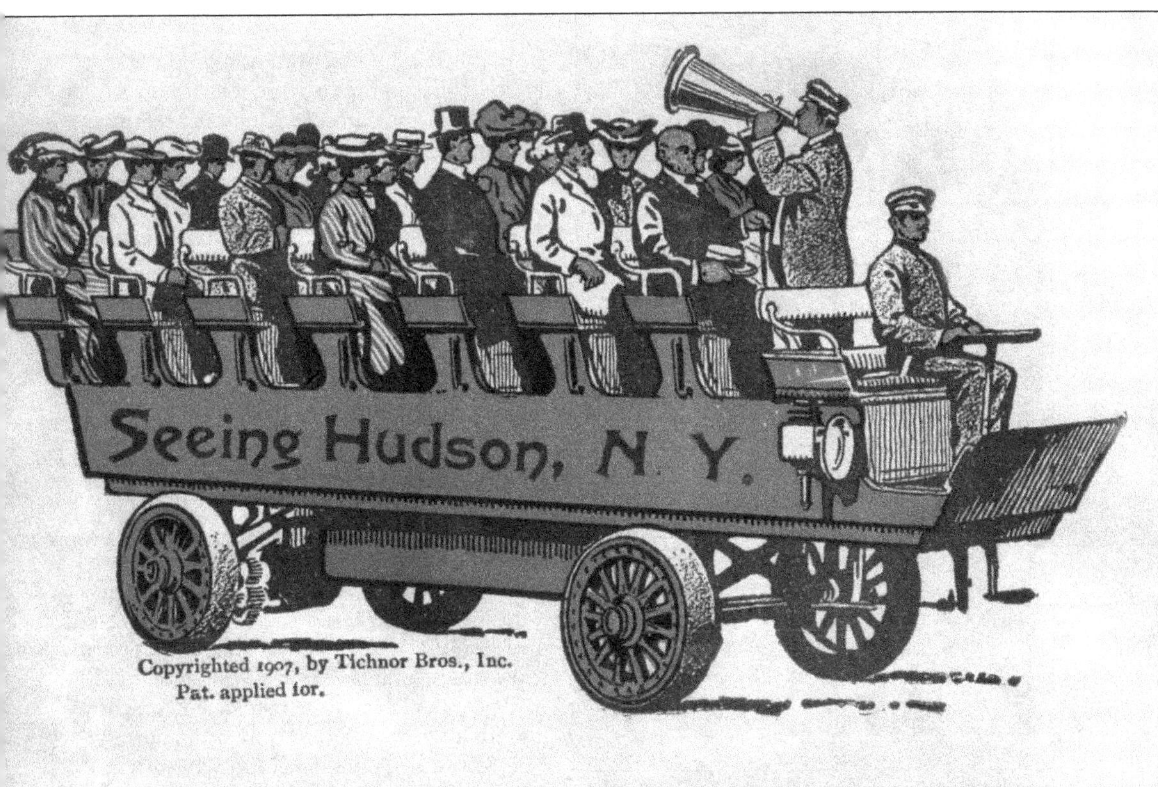

This 1907 postcard shows sightseers in Hudson, possibly taking in a parade or seeing the shops along Warren Street. Prior to 1898, only US Post Offices could manufacture and distribute postcards, which were later produced by private printing companies. (Courtesy Mary Howell, Columbia County Historian.)

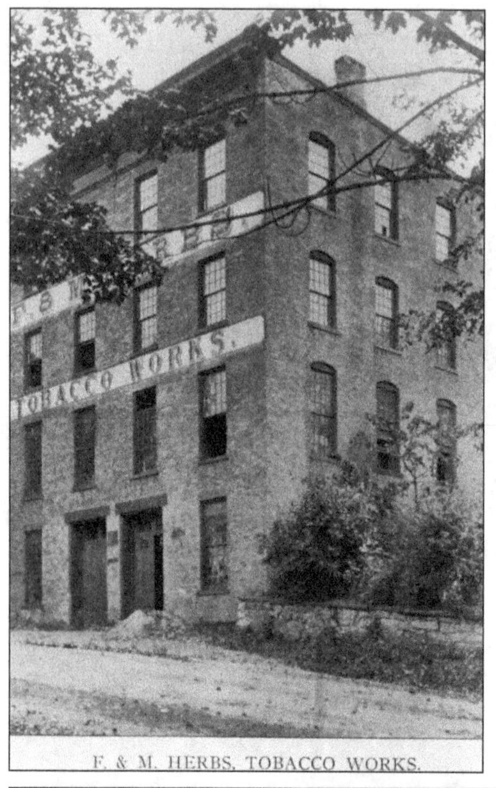

F. & M. HERBS. TOBACCO WORKS.

Seen at left is an exterior photograph of Herb's Tobacco Factory on Prospect Street, across from the current Columbia Memorial Hospital. According to Capt. Franklin Ellis in 1878, "The business was commenced by the present proprietors, Messrs. F. & M. Herbs & Bro., in the summer of 1875. Their factory building (four stories high) was commenced in August of that year, fitted with machinery, and occupied by the business May 1, 1876. The power is a fifteen-horse steam-engine. The raw tobacco is brought from Kentucky in hogsheads holding from 1200 pounds to 2000 pounds each, and about seventy-five of these furnish a year's supply of stock. The revenue paid to the government is about $3000 per month." The photograph below shows the interior and the working conditions of Herb's Tobacco Factory, with workers rolling cigars. Adorning walls behind the workers are posters and turn-of-the-20th-century sheet music for show tunes. The factory was sold in the 1920s or 1930s to a Pennsylvania tobacco company and no longer stands today. (Both, courtesy Mary Howell, Columbia County Historian.)

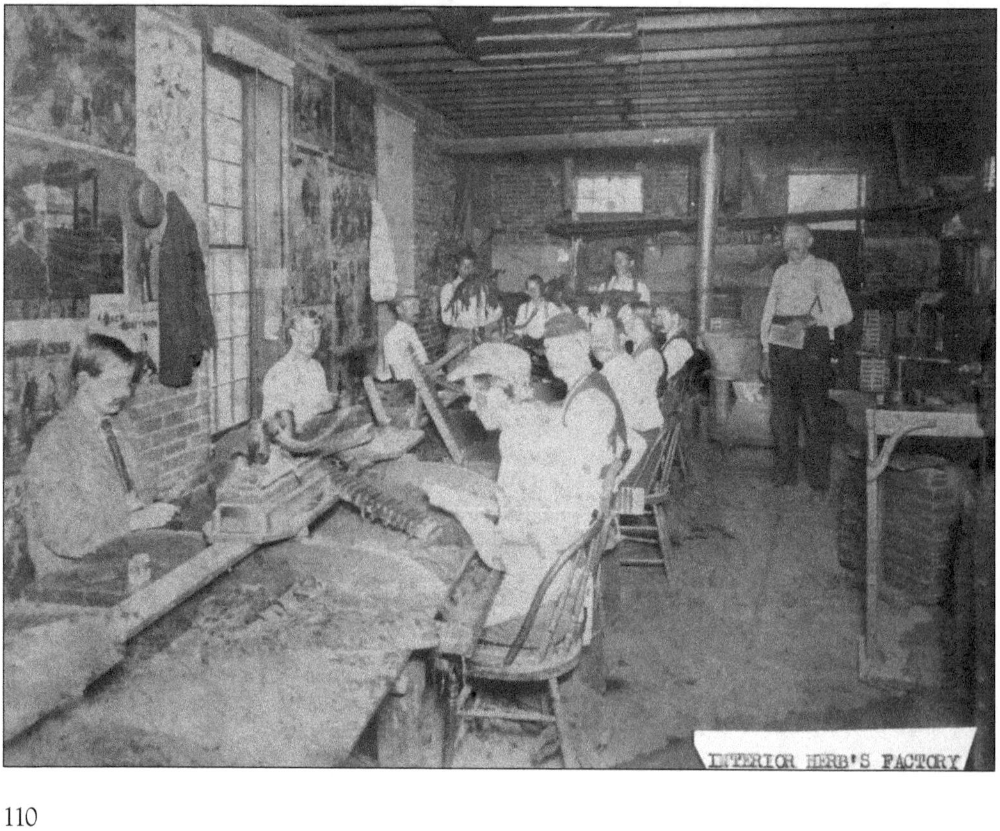

INTERIOR HERB'S FACTORY

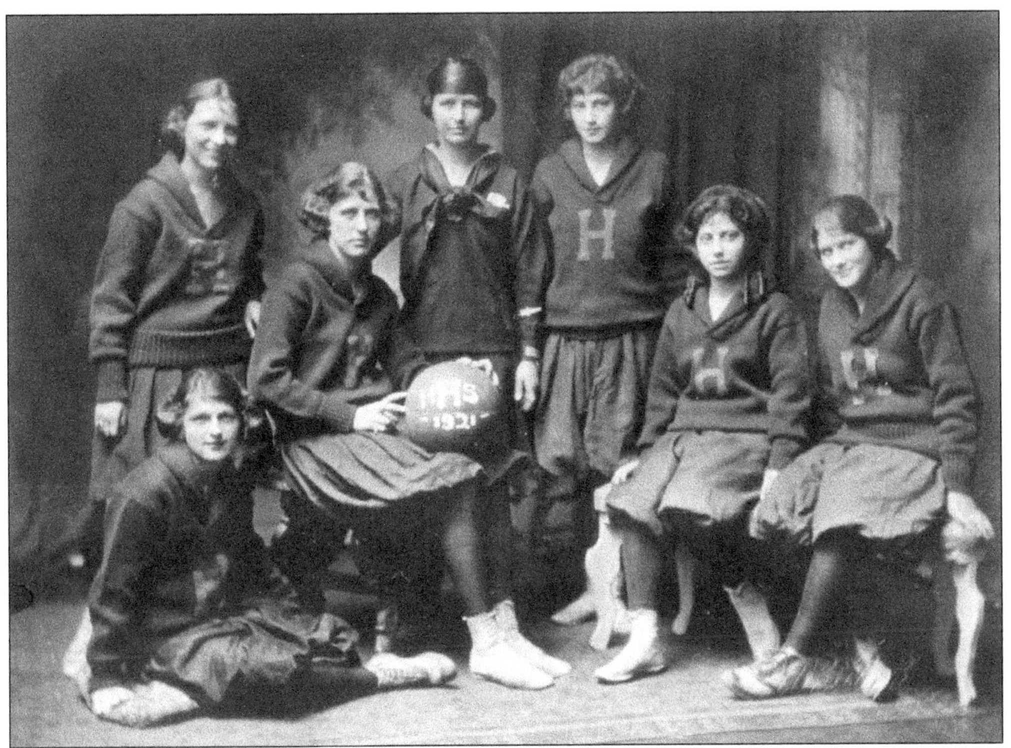

This is a 1921 photograph of the ladies' basketball team at Hudson High School. Hudson High School is also now the site of the Hudson Childrens Book Festival, drawing 5,000 visitors annually.

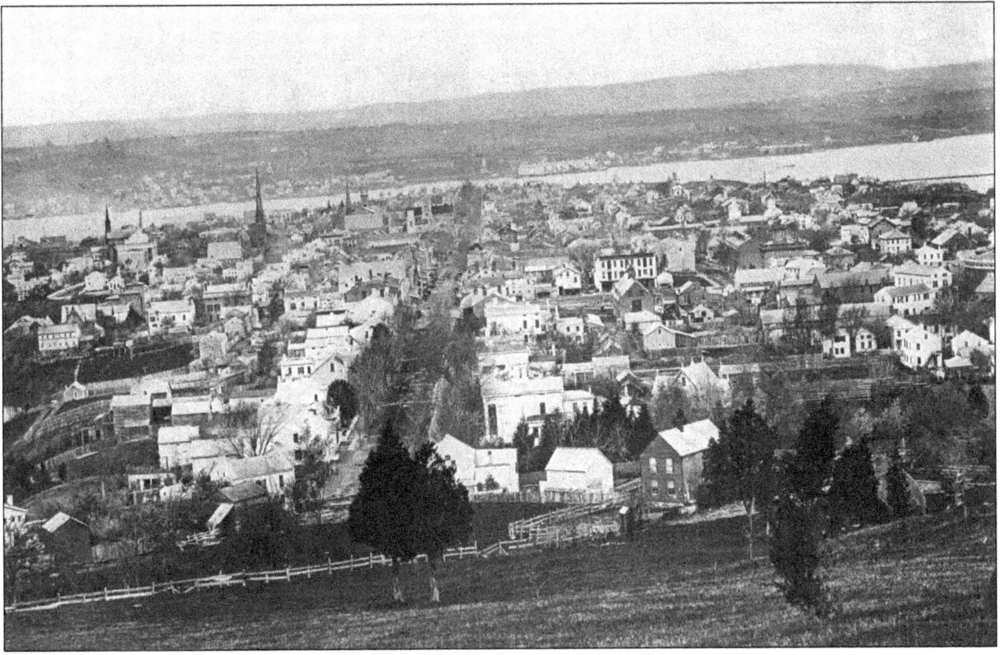

This 1867 Frank Forshew Studio photograph shows an aerial view of Hudson. The viewpoint is from Mount Ray (Rossman Avenue), looking west down Warren Street to the Hudson River. (Courtesy Mary Howell, Columbia County Historian.)

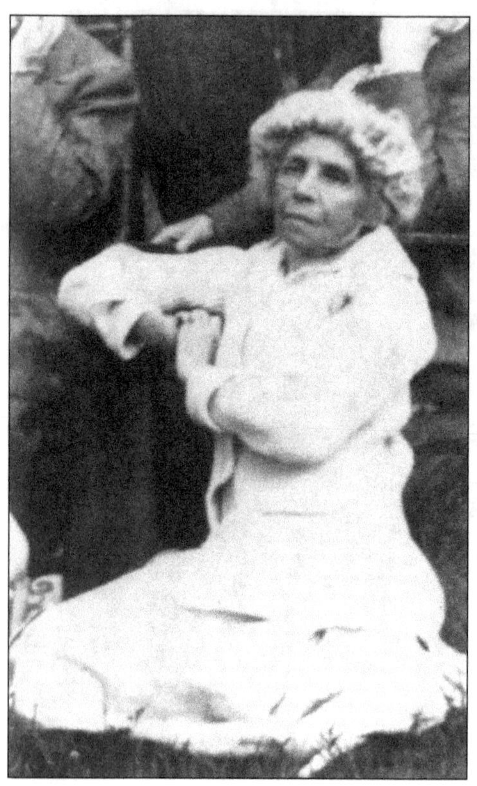

Kornelia Andrews and her niece Gretchen Fiske Longley were both *Titanic* survivors. On December 5, 1913, the *Hudson Republican* ran Andrews's obituary, stating that she had passed away the day before from pneumonia while living on upper Warren Street. She was on the board of trustees for the Hudson City Hospital and spent much time in her father's law office helping to prepare cases.

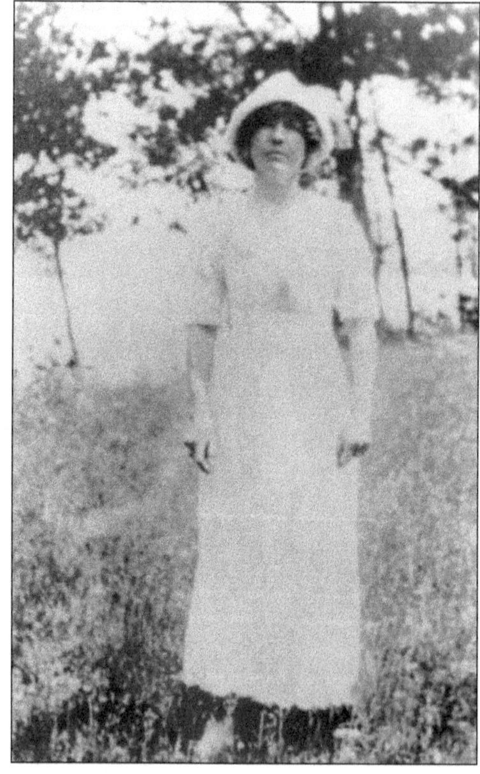

This is the passport photograph of Mrs. John Clinton Hogeboom, another aunt of Gretchen Fiske Longely and also a *Titanic* survivor. She was born in Livingston, the youngest of 10 children. The aunts lost their fortune in the stock market crash of 1929. (Courtesy Don Lynch and Phil Gowan.)

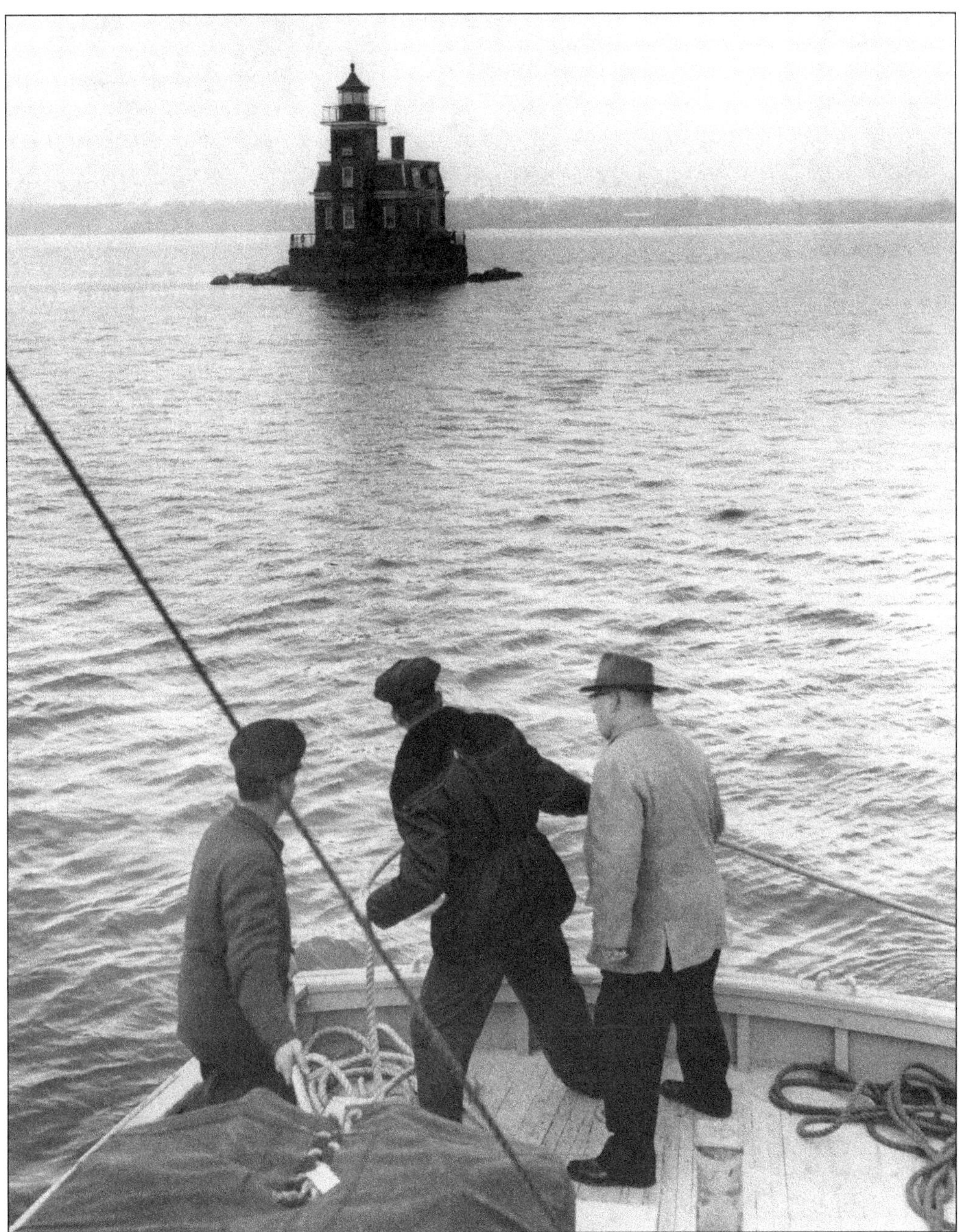

The Hudson-Athens Lighthouse, on its granite base, is also known as Stepping Stones Lighthouse. This 1958 image shows three men in a boat appearing to be leaving the lighthouse. It is now listed in the National Register of Historic Places and is also now a museum chartered by the State of New York. The navigation light, now solar-powered, still serves to warn of a nearby island called The Flats where shipwrecks have occurred with losses of life. Managed and lived in by a lighthouse keeper and his family until 1936, the Second Empire–style building has eight ample rooms. After 30 years empty, citizens formed the Hudson-Athens Lighthouse Preservation Society (HALPS) and purchased the house. Restoration work was completed by HALPS members. Public tours are held during boating season on Saturdays from June through October.

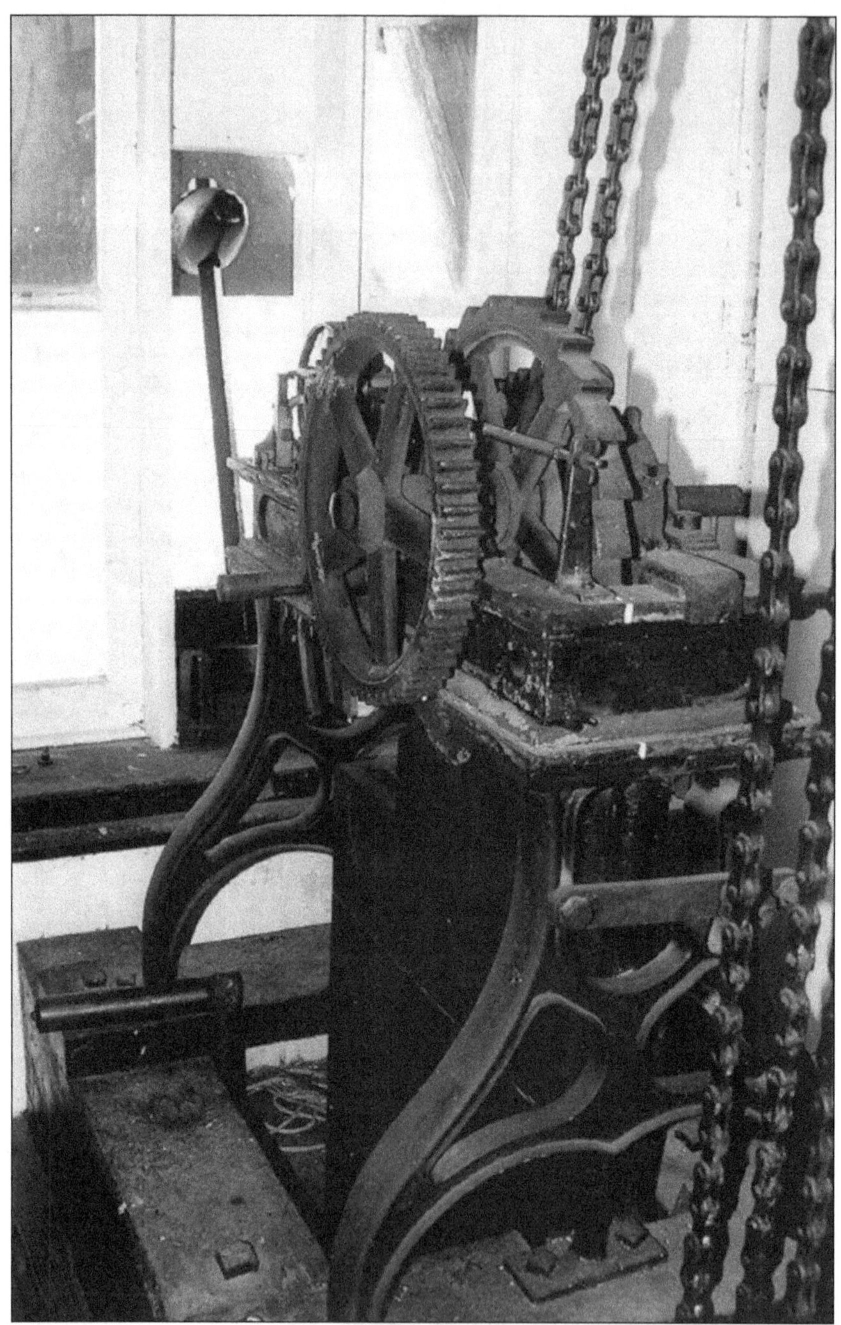

The fog bell mechanism at the Hudson-Athens Lighthouse is seen here. It would ring every 20 seconds for hours, warning of thick fog. The bell alerted ships to orientation and limited visibility when the lighthouse light was not enough. The lighthouse keeper would have to get up in the middle of the night to wind it. The Hudson-Athens Lighthouse graced the cover of the December 28, 1948, issue of *The Saturday Evening Post*, with a drawing of Emil Brunner, the last civilian lighthouse keeper, and his children, who all lived there. In those days, the Hudson River would freeze completely over at times, making it possible to walk across the ice from Hudson to Athens. (Courtesy Hudson Athens Lighthouse Preservation Society.)

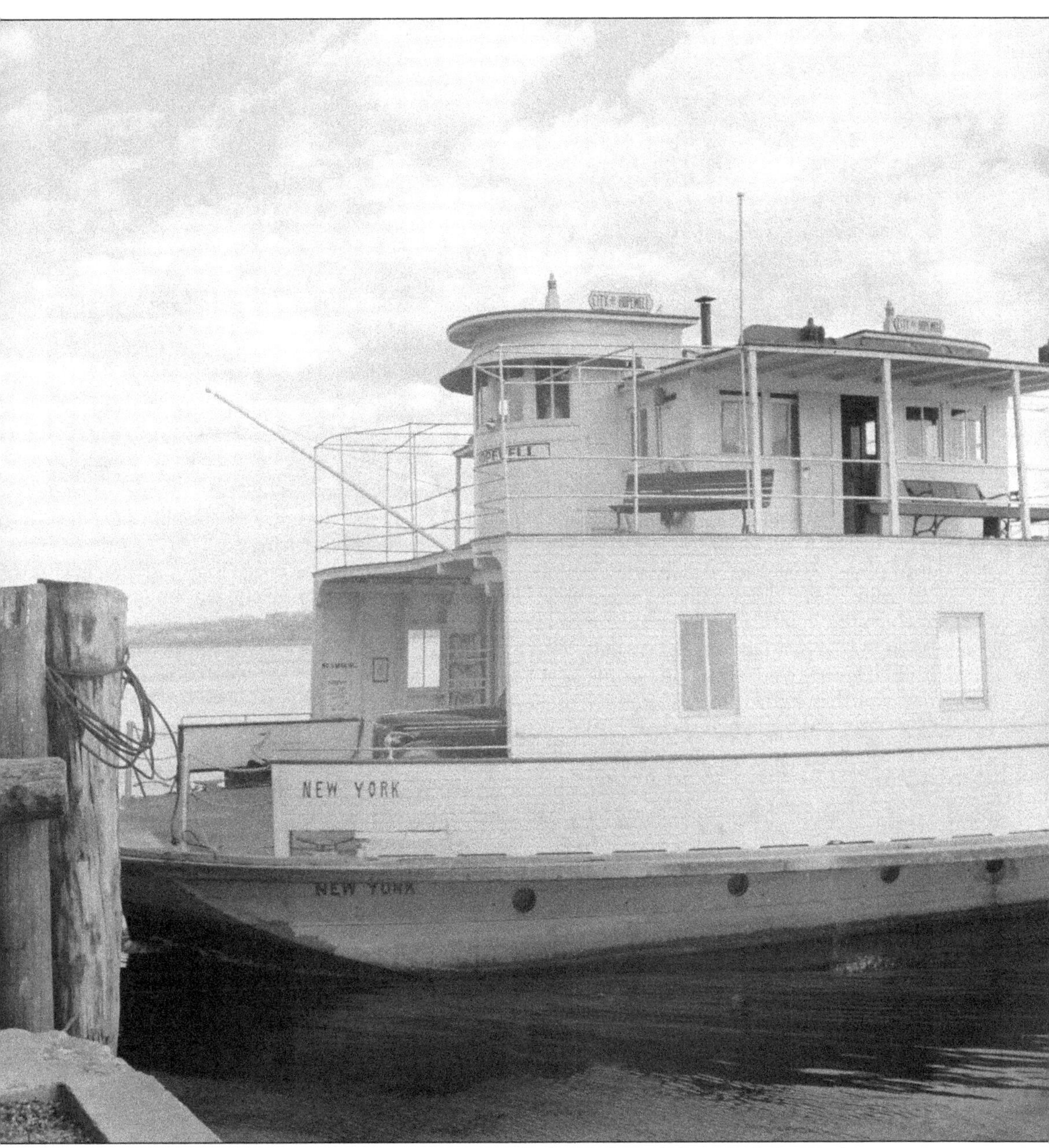

The Hudson-Athens Ferry works in conjunction with the Hudson-Athens Lighthouse Association to provide access to the lighthouse and tours. Completion of the Rip Van Winkle Bridge in 1935, several miles to the south of Athens, ended local ferry service across the Hudson River until the summer of 2012, when weekend ferry service resumed. The Hudson-Athens Ferry was portrayed in the 2005 Tom Cruise film *War of the Worlds*, in which Martians attacked the town, the ferry, and refugees from New York City who attempted to flee across the Hudson River.

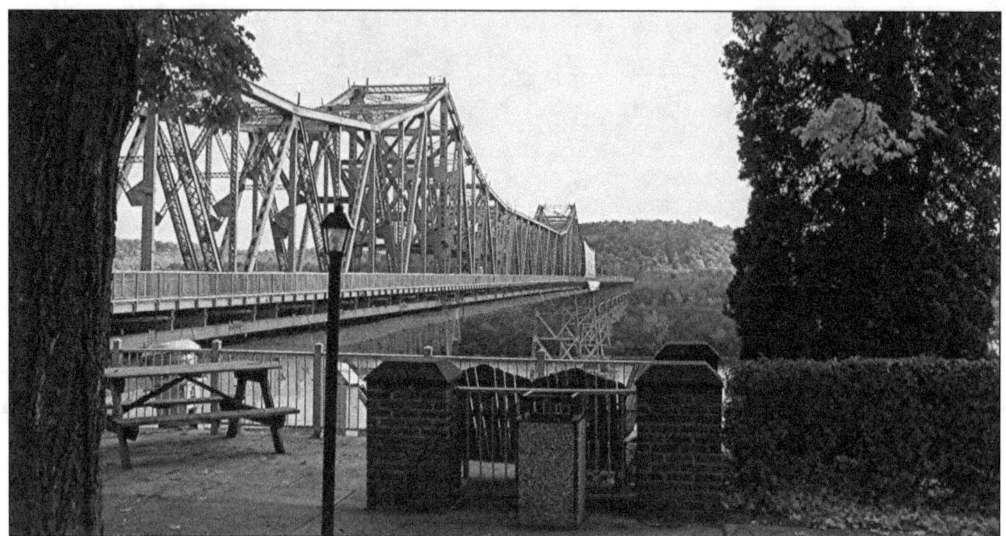

The Rip Van Winkle Bridge, spanning the Hudson River between Hudson and Catskill, opened on July 2, 1935, at a cost of $2.4 million. It was a toll bridge, with passengers paying a toll in the eastbound lane only, and there was a pedestrian walkway on the south side of the bridge that was open until dusk daily. The bridge was named after a short story of the same name written by Washington Irving, in which Rip Van Winkle fell asleep for 20 years in the Catskill Mountains after an encounter with the ghost of Henry Hudson and his men. This is one of America's oldest and most beloved folktales. In 17th-century Dutch times, Kaatskill, as it was then known, meant "Cat Creek." Catamounts, as they were then known, were the mountain lions inhabiting the region.

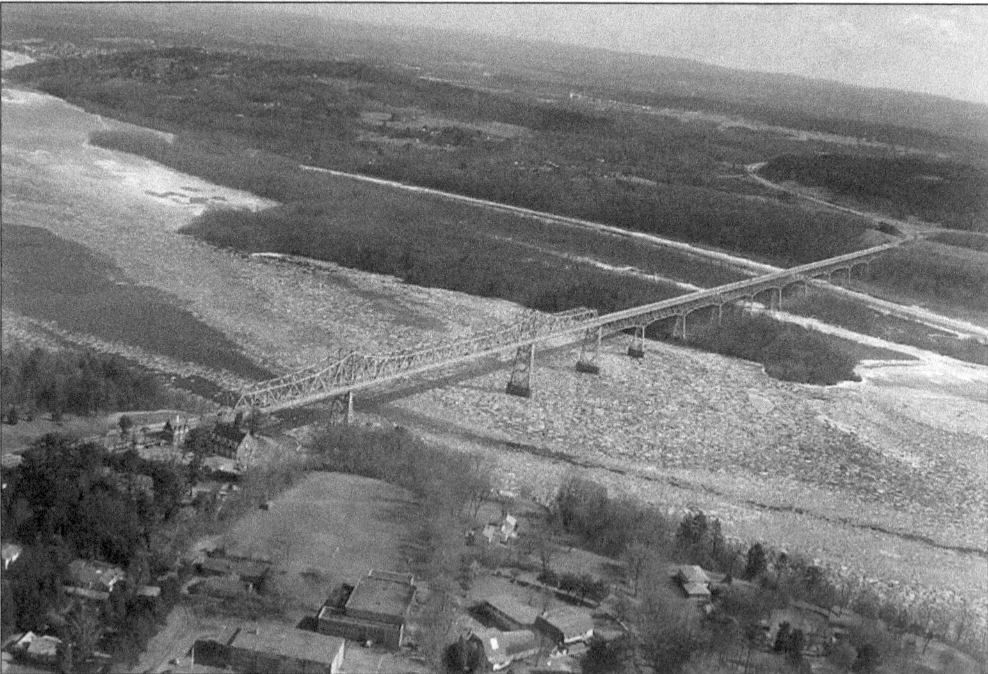

This is an aerial view of the Rip Van Winkle Bridge, showing portions of Catskill, Greene County, and the icy Hudson River, as well as Hudson, Columbia County, and the Taconics and Berkshire Mountains in the far distance. (Courtesy New York State Bridge Authority.)

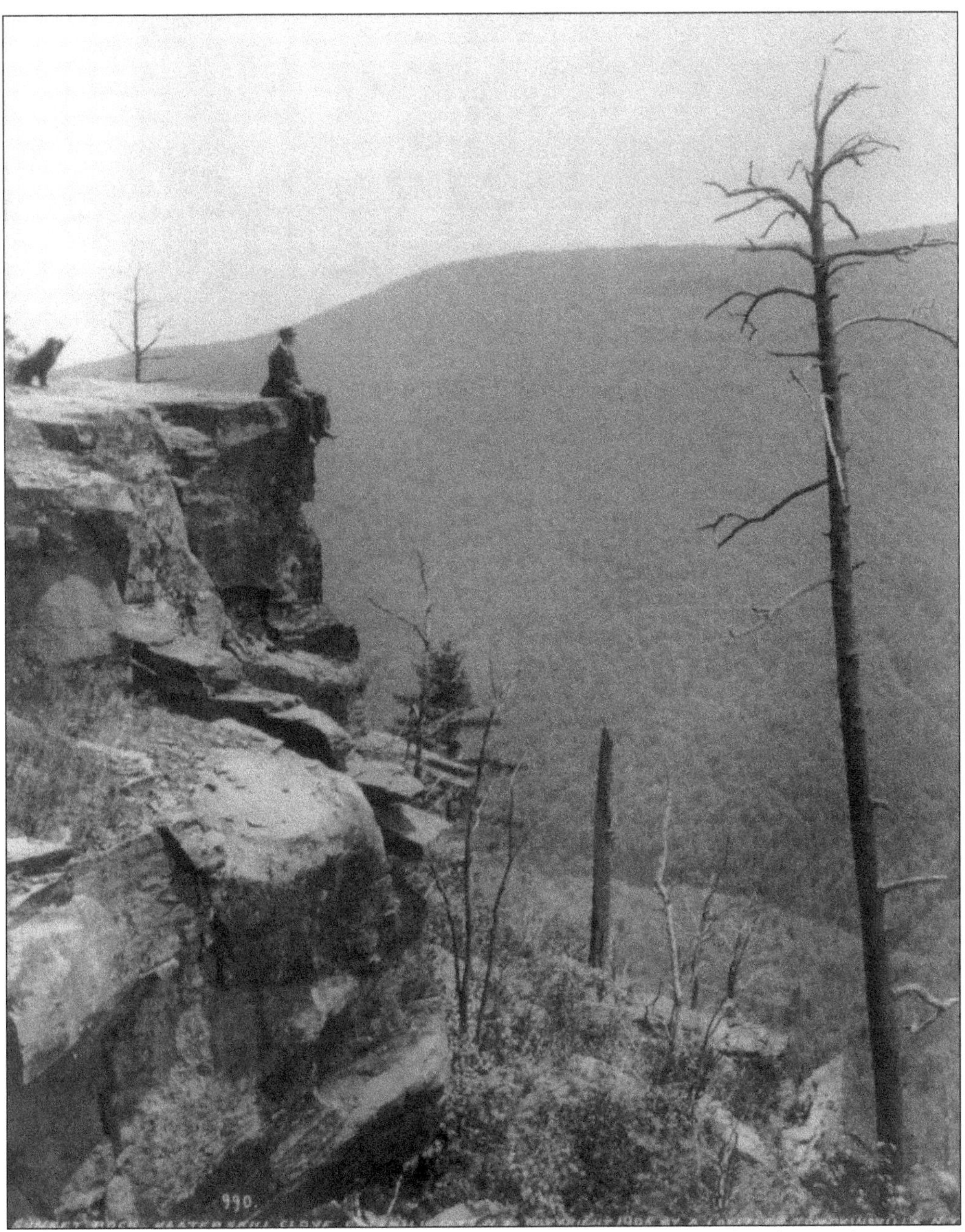

This 1902 photograph shows a man seated on rocks (Sunset Rock) with a dog in the Catskill Mountains. While the man faces towards Hudson, the Windham and Catskill Mountains are to his left. Washington Irving called the area "this spell bound region." One of America's best-known and beloved folk tales, Irving's *Rip Van Winkle* took place in this region, with Rip awakening from a 20-year sleep near the Kaaterskill Falls, the highest waterfall in New York State.

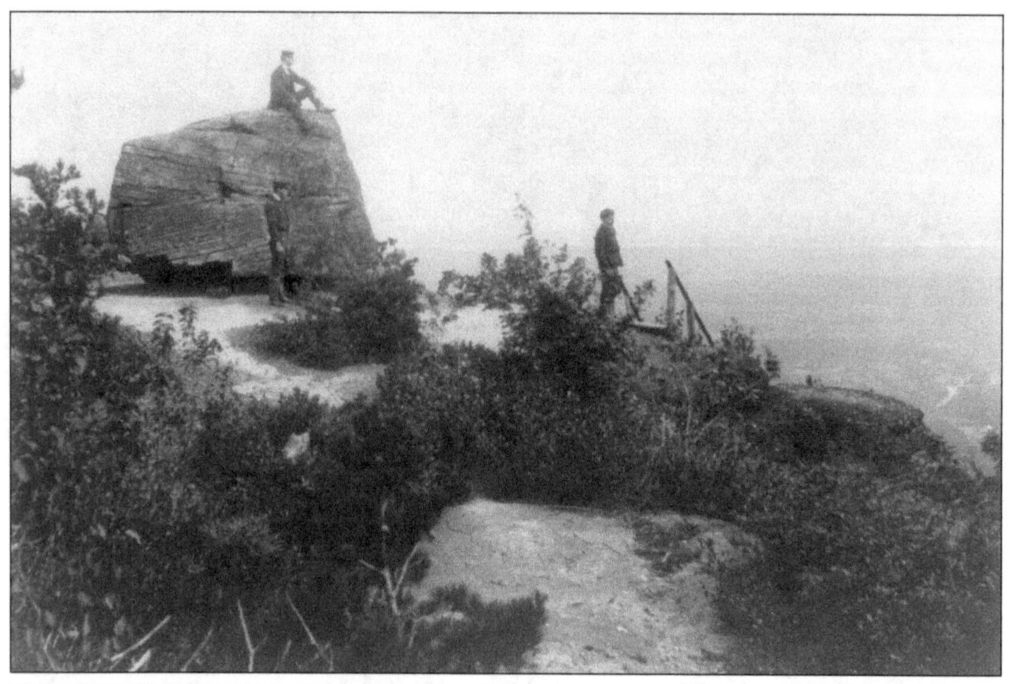

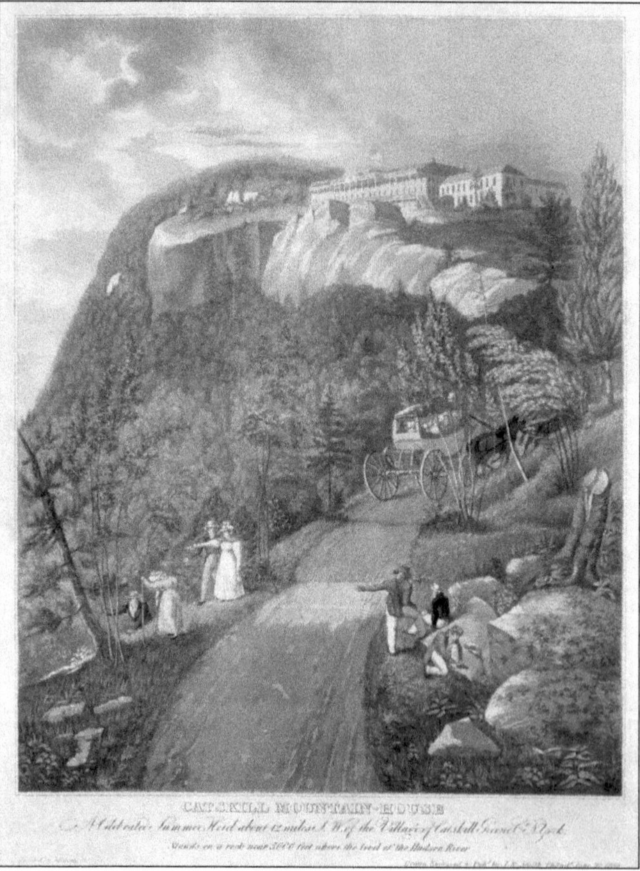

This is a 1902 photograph of three men on South Mountain in the Catskills, at the five-state lookout point. On very clear days, from this vantage point, parts of Vermont, New Hampshire, Massachusetts, Connecticut, and New York can all be seen.

The former Catskill Mountain House resort overlooked the Catkills, the five-state lookout, and Hudson. Still a popular hiking spot and an inspirational place for artists and painters, it was written about by Washington Irving and James Fennimore Cooper, author of *The Last of the Mohicans*. Built on the edge of a cliff in 1824 near Palenville, it was visited by three American presidents and the elite of society of the day.

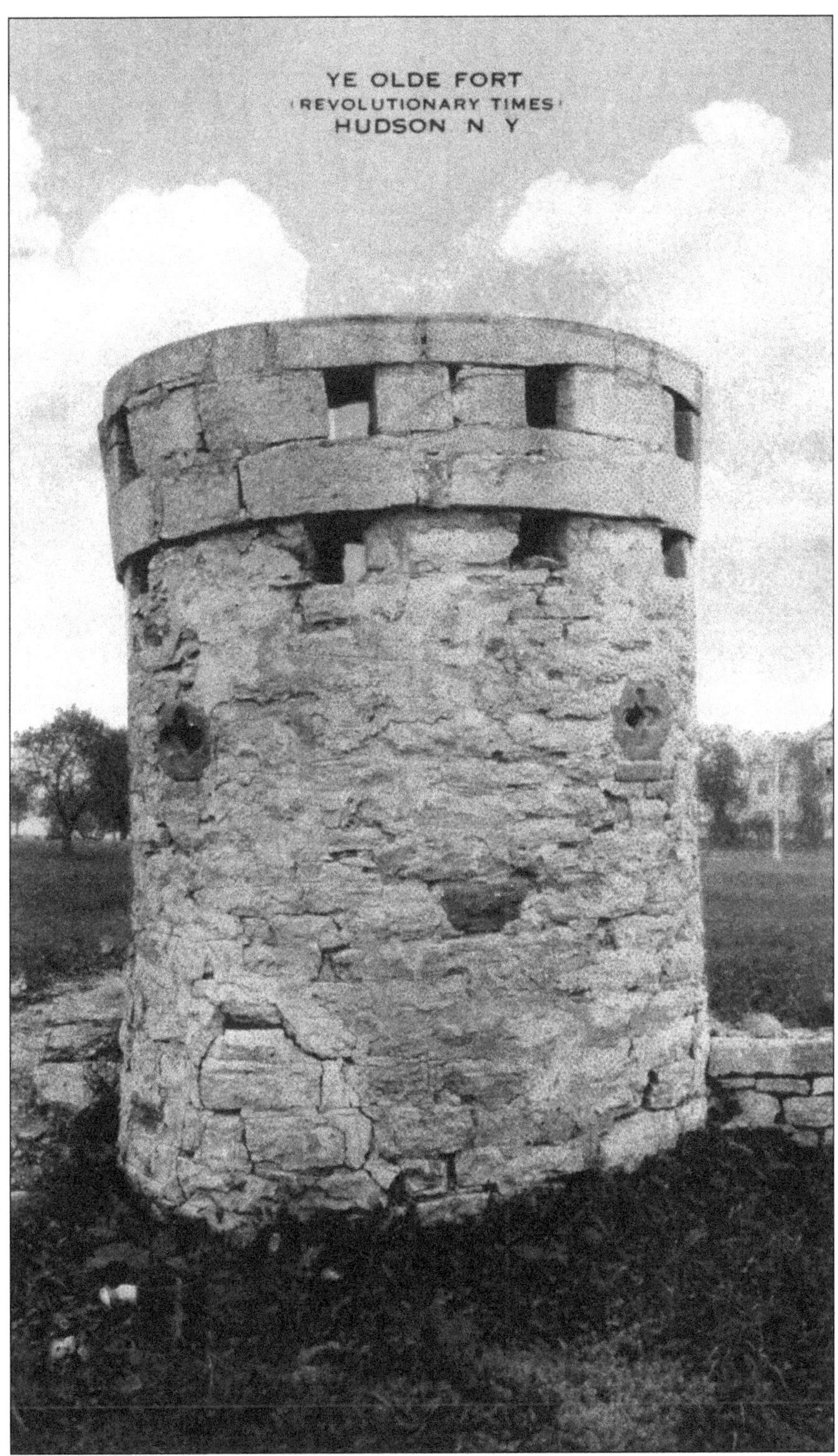

This is a postcard depicting Ye Old Fort in Hudson during Revolutionary times. The fort was situated on what is now Aiken Avenue.

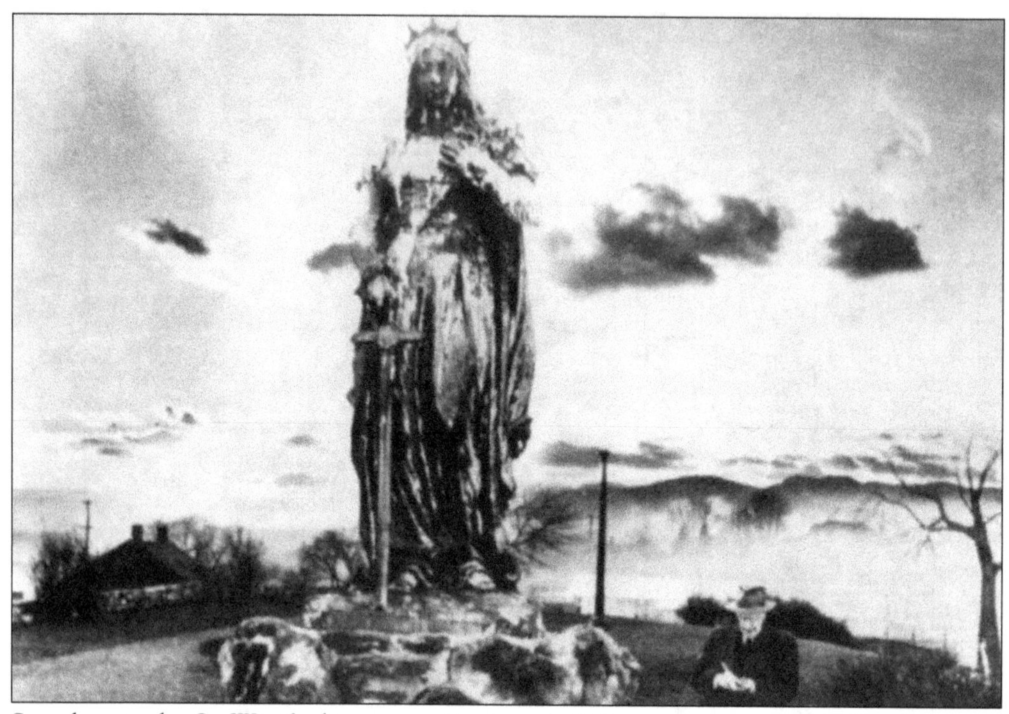

Seen here is the St. Winifred statue on Promenade Hill, overlooking the Hudson River. St. Winifred was a noble British maiden beheaded by Prince Caradoc for rebuffing his advances. Her head rolled down a hill, and where it stopped, a spring flushed forth, in Flintshire, Wales, which is still famous as a place of pilgrimage. Caradoc was called Caractacus by the Romans. Gen. John Watts de Peyster presented the statue to Hudson in 1896 and stated at the time that he "knew there were many saints in Hudson," but he "hoped there was room for one more." She wears the martyr's crown and holds the sword that beheaded her. Also in this photograph is a journalist, possibly from the *New York Times*, who ran a story of the unveiling. (Courtesy Mary Howell, Columbia County Historian.)

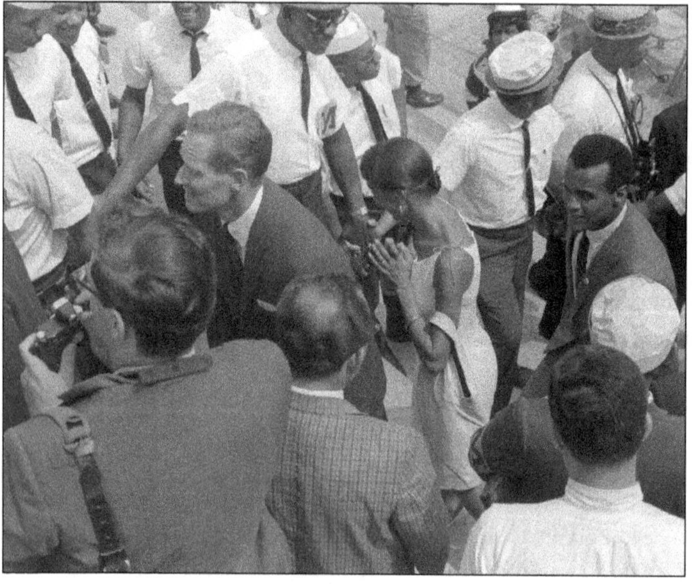

Harry Belafonte is an American singer, songwriter, and social activist best known for "The Banana Boat Song," with its famous "Day-O" lyric. He starred in *Odds Against Tomorrow*, a 1959 film noir shot in many parts of Hudson, including down by the waterfront. Other major motion pictures filmed in Hudson include *Nobody's Fool*, starring Jessica Tandy and Paul Newman, and *Ironweed*, starring Jack Nicholson and Meryl Streep.

Martin Van Buren (December 5, 1782–July 24, 1862) was the eighth president of the United States, from 1837 to 1841. He was the only president not to have spoken English as his first and primary language. He first spoke Dutch, and he was the first president from New York. A year after their marriage, Van Buren and his wife, Hannah, moved from Kinderhook to Hudson, the county seat.

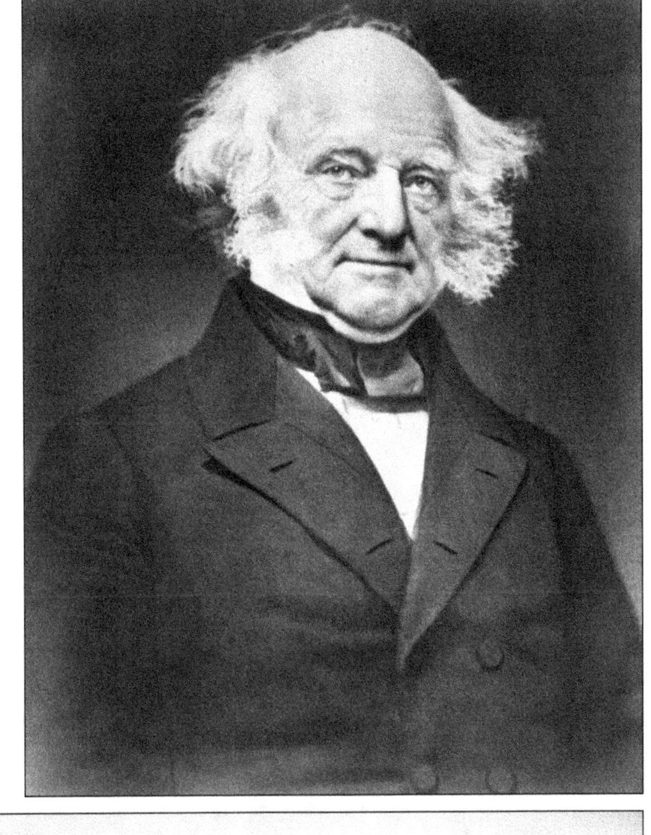

Lindenwald (German for "linden wood") is the 36-room Kinderhook house of Martin Van Buren, which served as his home and farm during retirement. As a widower for the first year and a half of his presidency, there was no first lady in the White House.

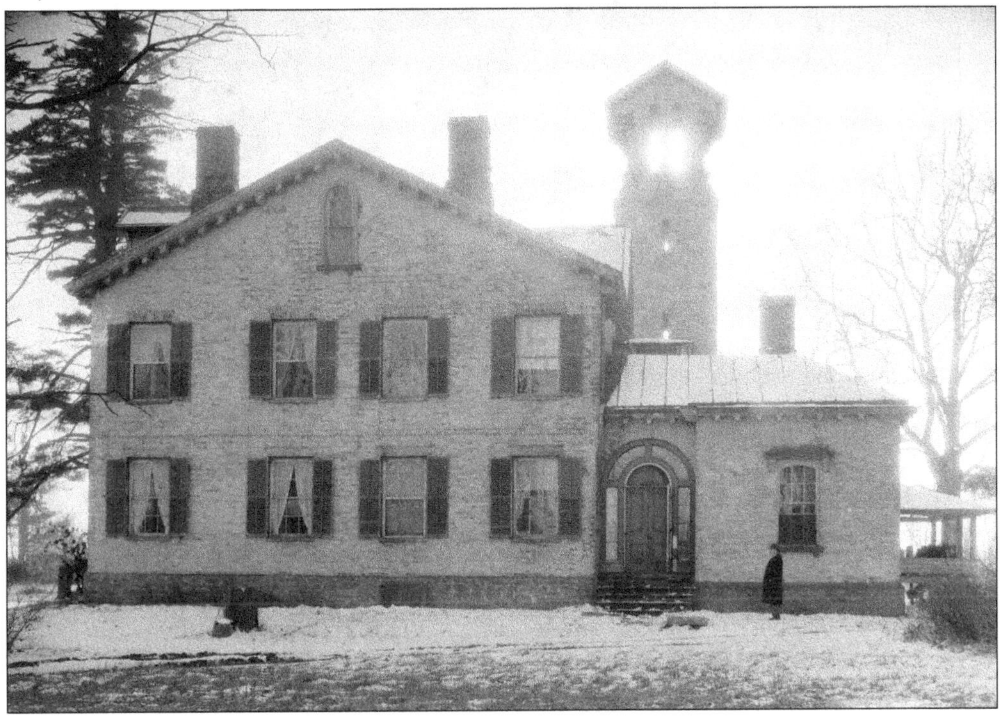

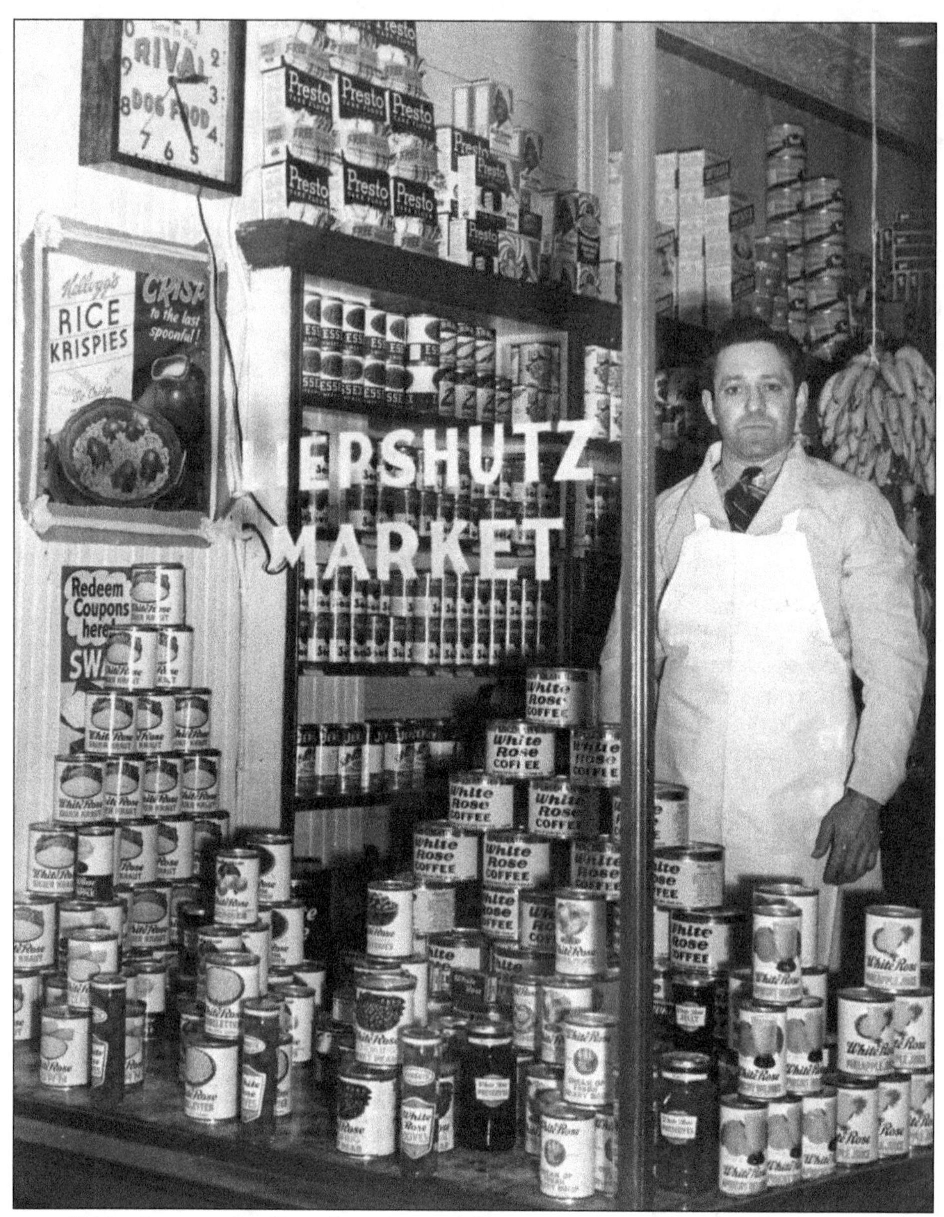

This is a 1940s photograph of Liepshutz meat and grocery store at First and Warren Streets. The store was opened by Samuel Liepshutz, a member of the Hudson High School class of 1925. Liepshutz also opened a slaughterhouse near the river that was in operation until 1962. The slaughterhouse and the National Biscuit Company were located in the Benedict Building on the northwest corner of Ferry and Water Streets. A February 16, 1962, *Register Star* article described Samuel Liepshutz as "an energetic man who almost seems to bounce as he strides purposefully along. Sam is fond of mentioning that the nucleus of today's Hudson Boys Club started at Washington Hose Company, Warren and Front Streets when he was 10 years old. He was elected first president of the club." Born in Brest, Russia, Liepshutz arrived in Hudson in 1911. His father, Jacob, was working on a Kinderhook farm for a monthly salary of $7 and a pair of shoes, and he later became the owner of Clermont Ice Company. Both were highly ambitious men that embodied Hudson's entrepreneurial spirit. (Courtesy Linda Russo Liepshutz.)

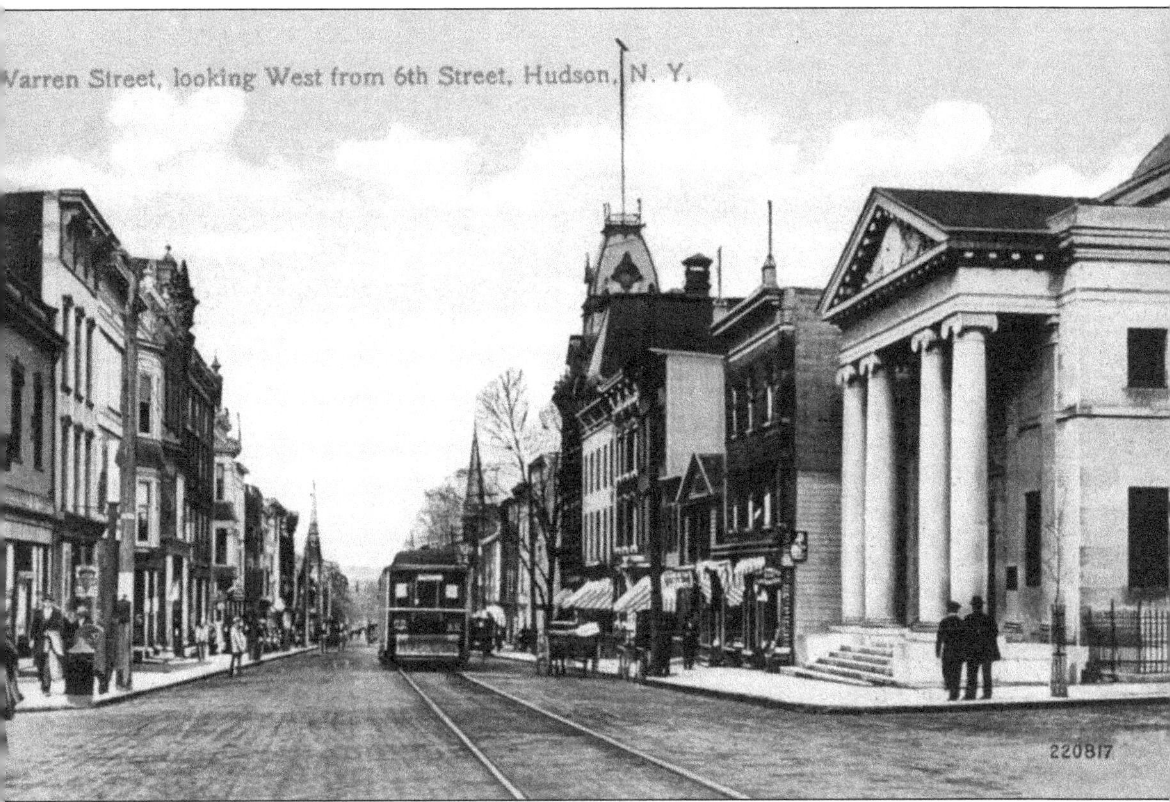

This is a 1918 postcard of unpaved Warren Street looking west from Sixth Street, showing the trolley and trolley track. The 1890 population of Hudson was 9,970. According to *Commercial and Financial Chronicle: Supplements, Volume 69, Part 2*, "Albany and Hudson Railway and Power is a consolidation of Hudson Street Railway, Hudson Light and Power Company, Kinderhook and Hudson Railroad, and Citizens Electric Light and Power of Hudson. Hudson Light and Power Company in June 1899 changed its name to Hudson Light & Power & Railroad Company so as to absorb the Hudson Street Railway." (Author's collection.)

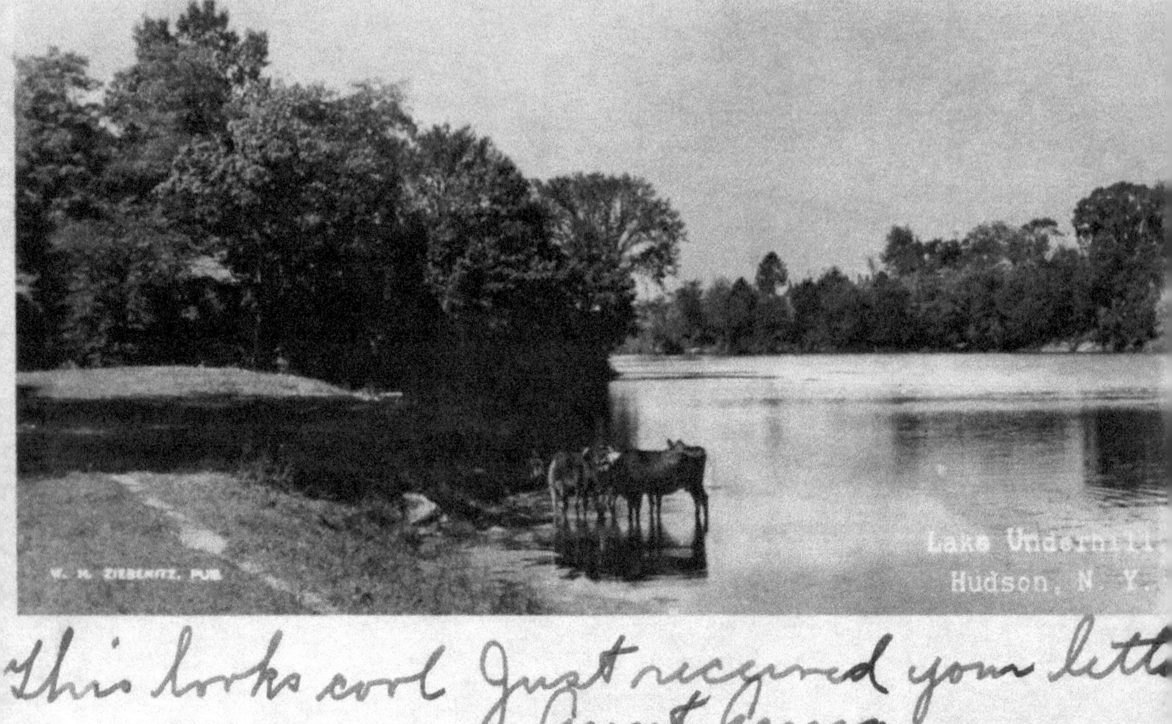

This 1907 postcard shows Lake Underhill in Hudson, with cattle in the water. The land around the lake is owned by the City of Hudson, was formerly owned by an ice company. It includes swimming privileges, a small beach, and a concession area. An inspection made on January 9, 1918, by the New York State Department of Health showed pollution to the water due to the operation of a sewage disposal plant nearby, serving a section of the city known as Fairground Boulevards. The Clermont Ice Company controlled the lake in winter for ice harvesting at a time when iceboxes were used in homes, before the advent of refrigerators. (Author's collection.)

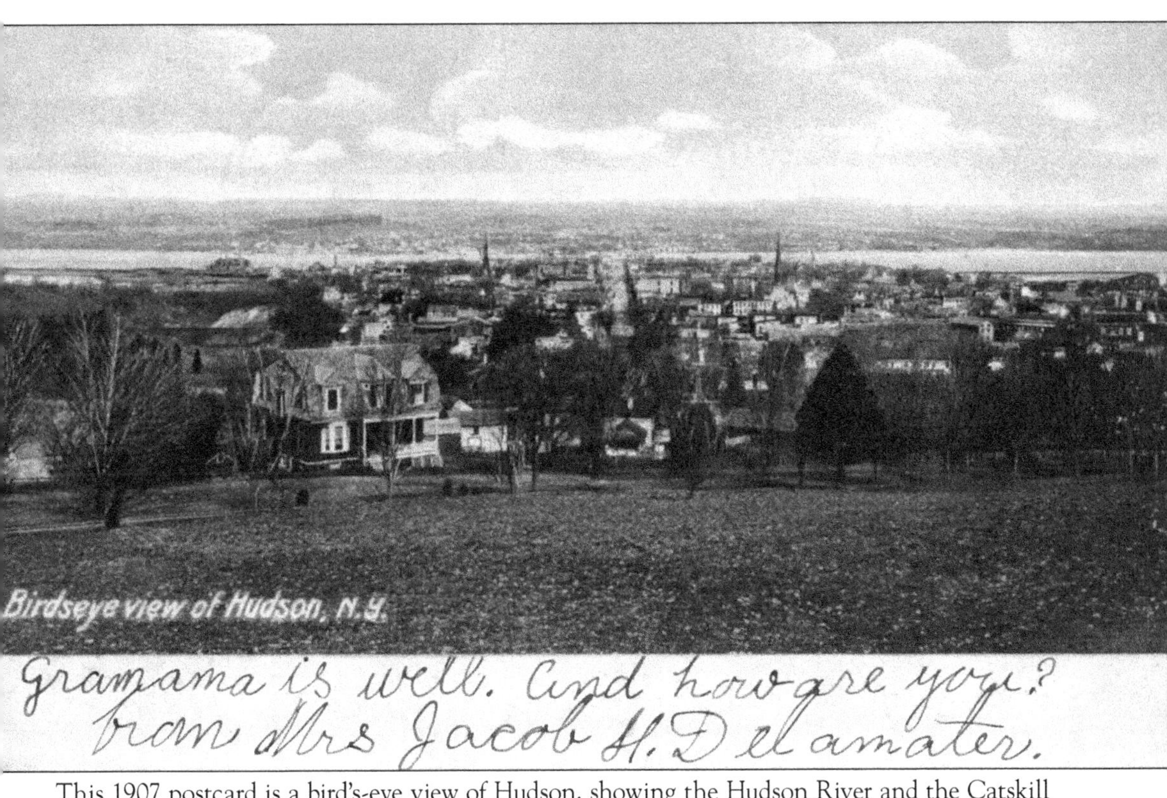

This 1907 postcard is a bird's-eye view of Hudson, showing the Hudson River and the Catskill Mountains in the distance. (Author's collection.)

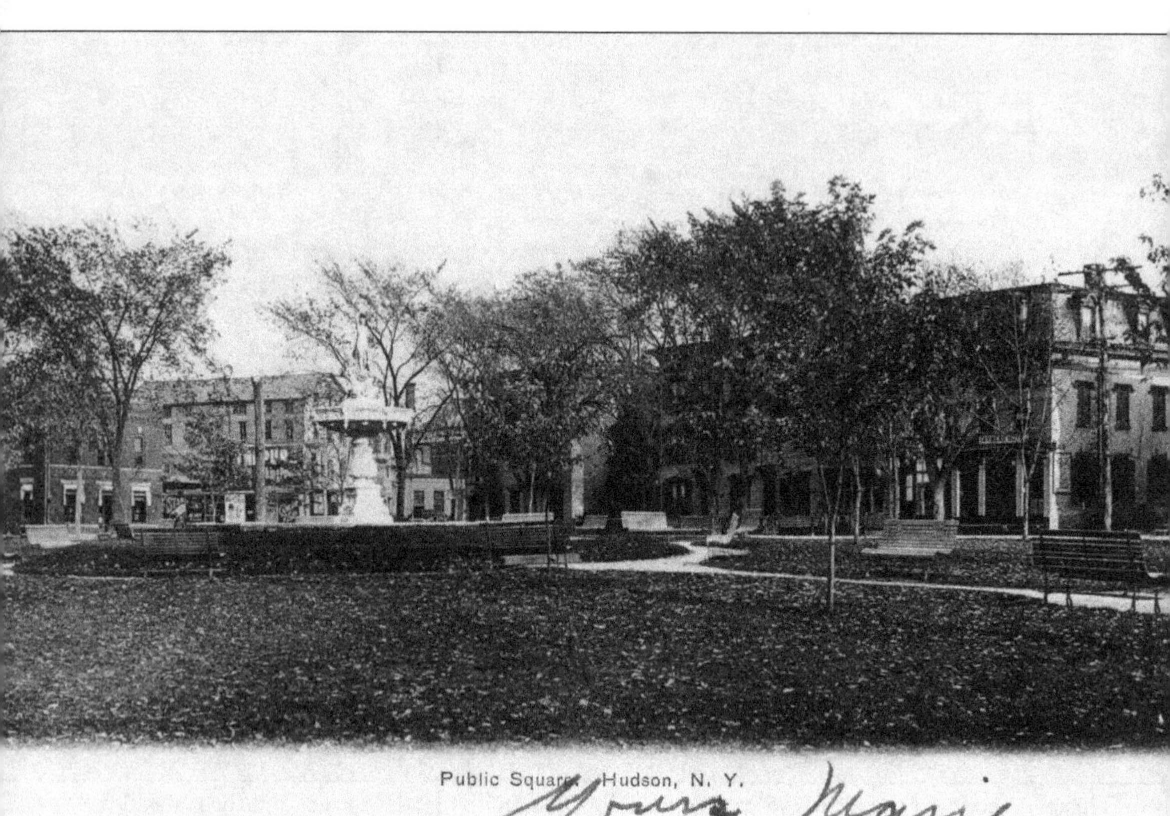

This 1906 postcard shows the Public Square, now commonly known as Seventh Street Park, with its statue of Venus and young trees but without the iron fencing seen today. The statue of Venus no longer resides in the park; it is in an undisclosed location and in need of restoration. The Farmer's Hotel, seen on the far right, no longer stands. The site is now the location of the St. Charles Hotel. (Author's collection.)

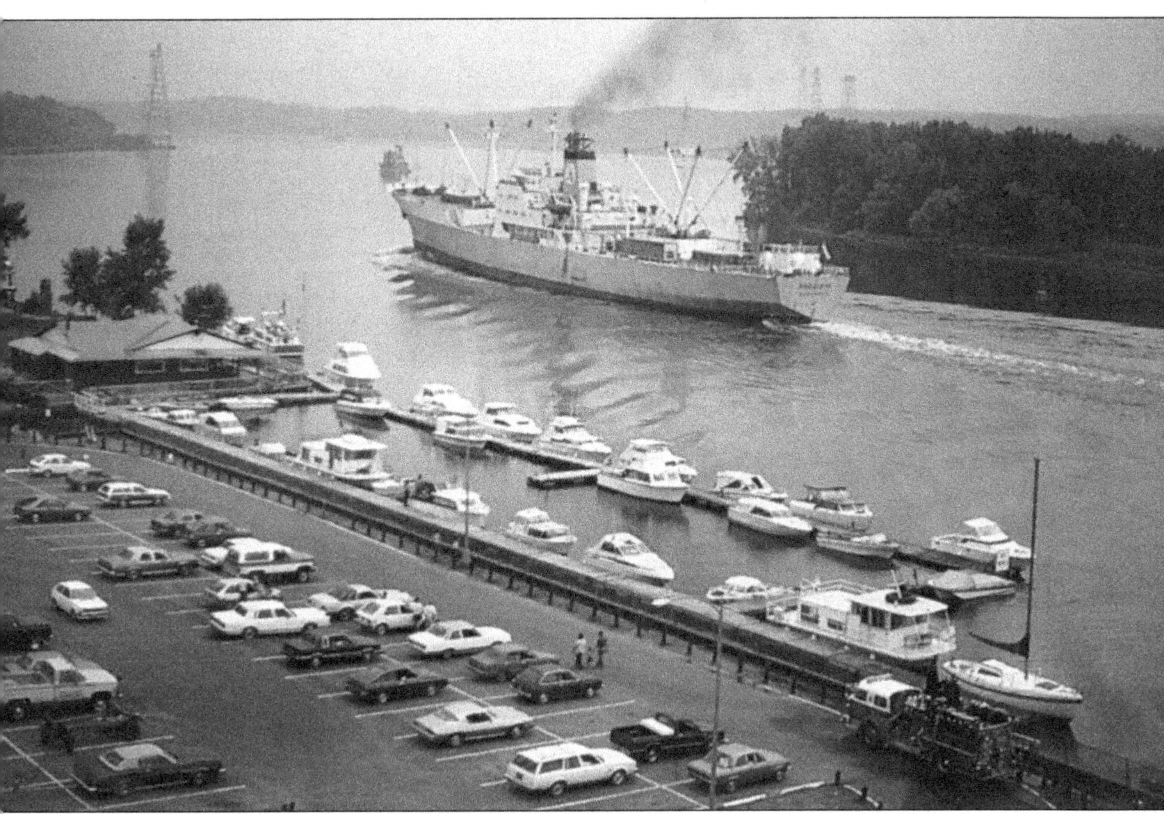

This postcard shows a Ken Bovat photograph of the Hudson Boat Launch with an extensive view of the Hudson River; the Hudson-Athens Lighthouse, in the near distance near the ship's front tip; and the Catskill Mountains in the far distance. Hudson was the first chartered city in the United States in 1785, after the signing of the Declaration of Independence. A whaling port from 1784 to 1845 and a port of entry from 1790 to 1815, the city has fallen, only to rise again many times. (Author's collection.)

www.ingramcontent.com/pod-product-compliance
Lightning Source LLC
LaVergne TN
LVHW081544100826
845153LV00004B/307
* 9 7 8 1 5 3 1 6 7 3 9 0 1 *